REVIVAL

Rodney Howard-Browne

River Publishing

REVIVAL

Published by River Publishing
P.O. Box 292888, Tampa, FL 33687 USA

ISBN: 979-8-88955-134-8

Printed in the United States of America

CONTENTS

INTRODUCTION

God called my wife and I as missionaries to America from Africa in 1987 and told us that He was going to bring a Great Awakening to this land. Since the day we landed here, we have not stopped preaching this message of revival and preparing the Church for the coming "Great Awakening." In 1989, in upstate New York, the power of God fell in a mighty way, and the Holy Ghost has been pouring out in our meetings ever since.

This book has been written using material originally preached in 2005. Much of it is prophetic, and as you read it, you will be amazed at how God was speaking then to prepare the Church, and how relevant it is to today.

Our message has not changed over all these years. America and the Church are not ready for what is coming. The events of 2020 have already proven this, and the need for revival is greater now than at any other time in our history as we prepare to usher in the soon-coming return of the King.

The Church has been so blinded by religion and tradition, and it is only revival that will break that open. But it has to start in the heart of an individual who crics out and is willing to humble themselves to receive from God. Many people are crying out for change, but they don't understand that change starts on the inside and then happens on the outside.

A change in leadership, a change in circumstances, a change in president, a change in external things will not make a difference. It's the revival change in your heart that will bring about a change to your family, your neighborhood, your town, city, your nation, and to every nation of the world.

It starts with you. *You* can carry the revival fire of God. *You* can bring the oasis to the desert because *you* are the carrier of the presence of God. God has called us to set at liberty those who are bound, to heal the sick, open the eyes of the blind, and bring hope to a lost and dying world.

In this book, I will show you how you can be the one to make a difference and to carry the fire of God where you are called. I will teach you how you can continue to be used by God and not let that flame be extinguished. This is not for the fainthearted; this is for those who are called, chosen, set apart, and who have a desire to see revival sweep across this land and to see the mighty harvest of souls come in.

The attack on the Church at this time is unparalleled in history. The devil knows his time is drawing near, and he is doing all he can to destroy God's people. But those who live in the fire, who walk in the fire, and who carry the fire will rise up triumphantly, having counted the cost, and will be the glorious Bride made ready for her Groom. This is the time for signs, wonders,miracles, and for the supernatural power of God to be seen. But God needs submitted, yielded, and purified vessels to be the carriers of this anointing.

There is no room to be lukewarm. Today you must choose whom you will serve and if you are going to be hot or cold. If you want to be red-hot on fire for Jesus, the revival must start in you.

I pray that you will be stirred up, fired up, and readied for revival as you read this book.

1

THE RIVER OF OFFENSE IS THE RIVER OF DELIVERANCE

The Roadblock of Pride

Have you ever been offended? Look at 2 Kings 5:1-10, Naaman was a great man, but he had leprosy:

Now Naaman, captain of the host of the king of Syria, was a great man with his master, and honourable, because by him the Lord had given deliverance unto Syria: he was also a mighty man in valour, but he was a leper. And the Syrians had gone out by companies, and had brought away captive out of the land of Israel a little maid; and she waited on Naaman's wife. And she said unto her mistress, Would God my lord were with the prophet that is in Samaria! For he would recover him of his leprosy. And one went in, and told his lord, saying, Thus and thus said the maid that is of the land of Israel. And the king of Syria said, Go to, go, and I will send a letter unto the king of Israel. And he departed, and took with him ten talents of silver, and six thousand pieces of gold, and ten changes of raiment. And he

> brought the letter to the king of Israel, saying, Now when this letter is come unto thee, behold, I have therewith sent Naaman my servant to thee, that thou mayest recover him of his leprosy. And it came to pass, when the king of Israel had read the letter, that he rent his clothes, and said, Am I God, to kill and to make alive, that this man doth send unto me to recover a man of his leprosy? wherefore consider, I pray you, and see how he seeketh a quarrel against me.
>
> (VV. 1-7)

In other words, the king of Israel thought Naaman was just looking for a fight.

> And it was so, when Elisha the man of God had heard that the king of Israel had rent his clothes, that he sent to the king, saying, Wherefore hast thou rent thy clothes? let him come now to me, and he shall know that there is a prophet in Israel. So Naaman came with his horses and with his chariot, and stood at the door of the house of Elisha. And Elisha sent a messenger unto him, saying, Go and wash in Jordan seven times, and thy flesh shall come again to thee, and thou shalt be clean.
>
> (VV. 8-10)

Imagine that it was some person high up in the military who had shown up: the last thing you would expect if he pulled up outside the house is for a servant to come out and greet him! Of course, if that happened today, ministers would be out there with the television cameras interviewing him in case he got healed so they could have another "notch under their belt," another one "up on the chart!"

But the prophet didn't even come out of his house. He sent his servant. Talk about getting offended! Naaman said, "The least he can do is come out and greet me!" That's the first mark of offense. The Bible says, "Naaman was wroth and went away," because the servant told him to go and wash in the Jordan seven times. Naaman thought,

"He [the prophet] will surely come out to me, and stand, and call on the name of the Lord his God, and strike his hand over the place, and recover the leper" (2 Kings 5:11).

Many times, when we come to God and ask Him for something, we have preconceived ideas in our minds and hearts about how God is going to do it, but that doesn't mean God is going to do it that way.

People come around the move of God with a preconceived idea of the way God is going to move. "I'm going to go there; the preacher's going to call me out. He's going to have me on television. He's going to wave his hand, and everything's going to be great." Or, "The preacher's going to come out, he's going to meet me, he's going to open the door, and favor is going to be over me. Everything's going to be great," and then it doesn't happen that way! Along the way there are going to be many obstacles. There are going to be many places where you can get offended. And those obstacles, if you allow them to, will stop you from entering into the blessing that God has for you. You have to get past your offense.

EVERYTHING THAT COMES FROM GOD HAS AN OFFENSE ATTACHED TO IT

> RIGHT AT THE DOORWAY TO THE GREATEST BLESSING, IS A ROCK OF OFFENSE. GOD WANTS TO GET YOU PAST YOUR POINT OF OFFENSE, BECAUSE THAT'S WHERE YOUR DELIVERANCE LIES.

There are so many people in the Body of Christ who are in a place where they are going no further because they are locked in a place of offense. Somebody offended them. They came to church, the usher didn't greet them properly, they didn't get the seats they wanted, somebody stole their parking spot; the pastor didn't smile at them the way they thought he should have, somebody didn't shake their hand, something went wrong, and they got offended. Meanwhile, "back at the ranch," the truth of the intention behind those incidents was nothing along the lines they thought. But some people are an offense going somewhere just to get offended. There are people who come to services looking to get offended—"I'm going to go there and see if I can tolerate another service before I get offended!"

If the music doesn't offend them, then the offering will offend them. If that doesn't offend them, then I'll offend them. If that doesn't offend them, then they will get offended by the time they hit the parking lot, or it will be the traffic officer outside, patrolling the street who will offend them. They are going to get offended!

But one thing I found out about the Lord is that many times, right at the doorway to the greatest blessing, is a rock of offense. Everything that comes from God has an offense attached to it.

Somebody says, "That doesn't even sound right," but only the humble person will be able to enter in. You have to let go of offenses and walk in forgiveness to enter in.

Naaman was upset because he was told to go and dip seven times in the Jordan. "Why should I go and dip seven times in the Jordan? It's a muddy, dirty river, the rivers of Abana and Pharpar, the rivers of Damascus, aren't they better than all the waters of Israel? They are clearer waters" (v. 12, paraphrased). Today people say: "Why do I have to come down to The River Church and get touched? I want to get touched at my denominational headquarters."

"Why would God make me do that? I'm not going to go down there and roll on the ground and make an idiot of myself."

"I don't want to sit there and get hit by the power of God! Whatever will people think?" But if they had humbled themselves, they would have received a touch from God. Naaman said, "May I not wash in [the Syrian rivers), and be clean?" (2 Kings 5:12). So, he turned and went his way. He was angry. You cannot believe how many people have left services in the same way—mad and angry. They've run out the door and said, "I'll never go back near that Howard-Browne character!" Meanwhile, if only they had just stuck it out, they could have received the breakthrough they needed.

Somebody says, "Do you purposely try to offend people?" Yes! You are right about that! The services are designed to offend the religious. You'd better believe it! My meetings are not designed to make people comfortable. God wants to get you past your point of offense because that's where your deliverance lies.

PRIDE BLOCKS DELIVERANCE

Naaman didn't want to dip in the Jordan because it was dirty. But the Jordan held the key to his freedom and his deliverance. Sometimes, the very thing you don't want to do is the thing God wants you to do. He wants you to come to the place where you humble yourself totally before Him and put aside your pride. It would take somebody putting aside his pride when he was the captain of an army, to go and dip in the Jordan when he had rivers back home that were cleaner.

Thank God for Naaman's servants! Look at verse 13: "And his servants came near, and spake unto him, and said, My father, if the prophet had bid thee do some great thing, wouldest thou not have done it?" In other words, if the prophet told you to do something hard, wouldn't you do it? Sometimes we want to do something hard. The servants said, "How much rather then, when he saith to thee, Wash, and be clean?" (v. 13b). They said, "What's the problem here? He said to dip seven times and be clean. If he'd told you to do something hard, you would have gladly done it."

The Bible says, "Then went he down, and dipped himself seven times in Jordan, according to the saying of the man of God: and his flesh came again like unto the flesh of a little child, and he was clean. And he returned to the man of God, he and all his company, and came, and stood before him: and he said, Behold, now I know that there is no God in all the earth, but in Israel" (vv. 14–15).

Naaman was so blessed that he took a portion of the earth so that when he got back to Syria, he had the ground from the banks of the Jordan (v. 17); that's how touched he was! He humbled himself and he received his miracle.

PRIDE BLOCKS SURRENDER

Naaman was a great man, but he was a leper. There are people all over the world whom God has used in an awesome way, but they have a problem. Leprosy is also a type of sin and there are many great people whom God has used in an area of the ministry and yet, they have opened themselves up and they are bound in a certain area of their lives. God wants to set them free, but they are too proud to come and dip in the river of God.

I heard the story of a pastor who was attacking what God was doing in the meetings where the power of God was falling and people were getting hit with the joy. He said, "All that stuff is ridiculous; it is rubbish! All you people being hit by the power of God, being drunk on the new wine of the Holy Ghost." And the saddest thing was that eighteen months later, he was admitted into an alcohol center for rehabilitation.

When I heard it, I thought, *My! If he had just not fought it, if only he had come and surrendered to the Lord and let God touch him, he would not have had a problem with alcohol.* But he thought the "river" looked dirty. It looked muddy, and it takes a humble person to obey the Word of the Lord and jump in and be clean.

Pride also blocks when people come with preconceived ideas about how God's going to move—but you don't know how God is going to move. You have just got to open your heart. Do you have a need today? Are you desperate today? Then you cannot come with preconceived ideas. You cannot tell God how He's going to do it or how He's not to do it.

PRIDE BLOCKS YOUR BREAKTHROUGH

God requires something of you. We see this throughout the Word of God. For example, in John 9, a blind man came to Jesus, and Jesus spat on the ground and made clay and put it on the man's eyes and said, "Go, wash in the pool of Siloam" (vv. 6–7). That man could have been offended. He could have left with mud on his eyes and said, "Jesus spat in my eye!" He could have been totally offended—"I went to that meeting, and the preacher spat on the ground and made clay and put it in my eyes. Can you believe it? What a disgusting ministry! And this offends me because I came and I was blind and clean, but now I'm blind and dirty!"

Many times, the key to our breakthrough is obeying what the Lord tells us to do, and *only* what He tells us to do. I know that the thing that He tells us to do sometimes looks difficult, but it's not. If you can get past the offense, there lies your deliverance.

Another example is the rich young ruler in Mark 10. When Jesus said to him, "Sell whatever you have and give to the poor" (Mark 10:21 NKJV), he couldn't get past his offense—"What do you mean? Are you telling me that you want me to sell everything I've got and give the money away?" Do you think Jesus was trying to make him a poor man? No! Jesus was trying to break him into the rest of his life. But the young ruler could not do it because his possessions were great. He could not part with them because *they had him; he did not have them.* His offense blocked his deliverance.

Today, people come to a meeting and when I talk about giving, they get upset. They get offended and leave, "Well, all he does is talk about money." They get mad and go home and watch *Who Wants to Be a Millionaire?* They had come into a meeting, the joy of the Lord was bursting out all over the place, people were getting hit by the joy of the Lord, but they had gotten mad and left to go back home—probably to swallow a handful of Prozac because they have depression!

We deal with this all the time. People have a preconceived idea, "Well, the preacher's going to come out, and this is how it's going to happen," but then the Lord doesn't do that and instead, He sends some little old grey-haired lady to come lay hands on them. But because this doesn't meet their criteria of what they think God should do, they don't receive.

Then there is the example of the SyroPhoenician woman in Mark 7. When she came to Jesus and she wanted healing for her child, Jesus said, "It is not meet to take the children's bread, and to cast it unto the dogs" (v. 27). He called her a dog!

But she did not let that stop her. She did not let it go. She came for a miracle for her child and she was going to get it. Basically, what she replied was, "You know, I might be a dog, but even the dogs eat the crumbs that fall from the table. So, listen: I'll just get whatever crumb I can get, and I'm not leaving." She came past the place of offense. She could have been offended right in that place but she chose not to be.

If you get offended, do you know what's happening to you? Pride is being dealt with right at that moment. Somebody says, "I don't like this, now I'm getting offended." Why? Because we are messing with your pride. The only way to receive from God is with humility. The *only* way to receive from God is to come in *total humility.*

In John 6, when Jesus preached the sermon "Unless you eat the flesh of the Son of Man and drink His blood, you have no life in you" (John 6:53 NKJV), the whole crowd left him. Talk about a sermon that bombed! Jesus preached that message and they took off. Somebody probably said, "He's preaching cannibalism now!"

Offended, they left Jesus and He turned to His disciples and said, "Are you going to go too?" And they didn't know what to do. So they said, "Where else would we go?" (John 6:67–68, paraphrased). Which sounds like if there was an option, they would have left as well!

In John 11, Mary and Martha were upset with Jesus because He didn't come on time and Lazarus died. Martha said, "If You had been here, my brother would not have died!" (John 11:21 NKJV). The sisters were offended, they were upset because He wasn't there when Lazarus died. But it didn't matter because the miracleworker, the blind-man-healer, the water-walker had arrived, and He who gives life to the dead had now come!

OFFENSE STOPS YOU FROM PRODUCING FRUIT

> THE MOVE OF GOD, REVIVAL, AND ANYTHING TO DO WITH THE WORD OF GOD HAS AN OFFENSE TO IT IN THE NATURAL.

Mark 4:14–15 says, "The sower soweth the word. And these are they by the way side, where the word is sown; but when they have heard, Satan cometh immediately, and taketh away the word that was sown in their hearts." The devil will try to come and steal the Word that God puts in your heart the moment it comes to you, and he'll use offense. Be ready to protect the Word of God that comes to you, so that the devil, who is like a buzzard in the air coming down, doesn't come and steal the seed. Why? Because the devil is afraid that if it grows, it's going to produce a great tree, and much fruit will come out of it.

> And these are they likewise which are sown on stony ground; who, when they have heard the word, immediately receive it with gladness; and have no root in themselves, and so endure but for a time: afterward, when affliction or persecution ariseth for the word's sake, immediately they are offended.
>
> MARK 4:16-17

You might as well accept that this is just how it's going to be. Persecution and affliction are going to come because of the Word. Period! If you don't want to be persecuted and you don't want to be afflicted or offended, then you don't want to have anything to do with the Bible. You had better go after *Reader's Digest* or the *Encyclopedia Britannica*.

But Mark 4 continues:

> And these are they which are sown among thorns; such as hear the word, and the cares of this world, and the deceitfulness of riches, and the lusts of other things entering in, choke the word, and it becometh unfruitful. And these are they which are sown on good ground; such as hear the word, and receive it, and bring forth fruit, some thirtyfold, some sixty, and some an hundred.
>
> (VV. 18-20)

You can get offended, or you can come into the place of production of fruit in your life. I've watched people get mad and leave the church and they go off to some other church, and two years later, they leave that church because they got offended there. Then they go to another church, and then two years later, they are offended there and leave! It's almost like the offense follows them around. They can even go from state to state and be sure that the thing that offended them at the last place is waiting for them at the next place.

So then they go to another state, where they get offended there too! People run around saying, "I'm looking for the perfect church." But they'll never find it! The day they show up—it just became imperfect! Remember this: some people take themselves with them wherever they go!

The move of God, revival, and anything to do with the Word of God has an offense to it in the natural. Just study the moves of God of the past. Look at what took place in 1906 on Azusa Street—the offense at that time was speaking in tongues. Do you know that speaking in tongues still causes an offense in some circles?

What if the only way you could get healed was through a man who spat on the ground and made clay? Would you die or would you go and get spat upon? What if the only way you could get healed was a spitting preacher? Would you choose to die, or would you humble yourself and live?

Naaman could have said to himself, "Any other river except the Jordan. Don't you know it is an offense for a Syrian to come down and get dipped in the Jordan? Why the Jordan? Please, not the Jordan—any other river but the Jordan!"

The blind man could have said, "Why did Jesus have to spit on the ground and make clay, and put it on my eyes?" The SyroPhoenician woman could have said, "Why did He call me a dog?"

WHAT OFFENDS YOU IS YOUR ROADBLOCK

> IF YOU GET OFFENDED IN THE NATURAL ALL THE TIME, THEN YOU'RE GOING TO GET OFFENDED IN THE SPIRIT. BECAUSE GOD, MANY TIMES, PROVOKES THE MIND TO REVEAL WHAT'S IN THE HEART.

I want you to just stop for a moment and think about what has gotten you offended recently. What's the thing that has really offended you in the recent weeks and months?

If you could find out what's offended you, you are probably going to find out what area the devil is trying to stop you from going into! Because he's put up some roadblocks for you.

Some of you get offended just driving on the highway! One time I was driving to Orlando. I was on the cell phone, talking, and I'm very animated when I talk. I had the earpiece in my ear, and I was driving and waving my hand as I was talking, and a guy in the truck ahead of me slowed down. Then I looked, and he had his hand raised with the "greeting" of a certain digit that was extended toward me. At that moment I could have gotten mad at him. I could have honked the horn. I could have accelerated away. But I just carried on with my conversation. I slowed down and his hand was raised at me as he was "worshipping his god." I just decided that I was not going to get offended. I carried on, and he slowed down for probably five minutes to block me.

I carried on, too busy with my conversation. Then as we got to double lanes, he pulled to the right and I pulled past. He rolled down his window and his hand came out with the digit extended toward me again. I just shrugged and carried on driving, and I took my cell phone and waved it at him. He had thought that I was shouting at him because he was in the lane in front, and so he'd extended his digit at me for about five minutes. But then, when he saw my cell phone, he felt embarrassed and just dropped right back!

I remained calm through the whole event and went through the other side, but I could have gotten offended; people get offended. Do you know that there are people who come to offend you? Family members come to offend you on a regular basis, especially at Christmastime!

What's offended you lately? Has somebody extended the "finger of greeting" toward you? What's offended you?

You might think that these natural offenses have got nothing to do with the spiritual, but some people get so offended in the natural that when it comes to the spirit, they can't even get off first base. If you get offended in the natural all the time, then you're going to get offended in the spirit. Because God, many times, provokes the mind to reveal what's in the heart.

Just stick around and you'll get an opportunity to get offended. Some people get offended because I walk around when I preach. "I wish he would stay back up on the platform where he belongs. Why does he keep walking around?"

In campmeetings, someone will say, "Pastor, it's the 7:00 p.m. service. We have a whole week of campmeeting services. Can't we wait till Wednesday night to go longer?

NO! God wants to touch you *now*! He wants to fill you *now*! He wants to bless you *now*! Not tomorrow, not next week, not next month, *now*! DIP! The Bible says, "There is a river, the streams whereof shall make glad the city of God" (Psalm 46:4). And that water is flowing right now. Don't wait, dip! You can dip right now as you're reading this.

Push past your offense; push past the thing that offends you.

OVERCOMING OFFENSE BRINGS FREEDOM

> IF YOU CAN OVERCOME WHAT'S OFFENDED YOU, THEN YOU WILL COME INTO GREATER FULLNESS OF THE THINGS OF GOD MORE THAN EVER BEFORE.

Every move of God has a rock of offense to it. Naaman made a wise decision and was made clean, and you have to make a decision. Maybe what you need to do is sit down and write down the things that have offended you recently, and realize that *they* are your obstacle. And if you can overcome what's offended you, then you will come into greater fullness of the things of God more than ever before.

If you don't, then you'll face the same offense year after year, and you will still be offended. So, it's time to deal with those things! The River of Offense is the River of Deliverance, and if you can come through that doorway, you'll be made clean; you'll be made whole; you'll be set free. The chains will be broken and the yokes will be destroyed (Isaiah 10:27).

And if personally, I have done anything to offend any of you, I want to ask you to forgive me, because it really wasn't intended. Sometimes people take things personally. I don't want to be the problem that's standing in the way of your breakthrough, but I want you to know I'm not your problem! I'm just here to point the way, and if you can ever get over the thing that offends, you will come right over to the place of breakthrough. But if you think offense is not going to come, you are deluded because offense will come! There is always a stumbling block of offense on the way to your blessing.

Naaman could have left and gone back to Syria and died of leprosy, but he did not. Thank God for his servants who persuaded him. "What do you have to lose? He said to dip seven times. Wouldn't you rather just dip and be clean?"

Wouldn't *you* rather just dip and be clean? Some of you have only dipped once, some of you have only dipped twice, some of you have only dipped three times, but he said, "Seven times." The River of Offense is the River of Deliverance! Is there anyone who wants to join the "Seven-Dip Association?"

There are going to be times when you feel like saying, "Do I have to? Do I have to go dip again? Do I have to?" Are you willing to let go of your offenses right now? Let's get rid of them! If somebody has offended you, I want you to forgive them right now. Because that offense is stopping you from walking into the fullness of the things of God. Naaman was a great man, but he was a leper. His offense could have kept him in leprosy. But because he humbled himself and he dipped seven times, he went away clean. Today, there is cleansing.

Just lift your hands to Heaven and say this out loud:

> Father, I forgive everyone who has ever offended me. Maybe because of something I was expecting from them—undue expectation, but I release them now. I owe no man anything other than to love them [Romans 13:8]. They owe me nothing, and I look unto You. I remove the offense. I forgive them and I release them now. And Lord, whatever You want to do, no matter how ridiculous I may look, You can do whatever You want to do. I'm not going to dictate to You how to deliver me. If You want to send a donkey my way, I'm totally open to whatever You want to do. I humble myself now because I realize that the River of Offense is the River of Deliverance. I'm not going to try to get it some other way. I don't want it some other, dignified way. I want it Your way or not at all. So come even now. Come by Your might; come by Your fire; come and do a work in me—a transforming work. Then I'll be able to say, "I'll never be the same again."

Now thank Him and praise Him. Thank the Lord Jesus, seven times. Seven times—not just once, but seven times. Determine to walk free of offense. It's coming to that place of surrender.

2

MOVING WITH THE CLOUD OF GOD

Following the Leadings and Promptings of the Holy Ghost

Father, we thank You for Your sweet presence. We thank You for utterance in the Holy Ghost that we might speak forth Your Word. Thank You that Your Word is quick and powerful and sharper than any two-edged sword, piercing and dividing asunder the soul and spirit, and of the joints and the marrow. And Your Word is a discerner of the thoughts and the intents of the heart (Hebrews 4:12). And even as Your Word goes forth, Your eternal purpose and Your eternal plan shall be wrought. We give You all the glory and we give You all the praise. Let every man be brought low, but let Jesus Christ of Nazareth be lifted up and exalted. We praise You for it. We thank You for it in Jesus' Name. Amen.

Look at Exodus 13:21–22:

And the Lord went before them by day in a pillar of a cloud, to lead them the way; and by night in a pillar of fire, to give them light; to go by day and night: he took not away the pillar of the cloud by day, nor the pillar of fire by night, from before the people.

Now, something that's very interesting here is that God was leading His people out of the land of bondage, and He uses what we could really term as a sign and a wonder. He used a pillar of cloud by day and a pillar of fire by night.

Remember: they were coming through the desert place, coming through the wilderness, and so the pillar of cloud would act like air conditioning in the desert. The pillar of fire by night, would firstly protect them. If you were an enemy of the children of Israel, the last thing you would want to do would be to come into proximity of the fire by night. Secondly, the fire would also warm them in the cold of the desert night, for as hot as a desert gets in the day, is as cold as it gets in the night! The cloud was a type of the Holy Spirit.

God was leading His people out of the land of Egypt into the Promised Land, and they knew that as long as they followed the cloud, they were fine. They knew that as long as they were with the cloud, God was with them and He was leading them and guiding them.

Exodus 40:34–38 says:

> Then a cloud covered the tent of the congregation, and the glory of the Lord filled the tabernacle. And Moses was not able to enter into the tent of the congregation, because the cloud abode thereon, and the glory of the Lord filled the tabernacle. And when the cloud was taken up from over the tabernacle, the children of Israel went onward in all their journeys: but if the cloud were not taken up, then they journeyed not till the day that it was taken up. For the cloud of the Lord was upon the tabernacle by day, and fire was on it by night, in the sight of all the house of Israel, throughout all their journeys.

If the cloud was taken up, then they journeyed. If the cloud stayed, then they stayed. This chapter is a message that I believe we should always keep very close and dear to our heart, "Moving With the Cloud of God."

THE CLOUD IS ON THE INSIDE OF YOU

The cloud was a type of the Holy Spirit. Now I want you to know that God does not lead His people under the New Covenant by an external cloud! You do not come to our meetings because you followed a cloud all the way down the highway. The only cloud you might have followed was somebody's motorcar that needed some desperate work and was puffing smoke. God doesn't operate that way under the New Covenant.

I'm not saying that there cannot be manifestations of the glory cloud. In fact, there have been times when people have seen the glory of God. Until recently, I hadn't seen it; I just walked by faith. But I can tell you that I have often felt it, and I've gotten lost in it. But on March 17, 2020, I had an open vision where the fire of God and the glory of God came into my bedroom, and it has profoundly touched me. I have not been the same since. But, I don't have to see and I'm not going around looking for something. I think you can get yourself into trouble that way! The Bible says, "Blessed are those who have not seen and yet have believed" (John 20:29 NKJV).

But the way that God leads you under the New Covenant is through the glory of God on the *inside* of you. We still have to follow the cloud, but it's the Cloud *within*. Romans 8:14 says, "For as many as are led by the Spirit of God, they are the sons of God." When the cloud moved, the people had to move. The biggest problem with people that we have to deal with is that they don't want to change!

God has to send a move, a revival, to shake them up and wake them up, and bring about a change. And it's uncomfortable, because in the early days of the shake-up and the wake-up, there's so much turmoil, conflict, and persecution that people long for the day when they can become accepted once again.

YOU HAVE TO MOVE WITH THE CLOUD

> WE CANNOT GET COMPLACENT, BECAUSE IF WE GET COMPLACENT, WE COME TO THE PLACE WHERE WE FEEL THAT WE'VE ARRIVED.

With every move of God there is a lifespan of that move. People come into it and they're running with God, and then they back off because of persecution and what others say. Part of this is because they want to become accepted, and that's the reason they back off. And then when the Cloud of God moves on, they stay behind!

I am convinced that out of approximately 2.5 million children of Israel, there were some that didn't feel like moving the day the cloud lifted and moved on. They probably said, "Man, we just moved. We moved last month. I'm not moving again." But I guarantee you that if they did lag behind, when that cloud lifted and started moving off into the distance, and the heat began to overtake them, they would have suddenly realized that their only protection was in the Cloud of God!

That's when they packed up their tent and they made a beeline for the cloud. Because in the Cloud of God is everything that you and I need. As long as we follow the Holy Ghost, as long as we follow the Cloud, the glory of God, we're going to be fine.

But people don't like to change, and then they end up in a rut—and a rut is a grave with the ends kicked out. In other words, they go through the motions; they do the same thing that they've always done.

Go back and study the revivals of the past. Why were people called "Quakers"? Because they quaked! But what happens when you don't quake because of the power of God? Then you just quake because that's what you used to do in church before, so you think you'd better do it now. You shake, quake, and bake, but there's nothing of God there. And that is called religion, and that is called tradition! We've got to follow the stirrings and the promptings of the Holy Ghost. We have got to follow the Cloud of God.

You cannot get complacent, because if you get complacent, you come to the place where you feel that you've arrived. Then, when that Cloud moves on, you are left high and dry and you wonder what happened! Because the thing that *brought* you into the move of God is the same thing that's going to *keep* you in the move of God. If you lose what brought you in, you'll find yourself on the outside and wondering,

What in the world happened? And someone will say, "God moved." Yes, God moved, and you did not move with Him.

YOU HAVE TO YIELD TO THE CLOUD

IF WE WANT TO SEE GOD MOVE AND WE WANT TO STAY IN THE MOVE OF GOD, THEN WE NEED TO COME WITH ANTICIPATION AND HUNGER EVERY TIME WE COME TO CHURCH. WE NEED TO COME READY, HUNGRY, AND THIRSTY FOR GOD TO MOVE AND DO WHATEVER HE WANTS TO DO.

You've got to be pliable. You have to be yielded, and you've got to be willing to submit to the Holy Ghost and do whatever He wants you to do, whenever He wants you to do it, and however He wants you to do it. Just follow Him, and don't try to put Him in a box.

That's why there are churches today that once had a move of God, but if you go there now with a spiritual magnifying glass, you wouldn't be able to find one little drop of it. There wouldn't even be a smattering of it. We went to places and had revivals; some of them lasted up to six weeks. Somebody says, "Well, why didn't you go on longer?" Because I knew when to quit! Some people just don't know when to quit, and they go on and on, and what was a revival then became a mess! But when I went back to those churches a year, two years, three years later, you couldn't even tell that we had ever been there!

But there are also places that I can still go back to today, that when we walk in the door, it's just like it was ten, twelve, fourteen years ago. Exactly the same and I just plug right back into high gear because they know how to move with the glory of God, and they know how to plug in to Heaven.

The problem with Sunday morning "Churchianity" in America is some people just want to come and just sit on their "blessed assurance," and they don't want to move with the Holy Ghost. They want to get in and out as quickly as possible. So even if God wanted to move, He couldn't move! The Spirit of God is restrained from moving in many places. It's like bathing with your socks on!

People don't come with the hunger and the anticipation that they used to, and if they do, they're waiting for some conference or some campmeeting to come with hunger and anticipation. But they don't come with that hunger and they don't show up with anticipation every time the doors of the church open. If we want to see God move and we want to stay in the move of God, then we need to come with anticipation and hunger *every* time we come to church. We need to come ready, hungry, and thirsty for God to move and do whatever He wants to do.

If people don't want to change, God is not going to sit by waiting for them. He's going to move on. But the best place to be is in the glory. The best place to be is in the Cloud of God, because in the Cloud is everything you need. In the Cloud is salvation, healing, deliverance, preservation, provision, all of His goodness, all of His blessings.

THE BEST PLACE TO BE IS IN THE CLOUD OF GOD, BECAUSE IN THE CLOUD IS EVERYTHING YOU NEED. IN THE CLOUD IS SALVATION, HEALING, DELIVERANCE, PRESERVATION, PROVISION, ALL OF HIS GOODNESS, ALL OF HIS BLESSINGS.

THERE IS REFRESHING IN THE CLOUD

There are times of refreshing in the Cloud, but Acts 3:19 starts with the need to repent and be converted, and that's part of the problem in the Church today. People are not repenting, and they're not being converted. Even preachers! There's a lot of unconverted preachers in the Church today. Acts 3:19 goes on to say, "when the times of refreshing shall come from the presence of the Lord." If you are dry and thirsty, you obviously have not been hanging around the Cloud. If you are parched, thirsty, dried, gnarly looking, sad, depressed, oppressed, plain pressed, it's because you have not been hanging around the Cloud.

THE CLOUD IS ALWAYS MOVING

The Cloud of God is moving. It's always moving. And we as the Body of Christ, His people, have to be sensitive. We have got to know when to move; we have got to do what He tells us to do, and we have got to obey instantly.

In the glory, in the Cloud, is everything you need. Outside of the Cloud is everything you don't need—religion, tradition, compromise—all of these things will stop the move of God. If somebody dies and their heart stops, and they fall to the ground, the first thing you do is call 911. The paramedics come and take the defibrillator out. They come over to the person; they rip open their shirt. They crank up the defibrillator which operates on high voltage, and then they tell the living to stand clear (because if the living don't stand clear, the living are going to be more living than they were before!). Then they use the defibrillator, to defibrillate the heart and get the thing beating again. They do not come with a 9-volt battery. You can't have a "9-volt" revival. You can't have an AAA revival.

A lot of people are not following the Holy Ghost, they are not following the Cloud. Instead, they are following each other. People are preaching each other's sermons, prophesying each other's prophecies, but I don't get my messages from television, I get mine from Heaven! People are running here, running there, running everywhere, trying to find out what God is doing. But what happened to the Cloud within you? What happened to the glory on the inside of you?

Jesus said, My sheep know my voice . . . The voice of a stranger will they not follow (John 10:27, 5 paraphrased). If you hear His voice, obey His voice, and follow Him, then He will lead and guide you by His Spirit. And there will never be a day, there will never be a week, there will never be a month, there will never be a year that you are not on the cutting edge of what God is doing, because you will always be constantly adapting and changing.

> THE CLOUD OF GOD IS MOVING. IT'S ALWAYS MOVING. AND WE, AS THE BODY OF CHRIST, HIS PEOPLE, HAVE TO BE SENSITIVE. WE HAVE GOT TO KNOW WHEN TO MOVE; WE HAVE GOT TO DO WHAT HE TELLS US TO DO, AND WE HAVE GOT TO OBEY INSTANTLY.

THERE IS REST IN THE CLOUD

Sometimes people think that all God is doing is charging flat out ahead. I've got news for you: sometimes Jesus says, "Come ye yourselves apart . . . and rest a while" (Mark 6:31). God will take you through times and seasons. You have to follow the Cloud of God; you have to obey the Holy Ghost; you have got to do what God tells you to do.

You can't run by popular opinion. You can't run by what somebody else thinks that you should be doing. If I listened to everybody's opinion on what I should be doing, I'd be confused—I'd be schizophrenic!

You have got to follow the promptings and the leadings of the Spirit of God, because He knows what He has planned for your life. And what He plans for one is different from what He plans for another.

In the times and the seasons of God, as you follow His plan and His purpose, and you follow the Cloud of God, He will lead you and guide you by His Spirit. You'll find yourself in that place of refreshing, and you'll find yourself in the place of rest, and the place of blessing. There will be provision, there will be direction, and there will be "This is the way, walk ye in it" (Isaiah 30:21). There shall be a boldness that will come to you, for you will know that this is what Heaven is telling you to do. And you won't walk around looking like a Canadian goose lost in a thunderstorm.

I've seen many people walking around like that. They don't even know which side is up, because they don't want to follow the Cloud. They don't want to move with the Cloud, and they are always running around, "I wonder what God's doing. What's God doing? What's He saying?" But God is doing the same thing as He's always done! He's saying the same thing as He's always said! He still saves, heals, sets free, and delivers. As long as there are people who need saving, we need to get them saved. As long as there are people who need healing, we need to get them healed. As long as there are people who need to be delivered, we need to get them delivered.

I think that part of the problem is that people have stopped following the Cloud and now they want to do scientific experiments on the Cloud. That's too complicated for me. I don't know about you, but when that Cloud starts moving, I'm just going to move. Glory to God!

EACH GENERATION MUST CONTEND FOR THE SUPERNATURAL

THE ANOINTING CANNOT BE TAUGHT, IT HAS TO BE CAUGHT.

Just because a place has revival today, doesn't mean it's going to have revival tomorrow. Just because a place had revival ten years ago doesn't mean it's going to have revival ten years from now.

John G. Lake went to southern Africa and pioneered 550 churches in five years. Do you know what it takes to pioneer 550 churches in five years? It takes a move of God! But if you went back to that denomination, in some places you'd find smatterings of what John G. Lake had, but in other places, you would think you were in the Dutch Reformed Church—because they wouldn't change and move on and follow the glory of God.

That's why in many cases, when the death of a leader comes, then also the end of the move comes, because there was nobody there to catch it. The move of God is not just passed down by name; the move of God has to be caught. The anointing can't be taught, it has to be caught. You have got to grab ahold of it for yourself, so that even if the person who was leading that move (or whatever God was doing through them) is gone, you are still plugged right in. Because you've been trained how to follow the Holy Ghost, how to flow in the Holy Ghost, and you won't back down for anything.

I was shocked back in 1990 at what I saw one time when I was preaching up in the city of Chicago, Illinois. I had heard about Zion City, Illinois, which John Alexander Dowie had built at the turn of the previous century, and what he called the Christian Catholic Church. Even though Dr. Dowie did not even operate in the baptism of the Holy Spirit as far as speaking in other tongues was concerned, God had given him great miracles. In fact, when the revival broke out on Azusa Street and people came to Zion City, they ran them off because they didn't want them talking in tongues around there. But Dowie had a manifestation in the gifts of healings that was unlike anything seen at that time in America, and he was arrested over a hundred times for, "practicing medicine without a license."

The walls of the tabernacle were lined with crutches, wheelchairs, neck braces, and back braces. God moved so awesomely in Zion City, Illinois, that it was a city that was devoid of any vice. Christians came from all over and were living there, and although everybody thinks that's the ultimate, it's not God's plan. If all the Christians in America lived in one city, that would be terrible, because we are called to be the light of the earth, the salt of the earth (Matthew 5:13–16).

If the whole of Tampa became a Christian city, then we should leave Tampa and go to the cities that are not Christian and keep witnessing until every city sees the light. God's plan for us is not to live in a city that's just all Christian. He hasn't put you to be hiding under some bush somewhere. He's called you to be a city on a hill, a light in the dark place (Matthew 5:14).

I had studied the move of God in the so-called Christian Catholic Church, Zion City, Illinois (it had nothing to do with the Roman Catholic Church, but "Catholic" meaning "Universal"), so I decided, whilst I was in the Chicago area, to drive up there and go and have a look around. Not because I thought maybe I would pick up some "spiritual thing" there, or get some kind of "impartation" standing around Dowie's grave, but I just wanted to see it.

I walked around the grounds and I could see evidence of the

influence of the time. As I was walking around, some staff told the leading overseer at that time that I was on the property. The revival had broken out in April 1989, and in 1990, I still wasn't widely known in America. Although we were conducting a revival in Chicago at that time, the overseer didn't know who I was. Today, he probably would send me away!

But the overseer met with me and we walked around, and I talked about Dr. Dowie. Then he brought me back and said, "Come have a look at the boardroom." On the walls of the boardroom were the pictures of the general overseers of the Christian Catholic Church. I went all the way back to 1900, and I looked and there was John Alexander Dowie.

You could see the little brass plaque right under his name, and it had the time period that he served as general overseer, and then it had the next man and the next man. As I was standing there, I was riveted. I thought to myself, *I wonder how much of what Dowie had in the Spirit was passed on to the next man, and how much of what that man had was passed on to the next man, and so on, all the way down to the current overseer standing right by me.* I said, "Sir, do you people pray for the sick here?" And he said, "We don't have the gift of healing like Dr. Dowie had, but we do have a little anointing-oil service once a month." I was shocked. I walked off that place, and I thought to myself, *How terrible is that? That God would send such a move at the turn of the century, and here we are, ninety years later, and they don't even pray for the sick except for once a month, and then somebody just dabs a little bit of oil on somebody's forehead!*

As I was leaving, I thought, *How great can a move of God be, and yet how far can people get from that move!* And the Lord spoke to me and He said, "Son, if I tarry another one hundred years from today, there will be many institutions that I once touched, that I breathed upon, that had My glory, that saw My anointing, but they will move so far away because they won't follow the Cloud. And they will be just as dead as this place." Each generation has to contend for the supernatural. Each generation has to be hungry and thirsty after the deeper things of God.

But what was so amazing when I looked at Zion City, Illinois, was that out of there, came Gordon Lindsay's mother and father, came F. F. Bosworth, Raymond T. Richey, and Lilian B. Yeomans and John G. Lake was influenced by what happened there. The early roots of the Pentecostal movement throughout the early part of the nineteenth century were all birthed in the fire of what came out of that. And it's the same fire today, it's the same Holy Ghost today.

NO COMPROMISING

> WE CAN'T BACK OFF THE MOVE OF GOD TO BECOME ACCEPTABLE.

We cannot compromise to fit into anybody's frame. We have to stay with the Holy Ghost, we have to move with the Holy Ghost. We've got to move with the Cloud and we have got to do what God tells us to do.

I know some people would like to say that Pentecostalism or being a Pentecostal is being part of a denomination, but I have got news for you: Pentecostalism or being a Pentecostal is not a denomination, but an experience. It is based on Acts 2, and the mighty rushing wind and the cloven tongues of fire, and we cannot back down off that.

There are also churches that I have seen where there was once a mighty move of God, and today, you couldn't even find a drop of it. I'm not telling you that every service you have to be swinging from the light bulb. I'm not telling you that every service you have to be jumping the pew, running around the building, doing somersaults and cartwheels, but you know that if you put your foot to the floorboard on the accelerator and nothing happens, then the thing is dead.

It's like driving a very high-powered motorcar. You don't go flying through a school zone at 120 miles per hour; you slow down. But if you ever need the power on the highway, it's there. That's one thing I appreciate about being at The River, because if we ever put our pedal to the metal, it is "Off we go," without any fear whatsoever!

Now there are some things that I have to do as a pastor because I have to feed people the Word of God and different subjects, but whenever you just plug in and you put your foot flat on the floorboard, then that thing is going to roar to life and you had better watch out, because we're flying down the highway.

Like a mighty rushing wind. We can't back off the move of God to become acceptable. So, I'm not even going to try. I'm called to preach, proclaim, and demonstrate. Preach, proclaim, and demonstrate!

NO APOLOGIZING FOR FOLLOWING THE CLOUD

GOD IS RAISING UP PEOPLE WHO ARE TOTALLY UNASHAMED AT WHAT HE'S CALLED THEM TO DO, AND THEY ARE NOT GOING TO BE MAKING APOLOGIES.

You might not even realize it, but that's what you are called to do—to preach, teach, proclaim, and demonstrate the power of the Holy Ghost to a lost and dying world. There's a whole generation of people who have never seen the power of God in operation, and if you don't demonstrate it, they won't even know that it's available. God is raising up people who are totally unashamed at what He's called them to do, and they are not going to make apologies.

How can we preach the gifts of the Spirit and then apologize for the gifts of the Spirit? How can we preach a mighty rushing wind and then apologize for the mighty rushing wind? How can we preach about cloven tongues of fire and then apologize when the fire falls and want to bring out the extinguisher?

I didn't even believe this was possible, but there are large churches in America that have several auditoriums and if you like worship that's just low-key, you go to the main building. If you want worship where there is a kind of "island feel," you go to the other service in a different building. And if you want a rock-type of worship, you go to another one. You think I'm joking, but this is happening. Well, why don't we just open up a supermarket and call it Supermarket Church? Or, The Church at the Mall, where you can go in there and then just invite all the different denominations? Put a Catholic church at one end, stick an Anglican next, a Presbyterian next, run them all the way down to the Baptist, and put the Pentecostals at the extreme far side. People can come there and take their pick of whatever they want to do!

I even know of a church where they have three services on Sunday morning. The first service, the music is below 90 decibels. The second service is below 100 decibels, and the third service, they blow it out of the roof. You can imagine who shows up at the first service—Rigor Mortis and his brother!

I don't know how it's possible that you can have dead preachers preaching dead sermons to dead people, and they think it's great. That would be like standing in a giant cemetery, Sunday after Sunday, and preaching to the tombstones and you are not getting any response. The only thing that's happening in the graveyard is the ivy and the weeds growing, and maybe somebody coming during the week and sticking a bowl of flowers down by the one tomb, but that's all. And then, all you really are is a caretaker of a huge cemetery.

STICK WITH THE CLOUD

> YOU WEREN'T CALLED TO BE PART OF THE STATUS QUO–YOU WERE CALLED TO COME AND TURN THE PLACE INSIDE OUT AND UPSIDE DOWN!

But Jesus said, "I am come that you might have life, and that you might have it MORE ABUNDANTLY" (John 10:10, paraphrased). I'm not here attacking denominations, but if you have been introduced to the Holy Ghost of the Book of Acts, then you had better stick with Him. And you had better follow the Cloud, and move with the Cloud, and stop raising your finger to try to check which way the wind is blowing.

You were never called to be part of the "Lukewarms," you were called to be part of the people on fire, full of the Holy Ghost. You weren't called to be part of the status quo—you were called to come and turn the place inside out and upside down!

You can just sit there and observe the fire of God falling, or you can enter in. The choice is yours. It's all based on your hunger and thirst. When God is moving, you have just got to jump in. You cannot sit and dissect it. You can't sit there and try to run it under a spiritual microscope. You have got to jump in.

THE NATURAL POINTS TO WHAT'S COMING IN THE SUPERNATURAL

Every time there's an upheaval in the natural, it represents what God is about to do in the spirit. The devil can't pinpoint it; he doesn't really know directly what's about to happen. He's doing everything he can, but he cannot stop what God's about to do in the earth. All God wants us to do is be sensitive to follow His promptings and His leadings and to trust Him.

We had a revival in Rockwall, Texas. The power of God hit that church and moved it across a lake. We had a revival in Fort Worth, Texas. Two tornadoes hit the place and moved the church four miles down the road. You never know what God is going to do. You never know what the Holy Ghost is going to do. But when He moves you, things are going to look different. It's not going to be "business as usual." It's not going to be the "same old, same old." When He moves, it's not going to be, "Snore, snore, yawn, yawn. How boring this is?"

In the natural, we've had a number of hurricanes over the state of Florida, and a giant tsunami that swept in the Indian Ocean. I know it looks like terrible things in the natural, but it's all just pointing to what's coming in the supernatural, because there's a move of God that will shake Florida. There's a move of God that will shake Asia.

The year 1906 saw the outbreak of Azusa Street, but also saw the great earthquake in San Francisco.

TRUST THE HOLY GHOST

But then there are times when the Lord will pull you aside and say, "Come here; let Me teach you. Come here; let Me show you something. Come here; just let Me pull you aside here. Let Me do a work in you." Every space shuttle that blasts out into space comes back, and then they do work on it and they add new equipment, and they repair certain tiles. Have you have had some of your tiles burned up? As you've come into reentry, have you had some of your tiles burned up? Well, God will just pull you aside and fix some of your tiles and put some new equipment in and get you ready for the next blast-off session!

There is nothing wrong with that. We know historically that a shuttle blew up over America because something was not repaired when it came in. They didn't repair it and a piece of tile came off and hit something on the tail piece which caused the problem on reentry. You have to allow the Spirit of God to pull you aside and do a work in you, and a repair, so that you can take the heat. Acts 3:19 says, ". . . that times of refreshing (of recovering from the effects of heat, of reviving with fresh air) may come from the presence of the Lord" (AMPC). Like a reviving with fresh air.

Somebody says, "No! I'm blasting off now. No! I'm leaving now!" You can't do that. Just chill; just follow the Cloud; follow the Holy Ghost otherwise you'll blow up and miss out on what God has for your life! That's why you have to trust the Holy Ghost. You have to trust Him. You have got to move with the Cloud.

I don't believe that you are reading this by accident. I believe you are reading this by divine appointment. I believe the Lord Himself has ordained that you read this and that God is doing a work in you. You might not even realize it right now, but it is going to show.

Sometimes what God does is routine. Sometimes the replacing of those tiles is routine. You say, "Well, I've done this before. I don't need that again." But if a space shuttle could talk, and it complained every time it went into the hangar for work to be done on it, it would become useless. It just has to be, and allow itself to be, shifted into place to be fixed up, then wheeled back out, taken right out to the launching pad, and blasted off on the next mission. And you have to be just like that. You have to yield yourself to the Spirit of God and allow God to do a work on the inside of you.

THERE IS NO LACK IN THE CLOUD

> THE POWER OF GOD REMAINS AT A CONSTANT; YOU AND I ARE THE ONES THAT FLUCTUATE.

I nearly allowed the burden of reaching the lost in the nations to kill me. But the harvest is not my problem, it is *His* problem. If He wants me to do it, I'll do anything He wants me to do. I'll go anywhere He wants me to go. He just has to say it, He just has to fund it, and He just has to make a way. If I'm funding it and making a way, then I'm not moving with the Cloud. When you are in the glory of God, you don't have to do anything in your own strength. When you are in the glory of God, you just lean on the Holy Spirit, because He's going to bring it to pass. When the children of Israel followed the pillar of cloud by day and the fire by night, He went before them, He made the crooked paths straight, and He's still the same now as He was with them (Isaiah 45:2).

He said to Joshua, "As I was with Moses, so I will be with you" (Joshua 1:5 AMPC), and then He says that to you and me today. He's still about us as a wall of fire. He's still with us every step of the way. He said, "I'll never leave you nor forsake you" (Deuteronomy 31:6).

We're getting ready! Sometimes I have to revert to tongues because I cannot put into the English language what I see that is about to happen. It's like the prophet of old said: "It's like fire shut up in my bones" (Jeremiah 20:9, paraphrased). This is it!

You are coming in with all guns blazing. You are coming in with all Heaven right behind you. You are coming in with the heavenly host. You are coming in with all the equipment to get the job done. When

He moves you, when He moves that mighty Cloud, that mighty glory of God, it's everything that you and I need. Nothing shall be lacking!

Get ready, get ready, get ready! The power of God does not fluctuate; it does not go up and down. It is at a constant. It's people that go up and down. There's never been a fluctuation in the power of God. Heaven's lights have never flickered one time during all of the crises on the earth. The power of God remains at a constant; you and I are the ones that fluctuate.

IT IS DEEP CALLING UNTO DEEP

You have to make a decision that you will move with the Cloud of God. You have a choice to make: you can either become acceptable to man, or you can be acceptable to God.

Somebody might say, "Brother Rodney, what happens if people think I'm crazy?" Well, that's a foregone conclusion, but they are going to have to put you in there with the likes of the Apostle Paul. They are going have to stick you in there with the likes of Peter, James, and John.

I'm not talking Old Testament things here, I'm talking New Testament. I'm talking Book of Acts. These are not the "Days of Elijah," as some people sing. No! No! No! Elijah would have given anything to have lived in this day and this hour. These are the days of the Holy Ghost! These are the days of the glory of God. Elijah, eat your heart out! These are the days of the wind of Heaven! These are the days of the mighty rushing wind! These are the days of the fire of the Holy Ghost!

The prophets of old couldn't even explain it. They didn't even know how to describe it, and I guess they just saw it like some kind of a wheel within a wheel (Ezekiel 1:16), but when that wheel starts turning . . . it's deep calling unto deep (Psalm 42:7).

And if the prophets of old couldn't even explain it, then who do you think you are, Mr. Theologian, to take your tongue and try to deal with it? There are not even words in the English language to describe the glory of that which is about to take place. This is it! The culmination of all that was prophesied.

I don't laugh with earthly amusement at this; I have a bubble of joy from within. It has got nothing to do with an amusement of your mind. It has got to do with an overflowing of the heart.

The foolish world around me, sage,
Thinks I'm drunk or mad with rage,
Drunk, doubtless yes, I'm drunken odd,
But drunken with the wine of God.

(1856 WELSH REVIVAL HYMN)

In 2 Corinthians 5:13, the apostle Paul said, "For if we are beside ourselves [mad, as some say], it is for God and concerns Him; if we are in our right mind, it is for your benefit" (AMPC).

JUST BE OBEDIENT

I know when we went to Madison Square Garden, New York, some people thought that we were moving away from our call. But how were we moving away from our call when God spoke to me in a dream to go to New York City, and then launch one of the biggest soul-winning crusades since the '50s? No! we didn't go away from our call. We followed the Cloud of God! We did what Heaven said to do, and the glory of God was mightily displayed there. There were 48,459 decisions in the city of New York!

When God told us to go to Soweto and go for the harvest, we just obeyed the Holy Ghost. Do you just sense the stirring of the Holy Ghost on the inside of you as you are reading this? It is not going to stop; there will be an increase so that God can do the work in you that He wants to, so that you can run over the next months with all the equipment you need. You might not realize it; you might be just sitting there right now thinking that nothing's happening, but I've got news for you: don't underestimate the work of the Spirit of God. There are things coming together in your spirit right now, things that God is stirring up in your spirit. It's in the divine atmosphere of Heaven that God will speak to you and give you direction for the coming months. Some of you have a big question, but you're going to get an answer. Allow God to do what He needs to do on the inside of you.

IN THE CLOUD IS PREPARATION FOR WHAT IS TO COME

> IF YOU GO WHERE THERE'S NO PERSECUTION, YOU ARE GOING TO END UP WHERE THERE IS NO ANOINTING. THE ANOINTING IS IN THE FIRE OF PERSECUTION.

I don't care who you are or where you are from, if you don't stay following the Cloud, the day will come when you will be high and dry, up the creek with no oar, sitting on the bank, stuck in the mud of religion and tradition, talking about the "good old days" of "I remember when . . ." We can look back over the years and reflect on what God is doing, but I can say with all honesty, that I wouldn't swap this very moment for any other moment in history. This is what we've been waiting for.

We have come through all of what we have come through, to get ready for what we are about to get ready for, and for what we are about to see the manifestation of. We couldn't have handled it fifteen years ago, twelve years ago, ten years ago, but God has been doing the work in us, and we have come right to that place. This is it. This is it! God hasn't quit moving.

You have to make the decision "I am staying with the Cloud. I'm moving with the Cloud. No matter what the cost, no matter what people may say, I'll not back down. I'm not going to compromise to become acceptable." Praise God! As you are reading, the Lord is speaking to several ministries that were contemplating backing off the things of the Spirit because of the persecution that they have been receiving. Sometimes that pressure is not just from the people in the congregation. Sometimes that pressure comes from other preachers.

Somebody says, "I'll have my ministry rebranded." You can't do that. You've already been on the Potter's wheel too long; you are not the one who fashions it. He's the One who fashions it. You can't take the line of least resistance. You can't back off to become acceptable to man. This is not a game. This is a matter of life and death, between the breakthrough and the future, and the continuance of your ministry to what God's really called you to do. Because if you go where there's no persecution, you are going to end up where there is no anointing. The anointing is in the fire of persecution.

The Church was not promised an easy road. The apostles were beaten with stones and imprisoned. The modern-day Church knows very little, if anything, about this, especially in America. The modern-day Church judges the anointing that they have by what houses they live in and what cars they drive. The apostles judged it by how many times they were imprisoned and beaten.

Some people think the anointing of God on their life is a license to do whatever they want. I've got news for you: if God didn't plan it for you, you don't want it. If God didn't ordain it, you don't want it.

I declare that from this moment, a fresh wind blows in your life and in your ministry. Just keep telling the story of the glory. Some started off telling the story of the glory, but now they have become nothing more than the *National Enquirer*. But keep telling the story; keep reporting miracles; keep reporting signs and wonders and what God is doing. That's what He's called you to do.

If they say that you are emotional, so what? You are! I'm emotional about Him. I've just seen Jesus; I tell you, He's alive! You're not going to turn me down. You're not going to quiet me down. I will not fashion my ministry to become acceptable to the sinners. What do they know anyway? And I'm sure not going to fashion it to become acceptable to the Church. In fact, I'm going to do only what the Holy Ghost says. If it tears up half of Florida and two-thirds of Oklahoma, then so be it.

I hear the Lord saying that there are ministries reading this that have felt, *Oh, God, have You forgotten me? It would seem like I've been on the back burner*. But the Lord would say, "No, I have not forgotten you. I have just been preparing you and getting you ready for what's about to happen. And you will no longer be on the back burner. But you'll be right on the front burner of what I'm about to do." For He has heard your cry. He's heard the cry of your heart as you've cried out to Him even in the night hour, and even on your bed, and even driving down the road in your car. And you've said, "God, I know that You prepared me for this day and for this hour, but it would seem like in some ways I have been sidelined." But the Lord would say to you, "No, I have just reserved you for this day and this hour, for it shall come to pass, even throughout the year, that there shall be an increase and there shall be launching in thy life and in thy ministry, and it shall just begin to escalate, and over the next twelve months, there shall be an increase in the anointing."

That's what I hear the Spirit of God saying. So don't feel for one moment that you've been sidelined or put on the back burner. Because God has just been getting you ready and preparing you for what is about to come, so that when it breaks forth in full measure, you will not fall by the wayside.

3

THE PURPOSE OF REVIVAL

Returning to Your First Love

If all the sleeping folk will wake up, if all the lukewarm people will fire up, if all the dishonest people will 'fess up, if all the disgruntled people will sweeten up, if all discouraged people will look up, if all the estranged folk will make up, if all the gossipers will shut up, if all the dry bones will shake up, if all the true soldiers will stand up, if all the non-tithers will pay up, and if all the church members will pray up, then we can have revival anywhere, anyplace, anytime! But one of the biggest questions that we could ask the Body of Christ is, "Does your church want a revival? Does it really?"

Revival is something that is so close to my heart, it burns in me. There is never really a waking moment that I'm not thinking about different aspects of revival and the move of God, in relationship to the Body of Christ. Not just here at home in America, but abroad in the foreign fields. What God has really called me to is to be a revivalist, to go into places and light fires. That's what I do.

SAME POWER, SAME HOLY GHOST

You deal with the same things, no matter what country you find yourself in, no matter what nationality they are. People think that somehow when you cross a national border, it is different there. They try to tell me, "Well, Brother Rodney, you have to understand; it is different here." But that's garbage! It's the same! They may drive on a different side of the road, speak with a different language, and have different kinds of food, but it is the same set of rules that have to be applied in every situation. Because if every place thinks that they are different, then they think that God has to come up with something unique. But the power of God is the same, the Holy Spirit is the same, and God doesn't change His rules. I don't care whether it's India, China, or Africa.

Now there are some places where it is a little harder to have revival and I would say the hardest place to have a move of God is right here in the United States! If you can have a move of God in America, you can have one pretty much anywhere on the planet.

REVIVAL BRINGS TIMES OF REFRESHING

> WHEN JESUS WALKS IN THE ROOM, IT'S NOT JUST LIKE MEETING AN ORDINARY INDIVIDUAL; YOU KNOW SOMETHING'S GOING TO TAKE PLACE!

Now I want to look at the purpose of revival, and I want to look at Pentecostal revival. Revival has a distinct purpose to it, just like taking a shower or having a bath has a purpose. And if you understand the purpose of the shower or the bath, then you'll understand the purpose of revival. I don't care who you are on this earth, how long you've lived, you are in constant need of a bath or shower. And likewise, we constantly need spiritual renewing, reviving, and refreshing.

I don't care how many degrees you have, I don't care how educated you are, you still need a shower. As clean as you might have been this morning, by tonight, you probably will need a shower. And the same principles that applied to you needing a bath or a shower this morning are also going to apply to you needing one tonight. Somebody says, "Well, I'm bored with that method." Well, come over here stinky; let's have a talk.

Look at Habakkuk 3 where the prophet is crying out. He says:

> O Lord, I have heard thy speech, and was afraid: O Lord, revive thy work in the midst of the years, in the midst of the years make known; in wrath remember mercy. God came from Teman, and the Holy One from mount Paran. Selah. His glory covered the heavens, and the earth was full of his praise. And his brightness was as the light; he had horns coming out of his hand: and there was the hiding of his power.
>
> HABAKKUK 3:2-4

Now, in the margin of my Bible, for "horns," it says, "Bright *beams* were coming out of His hands." When Jesus walks in the room, it's not just like meeting an ordinary individual; you know something's going to take place!

Now go with me to Acts 3:19, the first part of the verse talks about repentance: "So repent (change your mind and purpose); turn around and return [to God], that your sins may be erased (blotted out, wiped clean)," and then look at the second part: "that times of refreshing (of recovering from the effects of heat, of reviving with fresh air) may come from the presence of the Lord" (AMPC).

So revival brings times of refreshing. No matter how mature you are in the things of God, you are going to need to have a refreshing. How many of you in the heat of the day, look for something refreshing to drink? If you need that in the natural, then you need that in the spiritual. I don't know how people think they can get by without spiritual refreshing.

We are in a constant state of needing renewing, reviving, and refreshing from the presence of the Lord. I don't care who you are. People say, "Well, we've gone on from that. You know, we used to do that." But you can't go on from this, you can't go on from this! It's something you live by and you operate in. And the "times [plural] of refreshing" (Acts 3:19) come from the presence of the Lord.

We should never come to a meeting without expecting a refreshing. I'm going to get really personal, but if you go to a shower, the first thing you do is take your clothes off, because you expect water to come out of the shower. And in the spiritual realm, the first thing you have to do when you come before God is that you have to get rid of everything that you are carrying. Imagine if I arrived home in my suit and I walked in the shower with my suit and shoes on still, my wife would say, "What are you doing? Are you crazy?"

You have to get rid of the things that you are carrying, and you have to prepare. Why do you think that it's any different in the realm of the spirit? People are not seeing a continual refreshing, or a continual revival, because they haven't made preparation made for it. They think, *Well, I already had a 'shower.'* Yes, you might have had a shower yesterday, but it's time for another one today! We constantly need refreshing from the presence of the Lord.

REVIVAL BRINGS RELEASE

> SOMETHING HAS TO COME TO BRING ABOUT A RELEASE, AND IT'S ONLY THE REVIVING PRESENCE OF THE LORD THAT WILL COME AND GO WHERE THE KNIFE OF MAN CANNOT GO. IT WILL DO A DEEP WORK IN THE HEART OF MAN THAT NO ONE ELSE CAN DO, AND BRING A PURIFICATION AND A CLEANSING.

You have to be a contender for revival. Are you a contender? Your name has to be on the roster. You have to be the one crying out for yourself. Because if I'm revived, then when I walk into people's presence, I'm going to provoke them to get revived. You become that igniter. You become a self-starter that God uses to ignite revival. I don't go looking for revival—I'm not getting in a car and driving somewhere to look for revival. Revival is where I am. I have this habit of igniting it wherever

I am, because I'm putting together the necessary ingredients to have what it takes to have revival. I'm hungry and I'm thirsty *all the time.*

This has got nothing to do with what you know. Someone says, "I know all that. I know how it works. Well, you might know how the restroom works, but you still have to use it! No matter how advanced you get, you still have to use the restroom. When you are a baby, you have a primitive method of using a restroom; it's in the diaper stage. It's a kind of 'restroom-on-the-go.' But as you grow, you progress from that. But you are always going to need to use the restroom. Nobody has progressed to the place where they no longer make trips to the bathroom.

Someone says, "Come on, Brother Rodney. What has this got to do with revival?" It has *everything* to do with revival, because it's the same in the spiritual realm. Everyday, I have to make the choices in the natural to clean myself, brush my teeth, do my hair, and go to the restroom. Likewise, *every* day, *every* single day, when you wake up, you have to make the spiritual choice, "I am going to walk in the reviving power of God today." Revival is that integral part of your walk with God.

In the natural, you see some people who are smelly, their hair is all over the place, they haven't brushed their teeth, and they are really desperate to get to a restroom to clean up. In fact, if you travel to some parts of the world, like the city of Manila, Philippines, the traffic will jam up four, five, six, seven hours. And there are people on the streets selling little containers that you can use to go to the restroom in your car. Why? Because there's nowhere to park your car. You buy the container from the guy, and then you do what you have to do, sitting in the car.

There's nothing worse than being in a position where you really need to go and you can't go. And in the spiritual realm, I meet preachers like that all the time. They are in a desperate position to go, and they can't go anywhere. Why? Because there's no facility for them to go in. That's why they walk around and they are just plain "full of it!"

I know this is blunt, but you can't walk around with those continued attitudes, like *Somebody's done me wrong*. You need to flush it, buddy. You need to get rid of it. That's your problem, and you have to make the choice to either hang onto your stuff or get rid of it!

If the toilet's blocked, then we get a plunger. And I go to so many churches that have been blocked up for years. They are overflowing because of the blockages and stuff is running all over the place. So I go in to those churches to unblock them—it's a dirty job, it's a messy job, it's a smelly job, but somebody has to do it.

If you don't go to the bathroom regularly, then you end up being constipated. Constipation is not a good thing to live with over an extended period of time. There are people who have had extreme cases of constipation, and they have gotten seriously ill. I know some people are saying, "Oh Brother Rodney, what's this got to do with revival?" It's first the natural, then the spiritual. But you have to understand, that's why God sends revival—to stop the spiritual constipation. Because when all you are fed is spiritual junk food, you get constipated; you get blocked up.

When two-year-old children are constipated, there is nothing worse. They are always crying, whining, not happy, and they can't run and play like other kids. But when you apply medication to them, whatever needs to be done (normally in the form of a suppository), then the release comes! And a few hours later, they are running around and they are happy, and they are playing again like other kids.

And I watch believers running around irritated, cranky, sad, and depressed. Somebody says, "What's wrong with them?" They are blocked up, constipated. How do I spell relief? R-E-V-I-V-A-L! Revival will get rid of all the blockages. What's blocking *you* up? What is stopping *you*?

When someone is living in a state of revival, the storms come, situations come, but you always rebound. You always have a way of just coming through; you bounce back. But when revival is not there, it just compacts until you can't even function anymore.

There's nothing like a good "flushing" in the spiritual realm. You cannot walk around with that unforgiveness; you cannot walk around with that bitterness; you cannot walk around with that resentment; you cannot walk around with that critical attitude. You cannot walk around judging other people; you cannot walk around with that spiritual pride; you cannot walk around with that jealousy; you cannot walk around with that spirit of competitiveness. You CANNOT do these things and then expect to walk in the presence of God. The two do not go hand in hand.

Something has to come to bring about a release, and it's only the reviving presence of the Lord that will come and go where the knife of man cannot go. It will do a deep work in the heart of man that no one else can do, and bring a purification and a cleansing.

Just as you have to strip off everything to go in the shower, so, you have to stand "naked" when you come to the Lord. You have to strip off everything that you are carrying. In the natural we wear clothes to cover up, but when you stand before the Lord, you have to "strip off" everything spiritually. You cannot cover up anything and you cannot hide anything from Him.

It's about times of refreshing. Personally, I believe it's a daily washing—a daily cleansing, just keeping your heart right and keeping your heart pure. If something gets on you, then you get rid of it the moment it gets on you. Don't leave it for a week. Many people in the Body of Christ leave it for a week or a month, and then they walk around with it. No, you must *immediately* deal with it. Revival is dealing with the situation when it arises and getting rid of it so that it does not stay there as a continual hindrance in your walk with God.

NATIONAL REVIVAL

> GOD IS ALWAYS POURING OUT HIS SPIRIT, AND YOU HAVE TO DECIDE TO BE THERE, AND STAY THERE, REGARDLESS OF WHAT SOMEBODY ELSE IS DOING AND REGARDLESS OF WHAT THEIR ATTITUDE IS. YOU HAVE TO MAKE A DECISION: "IF IT'S POURED OUT, I'M UNDER IT."

Now that was relating to personal revival, and as far as national revival is concerned, it's still going to take somebody who is an instigator, someone who will stand in the gap on behalf of that nation. Second Chronicles 7:14 says, "If my people, which are called by my name, shall humble themselves, and pray, and seek my face, and turn from their wicked ways; then will I hear from heaven, and will forgive their sin, and will heal their land." A people that will rise up.

That's what happens when God comes and brings revival in the nation and begins to do a work in the land. Isaiah 59:19 says, "So shall they fear the name of the Lord from the west, and his glory from the rising of the sun. When the enemy shall come in like a flood, the Spirit of the Lord shall lift up a standard against him." I love that. You think God's not doing something, but He's raising up a standard. Because the Bible says, "Where sin abounded, grace did much more abound" (Romans 5:20). In Acts 2:17 it says, "And it shall come to pass in the last days, saith God, I will pour out of my Spirit." God's always pouring out His Spirit; it just depends on who's standing under the flow.

There are always fresh outpourings of the Spirit of God. When you make a decision, "I'm going to be under the shower," then when it turns on, you are going to get wet! Likewise, you have to make a decision, "I'm going to get under the spout, where the glory comes out." In the natural, there is not anybody in the world who can stop me from going to get clean. I will say, "Excuse me. I'll see you in a while. I'm taking some personal time right now. I need to go do some things."

Ladies often like walking to the restroom together but you never see a bunch of guys going to the restroom together. It's just not a guy kind of thing. The restroom is really a place that you need to go by yourself. And likewise, you have to make a decision for yourself that you are going to stay in God's presence. God is always pouring out His Spirit, and you have to decide to be there, and stay there, regardless of what somebody else is doing and regardless of what their attitude is. *You* have to make a decision: "If it's poured out, I'm under it."

You can position yourself. In Acts 2:17, the Lord said, "...upon all flesh: and your sons and your daughters shall prophesy, and your young men shall see visions, and your old men shall dream dreams." It's not only in a service, because many don't sleep in the service! We may have a couple of people drop off now and then, and they'll doze, but the dreaming of dreams normally takes place in the night hours, lying on your bed. Who could believe that the Spirit could be poured out as you lie on your bed?

But when you position yourself in that place, then you will dream dreams and you'll see visions. Acts 2:18–22:

> And on my servants and on my handmaidens I will pour out in those days of my Spirit; and they shall prophesy: And I will shew wonders in heaven above, and signs in the earth beneath; blood, and fire, and vapour of smoke: The sun shall be turned into darkness, and the moon into blood, before that great and notable day of the Lord come: and it shall come to pass, that whosoever shall call on the name of the Lord shall be saved. Ye men of Israel, hear these words; Jesus of Nazareth, a man approved of God among you by miracles and wonders and signs, which God did by him in the midst of you, as ye yourselves also know . . .

God's talking about an outpouring. He's talking about salvation taking place. He's talking about signs and wonders, and He's talking about prior to that "great and notable day of the Lord" coming. I believe that we are living in the last of the last days, this is the greatest hour of the Church!

And I'm not just in revival for myself. I have to constantly maintain revival for myself in my walk with God because I'm pressing in for cities, and I'm pressing in for nations. I'm pressing in to go and ignite fires and break whole nations open in revival—to go in there like a "Holy Ghost Green Beret." To light a fire in a nation so that when I leave, that fire will not go out, but will spread from one to another to another.

That's why we spent a lot of time in the nation of Finland. In 2004, the ministry did a ten-city tour across Finland. The fire is burning in

Finland and in places you wouldn't even believe. Will the enemy try to put it out? You'd better believe that he'll try to put it out. But that's why we have to keep stirring it up so that the fire will not go out. That's why we went to Norway. That's why we went to Sweden. That's why we went to Denmark. Great fires have been lit in the Scandinavian countries. That's why we went to Germany, and great fires have been lit in Germany. And that's why we are currently doing the 300-City Tour and going across Africa. I'd like to light fires everywhere, but you can't. You can only go where God sends you. That's why it's going to take more than one person to get the job done. Because all of us just have a portion of the ministry of Jesus. There's not any one person who's called to save the whole world.

I heard one preacher make the comment, "There's only three or four people in the world doing anything for God!" That's a lie! That preacher is deceived and is heading for a fall! There are more than three or four people in the world doing something for God. There are thousands of people in the world doing something for God. It's tens of thousands of people in the world doing something for God. They just might not be doing it all at the same magnitude as the next person, but that does not take away from the fact that they are doing something for God.

When I heard that, I said, "That person is going to fall." You can't put yourself up like you are the only person on the planet doing something for God! We each are just one of many. The prophet Elijah, when he was sitting under the juniper tree complained to God, "I'm the only one!" God said, "No, you're not. See, there are seven thousand others who have not bowed their knee to false gods." (1 Kings 19).

REVIVAL OUTSIDE THE WALLS OF THE CHURCH

> THIS NEXT WAVE OF GOD, THE REVIVAL WILL TAKE PLACE IN THE MARKETPLACE. THAT'S WHY SOME PEOPLE WON'T EVEN RECOGNIZE IT, BECAUSE THEY ARE NOT ABLE TO RELATE TO IT.

Do you think that He invests everything into one person? Do you think the Holy Ghost is asleep? No! The Holy Ghost is not asleep! He's very much awake, moving across the earth in an unlimited way. I've got news for you: God is not just moving in crusades. Some people think that if they are not having a crusade, then God is not moving. Did you know God is moving in the business workplace? This next revival wave of God will take place in the marketplace.

That's why some people won't even recognize it, because they are not able to relate to it. All they can relate to God moving is that it has to be in a meeting, with somebody up there on the platform with a song and a microphone. I'm so glad that God is not limited to a meeting with a song and a microphone. In fact, God's moving in many places, such as bars and nightclubs. Why? Because no Christian would go in there. But the Holy Ghost is in there, convicting and dealing with that person who is about to have another drink. They are about to shoot some more dope and snort some more cocaine, but the Holy Ghost is right in there, dealing with them, and He is not offended by where they are.

I remember years ago, when we were back in southern Africa, I was at the national conference for a certain denomination. There were probably about six thousand people there that morning, and I had to lay hands on them. So we took them outside and laid hands on them under the trees and on the grass. Some of the older ministers who had been in the ministry for thirty to fifty years, followed me as I was laying hands on people and said, "Oh, we can't believe this! God is moving outside under the trees. We thought He only moved at an altar!" I thought, *My, how limited their ministry is because they wouldn't believe that God would move outside.* That's the problem with a lot of people: they don't believe God would really move outside the walls of the Church. Some of the greatest moves of God that we have ever seen have been outside the walls of the Church.

I've been on a fishing boat in the Florida Keys, talking to the captain when the power of God hit him. Boom! He fell flat out under the power of God in the bottom of the boat. I was sitting there in the boat, with sharks swimming around and I was thinking, *My God! He had better recover out of this!*

I've been on a golf course where the guy fell out behind the golf cart, with a 3-iron stuck in his hand. It doesn't matter where we are: restaurants, shopping mall or an airplane. In our house, we have staff members falling out under the power of God in the kitchen.

We were sitting in our house around the dinner table with a female minister, who was hanging out with us for a couple of days after she preached at The River for a whole Sunday. She was sitting there eating food, and we were just talking and she suddenly started blinking and rolling her eyes and opening them wide. She said to me, "Did you put something in this food?" Then she looked at me and she said, "Oh, I forgot where I was!" Because people don't expect the power of God to fall at a meal place where you are sitting and eating. She was eating her food, and she was getting drunk in the Spirit.

The hardest place to have a move of God is in the Church. That's why sometimes you have to get rid of some people! Many places I go, we design the services to go long on purpose, just to get rid of some people. Because I know that the dead wood is going to leave at 9:00 or 10:00 p.m., but at 11:00 p.m., the desperate ones are still hanging on. And, BOOM! The power of God hits the place!

That's why The River at Tampa Bay Church is here, so we can have an atmosphere, an environment, where God can move, and we don't have to get rid of some people. Every now and then we have to get rid of one or two, but if you are hungry for God and you are blocked up, constipated with religion and tradition, and you are really desperate and need to go, then you know where to come to get a release!

REVIVAL IS RETURNING TO YOUR FIRST LOVE

> WITH THE FIRST LOVE COMES THAT JOY; YOU HAVE TO KEEP YOUR FIRST LOVE.

Revival is returning back to what you once had. Revival is returning back to your first love.

In Revelation 2:1–4, Jesus says:

> Unto the angel of the church of Ephesus write; These things saith he that holdeth the seven stars in his right hand, who walketh in the midst of the seven golden candlesticks; I know thy works, and thy labour, and thy patience, and how thou canst not bear them which are evil: and thou hast tried them which say they are apostles, and are not, and hast found them liars: and hast borne, and hast patience, and for my name's sake hast laboured, and hast not fainted. Nevertheless I have somewhat against thee, because thou hast left thy first love.

You can work hard, you can labor hard, you can have patience, you can know what's right, you can know what's wrong, but Jesus says, "I have somewhat against you, because you have left your first love." Your first love, that first love for Jesus, just like when you were first saved, that joy, that sparkle, you cannot lose that, no matter how busy you get. You cannot lose that joy. It's about Him; it's *all* about Him. It's about falling in love with Him all over again and loving Him more and more each day. First love, first passion. Don't sit and argue with me, "Well, I have the first love, but you know, I'm so busy. I'm running around . . ." No! You are *too* busy! You are too busy to be in love with Jesus.

With the first love comes that joy. Someone says, "How do I know I've lost my first love?" You've lost your first love because you've lost your joy! Watch a couple when they are dating and are just in love. They have only got eyes for each other. That's all the young man thinks about; he can't even function. His heart just bounces, beats in his chest—he has to turn the volume down because everybody can hear it. They can be in a roomful of people but it's as if there's nobody else in that room. He opens the door for her; there is nothing he wouldn't do for her.

Then they get married. Now she has to open the door for herself. Before, when she walked in a room, it was all eyes on her, just everything else blocked out. Now she walks in the room and he is ignoring her, switching TV channels with the remote. She says, "Honey?" He carries on changing channels. "Honey!" No response. What's happened? They've lost their first love.

You have to keep your first love. All of those things coming against you are designed by the enemy to do one thing and one thing alone—to take you away from your first love. When you fall out of love with Jesus, like the love you once had, the devil can rob you of the joy that you once had. Revival comes to bring us back to our first love, to restore back to us the joy of our salvation.

I look at some Christians and I don't see joy. I don't see joy in them. Their eyes do not shine; their eyes do not sparkle. There's very little life, like a battery that is running dry. If they were put as batteries into the 'Energizer Bunny', it wouldn't move!

Somebody says, "I can't live full of joy like that." Then it's contrary to the scripture, because it talks about your first love and the joy of your salvation (Psalm 51:12), and if you want to argue with me about that, then you probably need a good "suppository!"

There are no exceptions. Regardless of who you are, regardless of how long you been walking with the Lord, regardless of how long you have been serving God, regardless of how long your labor has been, regardless of your patience, you need to return to your first love. If you have lost your first love, if you have lost your joy, then Jesus says, "I've got somewhat against you, and you need to return!" (Revelation 2:4 paraphrased).

How do you return? You're going to drop everything else. You have to come to the place where there's nothing more important to you in the world. You'd rather give up your ministry; you'd rather give up everything you're doing, because you say, "I have to have my first love back. I have to fall in love with Jesus all over again. Jesus must become *number one* in my life."

YOU CAN LIVE IN REVIVAL EVERY DAY

IF YOU KEEP YOUR EYES ON HIM, HE CAN BRING YOU THROUGH EVERY STORM.

This is what the message of revival is about. We are dealing in the Church with Christians who move from on fire to lukewarm to cold to lukewarm to on fire. Today, on fire, six months from now, smoldering. Have you watched people go up and down like this? It's like they're riding a roller coaster at Busch Gardens, Tampa. At campmeeting, they are excited, happy, joyful, but three months later, they are depressed and sad. The only way for a person to maintain their first love and to maintain their joy, is to every day, constantly, allow the Holy Spirit to have His way in their life.

As I mentioned before, if you want to have a shower, you have to strip everything off. You have to get into the shower naked. Nothing hidden. In the natural, I do that every day, but I must also do that in the spiritual realm with the Lord every day.

When you strip away everything, you are vulnerable and you have to make yourself vulnerable. But to buy the devil's lie that you cannot maintain this first love, and you cannot maintain this joy, is to accept that, "Hey, I'm just going to be like this. I'm going to be a yo-yo Christian: one day on fire and the next, not; sold out one day and the next, not." And I don't believe that's God's plan for our lives. I believe that we can have that first love and we can have that joy. We can walk in His presence and we can walk in His glory on a daily basis, regardless of the circumstances that come and no matter what storms and trials of life come our way—because they will come!

But if you keep your eyes on Him, He can bring you through every storm. The Holy Spirit is here now. He is not here to a lesser degree, but He only gets involved in your life as you place a demand, or you make yourself available to Him. If you ignore Him, He'll ignore you.

If you want Him to come and do a work, He'll come to do a work. If you don't, He won't, He will never force himself on you. He's a perfect gentleman. He only comes where He's wanted. If you are ashamed of Him, He will be ashamed of you.

REVIVAL COMES WITH POWER

> REVIVAL BEGINS IN THE HEART OF A CONSECRATED INDIVIDUAL WHO IS IGNITED AND BECOMES THE ENERGIZING POWER BEHIND THE REVIVAL. IT IS IMPOSSIBLE TO HAVE REVIVAL WITHOUT POWER.

When you constantly allow the Holy Spirit to have His way in your life, you can become an instrument of revival—filled with revival power.

Remember that the Gospel is "the power of God unto salvation" (Romans 1:16), and you cannot have revival without power. It is *impossible* to have revival without power. Revival without power is an oxymoron, and if you believe you can have revival without power, you are just a plain moron! There is personal revival and there is corporate or city revival, and then there is national revival, which we are in desperate need of right now in the nation of America. We are desperately needing another Great Awakening.

Any time in history that revival has broken out, it's been in a time of deep moral darkness, and oh, how dark it is out there in the world right now. The lines have become so blurred. The Church has become so worldly, and the world has become so churchy, you can't even tell them apart.

Revival begins in the heart of a consecrated individual who is ignited and becomes the energizing power behind the revival. God always uses somebody. and it takes somebody who will stand in the gap and say, "Lord, here I am. I'm nothing, but I yield myself to You. Come and do what You want to do. Come and light a fire on the inside of me. Change me; transform me. I'm not worried about my reputation. I'm not worried about what other people think about me, but I yield myself to You. I'll do what You want me to do. I'll say what You want me to say. I'll go where You want me to go, and I'll be what You want me to be. Not my will, but Thine be done. I yield myself to You, Lord. If I die, I place myself in Your hands. Use me as an instrument."

YOU MUST DIE TO SELF

> YOU HAVE TO BE DEAD TO WHAT PEOPLE SAY. YOU HAVE TO BE DEAD TO EVERYBODY'S OPINION.

But how can God use you as an instrument of revival when you can't even take somebody's criticism? You get your nose all bent out of shape because somebody looks at you wrong! Touchy, touchy! If you can't even take the natural criticism that comes along, how will you handle the spiritual persecution?

You have to come to place where you totally die. If you go down to the cemetery to a particular grave site, and you read the tombstone, and then you get a megaphone and you start insulting the person lying in the grave, I guarantee you right now, no hand is going to come up through the ground and grab you by the ankle! Why? Because they are dead! By the same token, if you stand there and praise them, "What a wonderful person you were when you lived on the earth," no hand is going to come up through the ground and accept your praise. Why? Because they are dead And you have to be dead to what people think. You have to be dead to what people say. You have to be dead to everybody's opinion. Absolutely dead!

You have to be dead to their praise. You have to die. Because if you don't, you'll live a very painful life. I know that's easier to talk about, but I had to really walk through it. The revival broke out April 1989, and then began to pick up momentum from 1990 to 1993, and by the time I went to London, there were nine books in the UK that had been written about me! Nine whole books written about me! I thought, *They don't even know me, but they have written a book about me!* And none of it was the truth.

Then, one of the authors of the books wanted to meet me. So I said, "Fine. I'll meet him for breakfast." I went and sat down with a copy of the book and I said, "You wrote the book?" He said, "Yes." I said, "Let me tell you right now, the only thing that stops me from reaching over this table and grabbing you and knocking the stuffing out of you is the fact that I'm born-again and love Jesus with all my heart!" The guy started hyperventilating—I didn't realize he had asthma. I thought he was going to die right there! I said, "What right do you even have? You never interviewed me. You never even asked me, you just believed all the rubbish." "Well, I'm sorry," he said. I said, "Are you going to publish a book saying you're sorry? No! Because you are just in it for the money! That's the problem: you don't care what you print!"

But I learned that it's pointless to react because I don't have the time to run around the world and grab everybody who has written something about me, and have breakfast with them, and tell them what I would like to do to them if I wasn't saved!

The guy was sitting at the table wheezing. I felt so sorry for him. I said, "Are you going to be okay?" "I'll be fine," he said, taking some puffs on his inhaler. I said, "Don't worry; I'm not going to do anything to you. I promise you I'm not going to do anything. So, calm down; relax; eat your breakfast!"

So, eventually, after nine books, you don't even care, because it becomes a joke. If they write anything now, it's just a regurgitation of the same stuff that came out ten years ago. Some of the stuff that has been written—"Howard-Browne's daughter dies; what about his faith?" Or, "He goes to Madison Square Garden: no signs and wonders"—I laugh at it now because it's just funny. It is pointless even getting upset about it; it's just somebody's opinion, and it's not going to stop what we do. We just have to keep going and doing what God tells us to do.

But it's easy to sit where you are right now and say, "Oh, yes, I'll be okay," but let the fire of God come on you and let God begin to use you, and then you will have to face it.

Some of you might have already been facing it, and if you are not facing it, you are not in revival. You can judge your temperature by what you are stirring up.

We went to Soweto, South Africa, and we stirred up more devils than you can ever imagine! We had churches calling other churches, trying to stop the crusade by telling them that the crusade had been canceled. And I stood there and thought, *I'll send a lawyer's letter right now.* But then I said, "No, I won't! Father, forgive them, for they know not what they do. I forgive them right now in Jesus' Name. I just release them right now."

Because every day, you're going to have to make a choice, and every day is going to be a different set of things that come against you. You always have to deal with it. And when I say that in Soweto all hell broke loose, it was like the attacks of New York and Shreveport combined at one time. It is one thing when the attack comes from the world, but we had nothing from the world—it all came from the church!

I thought, *I'll just get in my car right now. I'll go down there and I'll sort them out. They already think I'm of the devil. I'll go down and I'll sort them out. Somebody needs to do this. Find me a jawbone of a donkey!*

But you have to release them. Otherwise, it takes away from what God has called you to do. You can't respond. You can't respond to emails; you can't respond to letters. Shredders work well! Many presidents have used shredders, so get yourself a very good shredder! Or have a very large bird, and put the papers at the bottom of its cage.

I don't know if some people want revival as much as they want fame, popularity, and fortune. I don't know if they *really* want revival, because there's a price to pay. Somebody says, "What is it going to cost me?" It might cost you everything!

Where revival is truly manifest, the Word is preached with power. The Word comes with the force of a sledgehammer, like a hammer that breaks the rock in pieces. You can't expect to have revival, true revival, with little namby-pamby motivational type preaching—to do with your "inner self," and it's all to do with the natural and the flesh. There's no dependence upon the Spirit of God in it. There's no humbling of yourself in it. A lot of that stuff is puffing oneself up with pride—"I can do this; I can achieve." There's no reliance upon the Holy Spirit, and there's no reliance upon the Lord. In fact, all it does is puff one up into more of a mode of sin and self, and the flesh and the natural. Jesus *has* to be the center of everything; otherwise, it's not Christianity—it's some other entity, but it is not Christianity.

WHERE REVIVAL IS TRULY MANIFEST, THE WORD IS PREACHED WITH POWER.

TRUE REVIVAL, TRUE WORSHIP

Where true revival is, there is power and there is always true worship, where you enter right into the glory of God without any trappings. I don't need somebody in a leotard, prancing across the front of the church. My God! I'm trying to get in the Spirit, and there's a heffalump running across the front of the church in a leotard!

Jesus said, "The hour cometh, and now is, when the true worshippers shall worship the Father in spirit and in truth: for the Father seeketh such to worship him" (John 4:23).

I don't need somebody running around with a flag. I don't need somebody blowing a shofar. Those are trappings! It's a distraction. "Rend your heart, and not your garments" (Joel 2:13). I've been in some meetings and I had to just close my eyes, bow my head, and pray, "Jesus, take me out of here right now!" I went to one meeting, walked down the aisle, and nearly had my eye poked out three times on the way to the platform with all the flags that were flying! I had to duck but I got stabbed in my head and my side! We went to another meeting and a woman came in dressed up—I thought she was part of a clan or something. Apparently, she was wearing some priest-like garment from the Old Covenant. She came forward with a bowl and put some incense on the altar, I thought, *My God, they're going to bring out a cow and slaughter the thing here in a few minutes!*

What was that? It was an excuse. It is counterfeit. It is not the real. I don't need that—get out of here! So, you have to make a decision—do you want the fake, or do you want the real? Do you want stuff that's going to leave a copper mark on you, or do you want to wear the real stuff? Why would you substitute brass for gold? (1 Kings 14) When gold is available, why wouldn't you have the real stuff?

REVIVAL BRINGS REPENTANCE

So with true revival, the Word preached in power, there is powerful worship, and there is repentance! Repentance is always the beginning. You have to have repentance. The problem in the American churches is that it is, "I'm sorry," but I do it again. "I'm sorry," but I do it again. "I'm sorry," but I do it again. So it's this game that's always going on. He is the God of the second chance, third chance, fourth chance, fifth chance, tenth chance, fiftieth chance, one thousandth chance! People just go from repentance back to what they were doing , but there is a time when you *really* need to get saved! You have to question if true salvation has really taken place in the life of people if they are constantly in a place of repentance and then doing it again, and then coming back to repent, and doing it again. Are they really, truly saved?

Some people say, "Well, yes, I am saved but I just have a problem with my flesh." Then you need to do something with your flesh. That's why the Bible says to mortify the deeds of your flesh (Romans 8:13). Put to death the deeds of your flesh. You've got to kill that sin; you've got to put it to death. And if you don't grow concerned about yourself, then who's going to grow concerned about you?

You can take a corpse, put a wig on it, put makeup on it, put collagen in it or whatever you want to do, but it's still dead. You can take a person, you can send them in for liposuction, and they can have all the reductions and enlargements they need done, but that change has to take place on the inside, no matter what it looks from the outside.

We don't have to get to a place of being sin conscious, where every day you are conscious of sin, but we have got to get to a place of being conscious of the righteousness of God, of who we are in Christ Jesus and of who He has made us to be (2 Corinthians 5:21). You cannot just put a covering over sin, you have to deal with it. Somebody says, "I'm in bondage." Well, why are you in bondage? What are you in bondage to? "I'm in bondage to this sin." Then when are you going to deal with it?

Whether the bondage is a bondage to drugs, or alcohol, or lust, or perversion, or anger (and I could list all the works of the flesh), these things have to be cut off at the root; otherwise, they will constantly plague the heart of man.

That's why I tell people the altar is open. If you've got to come here and stay on your face for ten, twelve hours a day until you get the victory, then do whatever it takes! Go and lock yourself in a room if you have to but you have got to cut the head of the giant off. Do whatever it takes!

REVIVAL BRINGS A RELEASE OF FINANCES

When there is a manifestation of true revival, there is always a release of finances. Finances flow because the Bible says people give freely in the day of His power (Psalm 110:3). There's always a release of finances. If you say, "Well, the people aren't giving," then you are not having a revival! There is always the release of finances, because where your treasure is, that's where your heart is going to be also (Matthew 6:21). So, when you get touched by revival, then your treasure is released and your treasure comes right in to where the move of God is.

> WHEN THERE IS A MANIFESTATION OF TRUE REVIVAL, THERE IS ALWAYS A RELEASE OF FINANCES.

REVIVAL BRINGS JOY

Revival brings an experience of exuberant joy and gladness among the people. I've never heard of a "sadness revival". I've never heard of a "depression move"—People don't say, "We had this evangelist come in for a month. We had a great revival move of depression! I tell you what, we sold out of all the books on mental illness. People went by our coffee shop and they bought Prozac like you wouldn't believe. We had to open up a special manufacturing plant just for the straitjackets! In fact, we had to open up one of the back rooms and have shock treatments daily!"

REVIVAL BRINGS DESTRUCTION OF IDOLS

In revival, you'll see the destruction of idols. In America, idols are television and cinema and sport, but you will see the destruction of these in revival. In the Welsh revival, the power of God was felt so strongly that soccer teams were disbanded because nobody wanted to play soccer.

That's why if you go to a Welsh rugby match even today, you will hear them singing some hymns. It's a fallout from the revival (traditional Welsh rugby song, "Cwm Rhondda" [Guide Me O Thou Great Jehovah], written by John Hughes in the Welsh revival). And boy, can the Welsh sing! I've got a little bit of Welsh in me. My second name is Morgan, and some of my ancestors came from Wales.

The destruction of idols comes, and religion is a terrible idol! And when true revival takes place, new hymns also come forth, songs of the Spirit, because that's an outlet for newfound joy. When songs come forth, you know that revival has returned; the song has returned.

When these things are made manifest, then Pentecostal revival will be the result. Somebody says, "Pentecostal revival?" Yes! I heard a founding pastor of a Baptist megachurch speaking on the subject of revival. I was shocked and I started weeping. He began to cite the Welsh revival and Azusa Street, and he called them two of the greatest moves of God since Pentecost.

I thought, *Here is a man in the Baptist realm who has publicly gone on record as saying that Azusa Street and the Welsh revival were two of the greatest outpourings of the Holy Spirit since Pentecost.*

I don't care who people are—whether they are Presbyterian or Methodist or German Lutheran—if you travel throughout America and you see huge churches that are there, then you know that at one time there must have been something there for these churches to have been built. There must have been a move of God that caused them to come about. But just because the building is there, it doesn't mean that the presence is there. Because the presence of God does not reside in a building. There is nothing holy about a building. People say they went to Israel, the Holy Land, and stood by the Wailing Wall and "felt the power of God." You can feel the power of God if you just stand by a wall in The River Church! I've got some walls back in my house where you can go stand and feel the power of God. God does not live in a building—that's idolatry—but buildings have been built to house and contain what God is doing.

I guess that's why the Lord just keeps moving on, because you are not housing Him! You can't build a building big enough; you can't build a building beautiful enough. You can't build a building where He can just hang around. He stays in the hearts of people, and He lives in the hearts of people, and as long as those hearts are turned toward Him, His presence will be manifested. The moment their hearts are lifted away, He's gone. He's gone!

I don't care how many millions of dollars you spend on your building; if He's not welcome there, you might end up with a lot of people there, but He won't be there. Neither will He be in manifestation. He comes to hungry and thirsty hearts.

> WHEN TRUE REVIVAL TAKES PLACE, NEW HYMNS ALSO COME FORTH, SONGS OF THE SPIRIT, BECAUSE THAT'S AN OUTLET FOR NEWFOUND JOY. WHEN SONGS COME FORTH, YOU KNOW THAT REVIVAL HAS RETURNED; THE SONG HAS RETURNED.

YOU MUST STAY HUNGRY AND THIRSTY

I know that some of these things you have heard several times, but we need to be refreshed concerning these things. Because it's not just about getting revival or having revival, it is about staying right in the move of God. You have got to stay hungry. You have got to stay thirsty.

The Lord is speaking to those reading this who have been touched by God, but who haven't been changed. God wants to change you, not just for the moment. He wants to change you completely from the inside out. Your walk, your talk, your lying down, your rising up, your coming in and your going out, your way of thinking—He wants to transform you. But you have to make yourself available and you have to be willing to allow Him to come and have His way. The older we are, the harder it is. That's why the Lord really impacts many young people and children, because they are so open. It's harder for adults and older folk to be changed. Someone says, "Oh, I got a touch," but I'm not talking about a touch, I'm talking about a change! "Well, I went flying through the air and did a somersault." I'm not talking about that either, I'm talking about a *change*.

I have prayed this prayer for years over people in every nation I went to and in every service. Close your eyes where you are, and lift your hands to Heaven:

> Now Father, You told me years ago that if I would give You an opportunity to move, then You would move. Lord, what I have shared is not my word, but it's Your Word. Only You can transform, only You can change, It's not by might nor by power but by Your Spirit, and I ask You even now, by Your fire, to come. I ask You even now, by Your glory, to come. Let the fire of God fall on all those reading this. Not only bring about a touch, but bring about a change and a transformation, a revolution on the inside of every man, woman, boy, and girl reading this, that the same fire that fell on the Day of Pentecost, now falls upon the hungry and upon the thirsty, in the Name of Jesus. It's only You, Jesus, only You. First love. First Love. Amen.

4

HAVING AN ENCOUNTER WITH GOD

Being Endued with Power

Revival is about having an encounter with God. Go to the book of Acts:

> And Saul, yet breathing out threatenings and slaughter against the disciples of the Lord, went unto the high priest, and desired of him letters to Damascus to the synagogues, that if he found any of this way, whether they were men or women, he might bring them bound unto Jerusalem.
>
> ACTS 9:1-2

It is amazing how there's always somebody out there looking to bind you up!

> And as he journeyed, he came near Damascus: and suddenly there shined round about him a light from heaven: and he fell to the earth, and heard a voice saying unto him, Saul, Saul, why persecutest thou me? And he said, Who art thou, Lord? And the Lord said, I am Jesus

> whom thou persecutest: it is hard for thee to kick against the pricks. And he trembling and astonished said, Lord, what wilt thou have me to do? And the Lord said unto him, Arise, and go into the city, and it shall be told thee what thou must do. And the men which journeyed with him stood speechless, hearing a voice, but seeing no man. And Saul arose from the earth; and when his eyes were opened, he saw no man: but they led him by the hand, and brought him into Damascus. And he was three days without sight, and neither did eat nor drink. And there was a certain disciple at Damascus, named Ananias; and to him said the Lord in a vision, Ananias. And he said, Behold, I am here, Lord. And the Lord said unto him, Arise, and go into the street which is called Straight, and enquire in the house of Judas for one called Saul, of Tarsus: for, behold, he prayeth, and hath seen in a vision a man named Ananias coming in, and putting his hand on him, that he might receive his sight. Then Ananias answered, Lord, I have heard by many of this man, how much evil he hath done to thy saints at Jerusalem: and here he hath authority from the chief priests to bind all that call on thy name. But the Lord said unto him, Go thy way: for he is a chosen vessel unto me, to bear my name before the Gentiles, and kings, and the children of Israel: for I will shew him how great things he must suffer for my name's sake.
>
> ACTS 9:3–16

I believe that if you had to pick out all the messages that I've brought on the subject of revival and said to me that I was only allowed to preach one, it would be what I'm going to share with you now, and that is, "Having an Encounter with God," because that's what revival is. You would be surprised how many people, even in the ministry, haven't had an encounter with God. Revival is having an encounter with God.

If you study the Book of Job you'll see something about Job in chapter 38. When God showed up in a whirlwind, the Bible says that Job fell on his face and God said to him, "Gird up your loins like a man; for I will demand of thee, and answer thou me." (Job 38:3). Job had been rambling and just talking rubbish and his three friends talked rubbish. The only guy who had any sense was the guy by the name of Elihu. As for Eliphaz the Temanite, and Bildad the Shuhite, and Zophar the Naamathite, boy, they are all you need as friends!

God began to reveal Himself to Job, and He said, "Where were you when I laid the foundations of the earth. Do you have a voice? Can you thunder like me?" (Job 38:4; 40:9). Well, Job did something that he probably should have done right at the beginning: he took his hand and he put it across his mouth. He said, "I put my hand to my mouth because obviously I've spoken things and I don't even know what I'm talking about" (Job 40:4–5, paraphrased). And then he made a powerful statement, "I have heard of thee by the hearing of the ear: but now mine eye seeth thee" (Job 42:5). It's one thing to read the Book; it's another thing to meet the Author of the Book!

REVIVAL IS HAVING AN ENCOUNTER WITH GOD.

AN ENCOUNTER WITH GOD TRANSFORMS YOU

Saul of Tarsus was on the road to Damascus, breathing out threatenings (Acts 9). I can just see him, hell-bent on destroying the Church of the Lord Jesus Christ. I know somebody will say, "Well, I don't understand. How come he had an encounter with God? He wasn't really hungry for God," but you'd be surprised, that sometimes, the people who fight the most, are really hungry. They are searching and they are looking.

It's not the one who's passive, just sitting there and not saying yea or nay. It's the person who's fighting and angry and lashing out, because he is so scared. He's sitting on the slippery creek bank, and he's about to fall in and he doesn't want to, so he's fighting. Sometimes, the people who fight it the most are those that are about to fall in. And who knows the attitude of a person's heart? He could be saying, "I'm going to kill them all, but if there's a God in Heaven, let Him reveal Himself to me."

You don't know what was going on with Saul. There he was,

hell-bent on destroying the Church of the Lord Jesus Christ. But what he didn't know was that he had an appointed time with destiny and that God had marked a spot on the road to Damascus. And that spot on the road to Damascus would be the place where the "suddenly" would take place. Suddenly, a light shone from Heaven and he fell to the earth. That light was so bright, brighter than the noonday sun, and it caused him to not see a thing for three days and nights (Acts 9:3, 9). He fell to the ground and God began to reveal Himself to Saul, some of which didn't even come out for about fourteen–sixteen years. And some of which he couldn't even talk about, because he said, "I knew a man in Christ above fourteen years ago, (whether in the body, I cannot tell; or whether out of the body, I cannot tell: God knoweth;) such an one caught up to the third heaven" (2 Corinthians 12:2).

God transformed the life of Saul and not only transformed his life, but also transformed his name. I love to say this: "God hit him so hard He knocked the *S* off and stuck a *P* there and made him Paul!" (And when I was young, I was always concerned that when God touched me, He would change my name from Rodney to Odney following the same pattern.) How is it possible that one of the greatest persecutors of the Christian Church, in what I call a head-on collision with the Holy Ghost, could be so transformed that he ends up writing nearly two-thirds of the New Testament?

But if you're going to write nearly two-thirds of the New Testament, you had better have had an encounter with God! Paul didn't walk with Jesus; he didn't talk with Jesus; he wasn't like the other apostles. What he received, he received by revelation. It was just as if he had been there, because he had met Jesus on the way. He even later on referred to it that Jesus appeared to him on the way (Acts 22:6 ESV). When he told the story time and time and time again, he could refer back to that Road-to-Damascus experience, and I believe that every single person needs to have a "Road-to-Damascus" experience.

GOD COMES TO THE HUNGRY AND THIRSTY

> WHEN YOU ARE HUNGRY FOR GOD AND YOU ARE THIRSTY FOR HIM, HE WILL COME AND STEP RIGHT IN THE MIDDLE OF THAT HUNGER AND THIRST.

Someone says, "I didn't see any bright lights." It's not about seeing a bright light. It's about the bright light shining *in* you, a head-on collision with the Holy Ghost and fire.

You might say, "Well, Brother Rodney, I'm not fighting the Church. I'm not out to destroy the Church." No, you might not be trying to destroy the truth, but you are not really going after God either! You have to have a passion, you have to have a hunger, and you have to have a desperation. Saul had a passion; he had a hunger. It might not have been for the things of God—he wanted to see the Church destroyed—but he had a hunger.

That's where God steps right in the middle. You've got to be hungry and you've got to be thirsty. If you study the lives of great men and women of God, you see that every single one of them before God ever began to use them, they had an encounter with God.

Look at Charles Finney. He was, a lawyer and at that time American law was based on the Scripture—what a novel idea! He would go down to the church house and listen to the Christians praying and he knew that they couldn't have been praying right, because he knew that the Name of Jesus had been given to the Church as a power of attorney.

He knew they weren't praying right because he took the Bible literally! So that drove him to search, and he found himself out in the woods, crying out to God, and Charles Grandison Finney had an encounter with God where the fire of God hit him. And God used him to spark a revival that shook America.

Some people search the Scriptures, but it's only to get the next message. They search the Scriptures just to get another revelation that maybe somebody else hasn't got. The only time they ever open their Bibles is to get a message. But when you are hungry for God and you are thirsty for Him, He will come and step right in the middle of that hunger and thirst.

For the Word of God declares, "If you hunger and thirst after righteousness, you will be filled" (Matthew 5:6, paraphrased), and "If you draw nigh unto me, I will draw nigh unto you" (James 4:8 paraphrased). I believe that there are hungry people reading this. You wouldn't be reading this book if you weren't hungry. But you have to learn how to activate that hunger. You have to learn how to come to that place of desperation and plug right in to what Heaven has.

AN ENCOUNTER WITH GOD CHANGES YOU ON THE INSIDE

Moses had an encounter with God. It's not called a "Road-to-Damascus" experience, it's called a "Burning-Bush" experience. It is amazing how different he was after he met the burning bush. Acts 7:20–29 says:

> Moses was born, and was exceeding fair, and nourished up in his father's house three months: and when he was cast out, Pharaoh's daughter took him up, and nourished him for her own son. And Moses was learned in all the wisdom of the Egyptians, and was mighty in words and in deeds. And when he was full forty years old, it came into his heart to visit his brethren the children of Israel. And seeing one of them suffer wrong, he defended him, and avenged him that was oppressed, and smote the Egyptian: for he supposed his brethren would have understood how that God by his hand would deliver them: but they understood not. And the next day he shewed himself unto them as they strove, and would have set them at one again, saying, Sirs, ye are brethren; why do ye wrong one to another? But he that did his neighbour wrong thrust him away, saying, Who made thee a ruler and a judge over us? Wilt thou kill me, as thou diddest the Egyptian yesterday? Then fled Moses at this saying, and was a stranger in the land of Madian, where he begat two sons.

A lot of people before their encounter with God, are really fearful and afraid, but there's something about an encounter with God. Something happens on the inside, and when that takes place, friends, family and loved ones, and people who have known you for years look at you and say, "There's something different about you."

I'm not talking about somebody standing up saying, "I think the Lord touched me." This is not about *thinking* the Lord touched you. When God touches you, you *know* He touched you. I listen to people who say, "The Lord spoke to me," and I look at them and say, "The Lord didn't speak to you! You were eating too much cheese pizza late at night!", because there is no sense of Heaven on what they are saying.

TALKING ABOUT AN ENCOUNTER CHANGES THE ATMOSPHERE

> WHEN GOD TOUCHES YOU, IT'S NOT GOING TO BE BUSINESS AS USUAL. WHEN GOD TOUCHES YOU, EVERYTHING IS GOING TO CHANGE; IT'S NOT GOING TO BE THE SAME OLD, SAME OLD.

People come and tell me that they just saw an angel. I look at them and say, "If you saw an angel, you wouldn't be standing here right now!" Some say, "Jesus walked in my room," but if Jesus walked in your room, whenever you relayed that story, the whole atmosphere of the room would change.

I hear people talking about how they were in a room and the Cloud came in and they were lost in the presence of God for hours, and I look at them and say, "No, you wish you were!" Because when that kind of thing happens, and people talk about it, the very atmosphere of the room changes. The reality of the presence of God comes in manifestation, and it's all relative to the touch, to the encounter.

In Acts 1:8 Jesus says, "Ye shall receive power, after that the Holy Ghost is come upon you: and ye shall be witnesses unto me both in Jerusalem, and in all Judæa, and in Samaria, and unto the uttermost part of the earth." Some people, say the power of God touched them, but they can't even get out of bed in the morning. He said, "Jerusalem, Judea, Samaria, and the uttermost parts of the earth," but they don't even want to leave their neighborhood!

When God touches you, it's not going to be business as usual. When God touches you, everything is going to change; it's not going to be the same old, same old. There will be a distinct difference between before and after. Just like when somebody loses a hundred pounds in weight and you have the before-and-after pictures. It's not the same old, same old.

Someone was in the revivals years ago, and I read the write-up about him. He was talking about the breakup of his marriage and he signed off his letter, "One sad drunk!" I thought, *He isn't drunk on the new wine. He might be sad, but he isn't drunk!* I'm talking about a transformation, where everything changes. Somebody said that his wife left him because she didn't like the anointing. No! It had nothing to do with the anointing! He was just a jerk.

It's amazing how people try to blame stuff on the anointing. It's one thing if she didn't want to serve God and left; that happens; but this guy said that the anointing was so strong on him that his wife took off! She probably got tired of him parting the water in the bathtub!

AN ENCOUNTER WITH GOD TURNS YOUR LIFE AROUND

Moses was on the backside of a desert. God had called him to lead his people out of the land of bondage but He tried to do it in the flesh. What you try to do in the flesh *before* the encounter, you will do by the Spirit *after* the encounter. The flesh is very costly because it ended up costing Moses forty years on the backside of a desert, looking after some sheep, thinking he had failed God. But after an encounter, everything changed.

Some of you feel like you've failed and you've missed God. You've been on the backside of the desert and you've been crying out to God, but don't forget: there is still a bush that can burn, and maybe, just maybe, today is the day that the bush will burn for you. Maybe, now is the time.

I can't dictate that, but I can stir hunger up in you. I'm here to stir you up to go after the deep things of God, to press in, because there's a place for you. You can touch the hem of His garment (Matthew 14:35–36). There's a place for you.

AN ENCOUNTER WITH GOD MAKES YOU BOLD

Acts 7:30:

> And when forty years were expired [I don't like that forty-year thing], there appeared to him in the wilderness of mount Sina an angel of the Lord in a flame of fire in a bush.

It wasn't just any bush. This was a bush inhabited by an angel, an "angel bush," and a fire was consuming this bush but it had not burned up. How was this possible?

Acts 7:31–34:

> When Moses saw it, he wondered at the sight: and as he drew near to behold it, the voice of the Lord came unto him, saying, I am the God of thy fathers, the God of Abraham, and the God of Isaac, and the God of Jacob. Then Moses trembled, and durst not behold. (Which means he shook and couldn't look. He shielded his face.) Then said the Lord to him, Put off thy shoes from thy feet: for the place where thou standest is holy ground. I have seen, I have seen the affliction of my people which is in Egypt, and I have heard their groaning, and am come down to deliver them. And now come, I will send thee into Egypt.

Could it be possible that the same man who fled the land of Egypt is now going to go and stand and take his finger and point it at Pharaoh's nostril, and say, "Let my people go?" What happened? What took place? I can tell you that when Moses stood in front of Pharaoh, and Pharaoh looked in his eyes, Pharaoh could see the flames flickering on the bush in Moses' eyes. It was still there. The imprint of that was burned into Moses' very being, and when he said, "Let my people go!" Pharaoh probably thought to himself, *I have never seen a man like this. I see a reflection in his eyes of something the likes of which I've never seen before.* Because he was looking into the face of God, and you cannot have an encounter with God and it not affect your whole being! Something happens!

YOU HAVE TO BE DESPERATE FOR GOD

Someone says, "But Brother Rodney, I prayed for an hour." Moses was there forty years! One of the problems of modern-day revivals is that people think it's a drive-through. They think it's a "Revival-Bell" where you pull up to the window. "I'll take three shakes and give me a roll." Or, "I'm going down there to 'Revival King,' I'm going down to 'MacRevivals!" They want everything instantly. If they don't get what they want from God the night that they pressed in, they quit pressing in. "I went to that meeting. I think I'll just stay home now and I'll come back Friday night and see maybe what I can get."

When you are hungry, when you are thirsty, when you are desperate for God, you'll be there before the doors open and you'll be the last one to leave. When you get so hungry and thirsty and so desperate for God, you won't care what it costs. You will press in and you will have a visitation from God.

Jacob wrestled all night with an angel and came out with a limp (Genesis 32:22–32). You might limp for the rest of your life, but you'll be marked. People will say of you, "I tell you what, they are nice people but a little strange. They love God with all their hearts, but they are a little different."

YIELDING TO THE HOLY GHOST

Do you think you're going to be normal after God touches you? Do you think for one moment that you're going to have an encounter with God and you're going to be normal? No! So stop trying to be normal and stop trying to make yourself normal. You're not normal and you're never going to be normal.

I would go and preach for certain preachers, and just before I would get to the platform, they would say to me. "Now, listen: I don't want you to do this, and don't do that." I'd say, "What are you looking for? You are just looking for another version of you!" They didn't do the stuff I was doing, so they didn't want me to do it. I'd say, "Why don't you just go out there and do it yourself? How can you tie my hands, tie my feet, and put a gag over my mouth? You can't have me come here for revival and then not want me to do this and that and the other thing. You have got to turn me loose, brother!"

The problem is, they don't know what I'm going to do next. But it's not that they don't know what *I'm* going to do next; they don't know what the *Holy Ghost* is going to do next! Someone says, "Boy, if we can just contain him, if we can just get him to do that." Well then, you might as well just do it yourself!

I went to one place where the pastor had been in my meetings and knew "the rules." We started the crusade Sunday night, and the service started at 6:00 p.m. and finished at 10:00 or 11:00 p.m. He then called me and said, "We need to have this Monday night service over by 10:00 p.m. also."

I said, "Start at 7:00 p.m. and finish at 10:00 p.m.? If the Lord's finished at 10:00 p.m., that's fine, but you cannot limit me. We may have finished last night's service at 10:00 p.m., but there are times I get lost and I don't know what the time is. I don't even look at my watch. We're not here to watch the clock."

If you go to a great restaurant to eat, you don't care about what time it is. Somebody says, "I know the steak is not here yet, but you know what? It's getting late, so I need to go." There is a steak house in Tampa where you sit the whole night, and then you go over to the dessert place, and you stay there longer. They have desserts that come out and they set them on fire right at your table! It's a whole-evening deal. Now, if you go to places and there's no food, the time stretches out. But when you are enjoying yourself, you don't sit and say, "My God, look at the time!"

So, when this preacher said to me, "It would be good if you can be through by 10:00 p.m.," I said to him, "I just can't do it. I will do my best to have the service over by 10:00 p.m., but I cannot promise you anything."

I did my best that night, and I squeezed it all in till about sixteen or seventeen minutes past 10:00 p.m. The power of God was hitting the place, but I shut it down and walked right off the platform. Then he called me and said, "Listen: I'm sorry. I'm sorry for doing that. Take as long as you want to; go till 2:00 a.m."

You cannot dictate to the Holy Ghost. Somebody says, "Well, it's up to the Holy Spirit." Yes, the Holy Spirit knows what He's going to do, but He might not tell you everything, and it is dependent upon you yielding to the Spirit. You don't know what God's going to do. Now, sometimes the Lord will show you in advance what He is going to do. Sometimes I know what the Lord is going to do before He does it, but other times, I don't. I'm just out there surfing, looking for a wave.

However, we've gone to some places, and there isn't a wave! I'm looking for something, crying out, "My God, send something! God in Heaven, send something!" I'll bring my own dynamite and try to blow up something in the distance, just hoping a wave will come! You do what you can do! Sometimes you get on the surfboard and just paddle in, and that's the best you can do, and people run around saying, "We're having revival!" Meanwhile, I'm thinking, *We haven't even gotten started here yet!* But they have had nothing before, so they think just paddling is revival!

AN ENCOUNTER WITH GOD BRINGS RESTORATION

I was in a meeting in 1991 in Louisville, Kentucky. We conducted about a three-week crusade, and a man and his wife came every night, and I saw him sitting over at the back of the church. All he did was sit and stare at me for two meetings a day, Sunday through Friday, like a Kentucky bullfrog in a hail storm.

I knew that he couldn't be against the meetings because he kept coming back every service, morning and night, just sitting back there, but that was it, there was no change of facial expression whatsoever.

We came up to the last Thursday night and I felt led to pray for all the preachers that night. So I said, "All those in the ministry, come and line up here," and the guy came walking out. I laid hands on him, and he just stood there looking at me. He didn't close his eyes; he just looked at me. It was like laying hands on a pillar or a refrigerator. There was nothing there to grab ahold of. I thought to myself, *Nothing is happening to this guy.*

I didn't waste too much time—you can work too hard just on one person, so I kept my hands on him for a while and then went on to the next person. Everybody else was flat out under the power whilst he was still standing, looking around, blinking. But Friday morning, when I walked into that church, there he was, sitting on the front row now, his face lit up, and I knew something was different. I couldn't even begin ministering, I had to find out what had happened to him. So I went over and said to him, "Sir, come up here. Tell the people what happened." He said, "Well, let me just say this: I've been in the ministry for many years, and I quit the ministry." I said under my breath, "Thank God you did! We're trying to help people. If he ministered under that condition, people would have been committing suicide in the parking lot! People come to a meeting to be uplifted. But you go to some meetings and it's like a form of torture, pulling out your toenails or removing your nose hairs with a pair of tweezers!"

He continued: "I've been coming to the meetings and sitting near the back, watching you." I said, "I know. I know you were watching me because I was watching you." And he said, "I came up last night and you prayed for me, and nothing happened to me." I said, "Well, obviously it did!" He said, "Nothing happened to me when you prayed for me, but I went home, and about 3:00 a.m. the whole bed started shaking. I woke up, I looked at my wife and I said, 'Stop shaking the bed!' And that's when she said, 'I'm not shaking the bed; you are!' and

I looked down, and my whole body was just shaking under the power of God! My wife said, 'I'm not going to be able to sleep if you keep shaking like this, so go in the next room,' so I got out of bed and I went through to the next room and I lay there and I shook till about 7:30 a.m. this morning!"

He said, "Whatever had hold of me, whatever was binding me, whatever was stopping me from doing the work of God, God shook it off me. I feel like a new man! I'm going back in to the ministry. The joy of the Lord hit me, and that's why I'm sitting here on the front row." I said, "It didn't take a rocket scientist to see something had happened. I can see it in your face, I can look in your eyes and I can tell you that something is different about you." This was not the same guy who had been sitting at the back there for three weeks, watching me.

Something must have happened to move him all the way from the back to the front. See, he was still in "Jerusalem;" he hadn't gone to "Judea and Samaria." But he had moved from the back row—you always know something has happened when people move from the back row.

I know everybody can't get near the front, and we understand that, but beware when people are always looking for back seat. Why? If they are always wanting a back seat, they might want to just stay at home and watch the services on the internet. Some people just want to slip in so they can slip out!

AN ENCOUNTER WITH GOD BRINGS RADICAL CHANGE

When you have an encounter with God, there will be a radical change in your life. It is so radical that there will be a marked difference that family and friends and loved ones who have known you for years, will see.

That happened to Smith Wigglesworth when he got baptized in the Holy Ghost. His wife was the preacher, and he would take the kids on pony rides outside the building, but one day he got baptized in the Holy Ghost. And when he got up and began to speak, she sat on the front row and shook her head and said, "I can't believe that's my Smithy. I can't believe that's my Smithy!"

In 1994, we were ministering at the Wembley Conference Centre in London, England, and a woman came to the meeting and the power of God hit her. She was so hit by the power that she didn't even know how to function. She managed to find her way back to the train station and she went all the way home. It was probably about a two-hour ride. She got off and she walked up the street and went back to her house. She climbed up the steps and opened the front door. Her husband was a drunken sailor who had been fighting God all their married life. She walked in, still under the glory of God, and couldn't even speak in English; all she had been able to do was speak in other tongues for hours.

Her husband came from out of the kitchen and walked down the passageway to meet her. He took one look at her and when she looked at him, he fell on the floor. The moment he hit the floor he was speaking in other tongues. Somebody says, "I don't understand that." Well, he got saved on the way down!

That doesn't fit with some people's theology. How's that possible? But how was it possible for Saul, "breathing out threatenings" on the road to Damascus, to fall and say, "Who art Thou, Lord?" (Acts 9:1–5). Talk about instant conversion! "Who art thou, Lord!" He asked the question and answered it himself!

AN ENCOUNTER WITH GOD BRINGS REVELATION OF HIM

So, the Moses who stood in front of Pharaoh was a different Moses from the one who had fled. He had a message. Pharaoh asked, "Who sent you?" and Moses replied, "I AM!" The reason why people fail in ministry and don't succeed is because they go in the name of the organization. That's all they have had a revelation of. But when you have had a revelation of God, it does not matter about the denomination or the organization. God revealed Himself to Moses and said, "I AM the God of Abraham, Isaac, and Jacob. And if they ask you who sent you, tell them, 'I AM'" (Exodus 3:14–15 paraphrased).

I AM is here! Do you know that I AM tomorrow will still be I AM tomorrow? Do you know I AM is now? I WAS is yesterday. I WILL BE is tomorrow, but "I AM THAT I AM" is always now (Exodus 3:14). Moses went in the power of "I AM." He didn't go there to negotiate the terms of release. He said, "Let my people go!" (Exodus 5:1). This is not even open for discussion. This is not even a limited release. Do you realize that that is what we are called to do? We go to set the captives free, and there's no negotiation with the devil.

AN ENCOUNTER WITH GOD ENDUES YOU WITH POWER

> IF THE DISCIPLES WHO WALKED WITH JESUS HAD TO WAIT UNTIL THEY WERE ENDUED WITH POWER, HOW MUCH MORE SHOULD WE, LIVING IN THE TWENTY-FIRST CENTURY, BE ENDUED WITH POWER?

We can look at different examples, but did you know that Jesus could and can, reflect to a point in His own earthly life when he had an encounter with God? Someone says, "But He was God." Yes, but He didn't do anything until the encounter. "What do you mean?" When He came down to the River Jordan, He was baptized by John, and when He came up out of the water, the heavens opened and the Holy Spirit descended like a dove, and God said, "This is my beloved Son, in whom I'm well pleased" (Matthew 3:17). It was from that moment things changed.

If it was important for Jesus, who was God manifest in the flesh, to be able to pinpoint the time when it took place, how much more for us? It's almost like the initiation; that's when it started. Somebody says, "I don't know when God touched me, but He did some time back; I can't remember when." No! No! When you have an encounter with God, you'll remember the date, the time, and the place. You'll even remember what shoes you were wearing. Especially when you have to take them off.

Jesus had been in preparation thirty years for His earthly ministry and had done absolutely nothing, but right after this encounter, all

Heaven broke loose, and the first miracle He did in Cana of Galilee was when He turned the water into wine. But he didn't do it until the encounter. And then when He was leaving the earth, He told the disciples to wait. They had walked with him; they had talked with him; they had even performed miracles, but He told them to go and wait. Wait for what? "Until ye be endued with power" (Luke 24:49). You think the rules have changed? Absolutely not! If the disciples who walked with Jesus had to wait until they were endued with power, how much more should we, living in the twenty-first century, be endued with power?

And fortunately for us, when that happens, it is the same power that filled the apostles. When the Holy Spirit came, it was a man called Peter, the one who'd denied the Lord on three occasions, who suddenly had an encounter with God and his whole life was transformed. He was the guy addressing the crowd on the Day of Pentecost. If it was up to me to choose who would have preached, I probably would have picked Thomas, even though he most likely would have doubted whether he had the ability to speak to the crowd! But it was Peter, the one who had denied the Lord, who was suddenly transformed with a boldness that he'd never had before, and he got up there on that day and said, "This is that which was spoken by the prophet Joel; and it shall come to pass in the last days, saith God, I will pour out of my Spirit upon all flesh" (Acts 2:16–17). I can just imagine somebody standing by saying, "Could that be Peter? Could that be the very one who denied the Lord Jesus? Something's happened to him! What has gotten into him?"

You'll hear people saying that about people who get touched. Some of the wives say, "What got into my husband?" Some of the husbands say, "What got into my wife?" Some parents say, "What happened to my child? They're not the same person; something's different about them!"

DON'T QUIT; KEEP PRESSING IN

It's a *radical* encounter, as radical as if you went and stood on I-75 and a Mack truck came down the highway at seventy miles an hour and hit you head-on and your friends and family peeled you off the front grille, and then they looked at you and said, "My, how you've changed! You look different. You walk different. You talk different. You're not the same person that we used to know!" How much more if God touches you? When the Creator of Heaven and earth touches you, your whole life will be changed and transformed.

Do whatever it takes and press in until you get it. Some of you have quit too soon; some of you have given up too soon and now you've just become observers. Evangelist Richard Moore will tell you this. He was first traveling with us, in 1988–89 and was supposed to be working in the ministry, but he was the first one up in the prayer line! And then, when the revival broke out in April, 1989, he said to me, "I want God to touch me and you say I've got to get hungry, but I am hungry." I said, "You've got to get hungrier." He said, "I am hungry. I'm desperate!" I said, "You've got to get hungrier and more desperate!" And I didn't let up on him.

He was so hungry I think he got saved about forty times. He was supposed to be helping me, and I'd give an altar call and he'd come in the altar call, and I'd think, *The guy has just driven me here. I'm getting my own driver saved! This is just phenomenal.* I'd introduce him to the pastors and say, "This is Brother Richard; he's helping me; he's been to Bible school and he's called to the ministry," and then I'd give an altar call, and he was the first one in the line! I'd think, *My God, he got saved last week in the last place we were at, and now he's back here getting saved again!*

And I watch hungry people come in the prayer lines. They get prayed for, then go to the end of the line and get prayed for again. Some people put on their sweaters; some people take off their sweaters; some put on their shades; they bring changes of clothing, and they run to the restroom and come out. I look and I think, *I've prayed for you before*; they changed their sweaters and ran to the end of the line to get prayed for again, but they are hungry.

IT MUST BE REAL!

You must be hungry for Him and not just hungry for a manifestation, and it must be real. I used to lay hands on everybody every service, but I stopped because everybody started having revival meetings and laying hands on everybody every service—except nothing was happening!

You go to some churches and everybody is being pushed in the floor. Some people, when they pray for you, are determined that you're going down whether you want to or not! Anointing or no anointing, you are going on the floor! You might have come there healed, but you are leaving with whiplash!

That's how ridiculous it got, and that's why I just quit doing that for some time. I said, "Lord, You are going to have to touch Your people regardless." That's why many times when I pray for people, I don't touch them. I just stand away from them.

It got so ridiculous that one time I went to a church and before I could even pray for the people, there were lines of people lying on the floor. I walked up to the first person and said, "What are you doing? It's not time to sleep; get up." They said, "We were told by the last preacher who came through town that if we don't feel anything, then just lie down in faith!" I thought, *I have come to pray, and the whole place is lying out there. What is this?* So, I went around saying, "Get up! Get up! Stand up on your feet. No time to sleep. If you want to sleep, sleep at home!" It is a *ministry* of laying on of hands.

Then churches started having what they called "prayer teams." There's nothing wrong with that as long as the people praying have something to give! The problem was that some of them were praying, and then were going outside for a smoke break and then coming right back to lay hands on people!

I'm serious. You think I'm making this up, but I'm not, and I warned those pastors where this was happening and said, "Be careful! Make sure that the people laying hands on people have something to give. If you don't, people are going to come and get nothing." Why would you come for five times in a line to get nothing?

This is holy. There's a price to pay. If you want to lay hands on people, then pay the price. And you don't just want anybody coming up to you and laying hands on you. You don't know where those hands have been! It's holy. These are holy things.

But the pastors didn't listen. I warned them. I said, "Please control this thing. Don't let it get out of hand." They said, "No, we are free here." I said, "Fine. Then the revival you're experiencing will dissipate and disappear." And that's exactly what happened. When they gave a call for people for prayer, the prayer team was standing by and nobody came forth because everybody knew they were not going to get anything anyway. If you look at the places that were involved in all of this, you won't find even a drop of revival today.

Then there was all the other crazy stuff that happened at that time. On one occasion, there were people falling under the power, and one guy started giving another guy mouth-to-mouth resuscitation, and it was supposed to be "*prophetic!*" He didn't realize it was *pathetic*! No wonder the move of God came to an end! There were even people even dressing up in frogman suits! A deacon was walking around with flippers and a snorkel on! Come on! That's not what the move of God is about. If I want diving instruction, I'll go get it. If I want to become a certified diver, I know where to get instruction—but that's not what I came to church for !

I know some of you think I'm making this up and that this didn't really happen and I'm just playing around with you, but these things happened. And the problem is that some of these people got up and said that they had come to one of my meetings! Yes, they might have come to one of our meetings, but they left right at the offering! But sadly, we did get the blame.

Let me tell you, if your pastor ever gave you mouth-to-mouth, it's time to leave! I don't care how he said it was prophetic—it's time to leave the church! Now, I can't say if that stuff is happening right now, but it all takes away from what God wants to do. You don't need a frogman suit; you have got to get hungry for God. You don't need mouth-to-mouth (unless you are dying and somebody's administering CPR!); you just need to get hungry and thirsty for God. "Where sin abounded, grace did much more abound" (Romans 5:20). You've got to get hungry. You've got to get thirsty. I'm not talking about hungry for a manifestation. I'm talking about getting hungry for Jesus. You've got to get hungry for Him. You've got to get thirsty for Him. You have got to want Him more than anything else.

ONE TOUCH AND YOU WILL NEVER BE THE SAME

> HE WANTS TO DO IT IN YOU BEFORE HE DOES IT THROUGH YOU. HE CANNOT DO IT THROUGH YOU UNTIL HE DOES IT IN YOU. ALL IT TAKES IS ONE MAN, ONE WOMAN SET ABLAZE, AND WHOLE CITIES WILL BE SHAKEN. JUST ONE TOUCH AND YOU WILL NEVER BE THE SAME.

Evangelist Richard Moore did get touched by God, it was January, 1990 in Apollo, Pennsylvania. When I ask him to tell what happened, he cannot tell the story without getting touched again like he did that first time. He was in meetings morning and night, six days a week, for four months and did not get touched, but then one morning, the fire touched him, and he has never been the same since.

We were in Buenos Aires, Argentina, and my interpreter fell out under the power. Pastor Lucy Van Volkenburg then came and helped me interpret, but then she also got touched and when I ask Pastor Lucy to tell what happened to her when she took over, it is the same story that she tells every time. She cannot put words to it, so she tries to explain with hand gestures how the power of God hit her, and it's the same every time. There's no way you can tell that story over and over and have the same result if it wasn't God.

And as she begins to tell it is it's just like the moment it first happened. That's what the witness is about. The witness is about bringing the past into the present, so that even ten years from now, it's still as fresh as it was when it happened. It reminds you and brings not only the remembrance of what took place, but also, the very display of the power that brought it into manifestation the first time.

My mother was in a meeting when the fire fell on a Friday night in February, 1991, and the fire hit her. Like Evangelist Richard, she could never put into words what happened. It was too glorious.

God touches everybody differently. Another pastor came to the meetings in 1994, when he had been diagnosed with lymphoma cancer and only had a short time to live. They brought him to me and his wife told me that he had cancer. I put my hand on his chest and the fire of God hit him and went through him, and the cancer left. But he cannot tell the story without being overwhelmed by that same fire touching him again. One touch, one touch from Heaven, one touch from the Master's Hand, one touch, and you will never be the same!

The thing that I want you to notice is that each of these were touched in different services, different times, different months and different years, but when they begin to tell what God did, the same anointing that touched them back then, comes back into manifestation. It's not just the telling of a story; it is bearing witness and it's just like the first time it happened.

That's what the witness is about—bringing the past into the present, so that even ten years from now, it's still as fresh as it was when it happened. It reminds you and brings not only the remembrance of what took place, but also the very display of the power that brought it into manifestation the first time. That's why you need the power to be witnesses, because when you witness, the power of *the* Witness will come into manifestation and the atmosphere changes..

When Paul told his story, I believe that many times he could hardly contain himself. Why did he say, "For whether we be beside ourselves, it is to God: or whether we be sober, it is for your cause" (2 Corinthians 5:13)? Because there must have been times when he was beside himself. I'm not talking about making something up. I'm not talking about pretending. I'm talking about when you begin to witness concerning that which God has done. Then the reality of what is done will come into the now. That's why when Moses stood in front of Pharaoh and said, "Let my people go; I AM sent me," Pharaoh didn't just see Moses; he saw a burning bush. That's what it's all about, an encounter with God.

So, all I can do is make you hungry. I can't press in for you. *You've* got to press in for you. I can't get thirsty for you. *You* have to get thirsty for you. I can pray for you, I can lay hands on you until you go bald, but you must be hungry and you must be thirsty,

When God touched me with His fire, I wasn't in a meeting. As a young man of eighteen years of age in July, 1979, I pressed in and cried out in desperation and the fire of God fell on me.

So I know God can touch you wherever you are, whether in your living room, in your bedroom; if you seek Him, you will find Him. The Bible says that Jesus returned in the power of the Spirit into Galilee (Luke 4:14). The Bible says that where the apostles ministered, the Holy Spirit gave witness with signs, wonders, miracles, and manifestations (Acts 2:43; 14:3; Hebrews 2:4). That's what you were born for. That's the power of the Gospel of the Lord Jesus Christ. But He wants to do it *in* you before He does it *through* you. He cannot do it through you until He does it in you. All it takes is one man or one woman set ablaze, and whole cities will be shaken. Just one touch and you will never be the same.

When the revival broke in 1989 and began to pick up momentum in 1990–1993 in central Florida, and then around the world in different places, all the excesses arose and things begin to wane. That's when God said to me in 1996 to start The River Church. He said, "Son, it will come full circle again, but I'm just taking you in a different direction at this point."

God told me to stop having extended meetings. He said, "It'll come again. I will speak to you about the city, the time, and the place, to have the first one." And God has already dropped the city on me, I know exactly where the city is. I believe in that city will be one of the greatest revivals that we've ever held. There's going to be a whole new batch of people that have never, ever been touched by the power of God, a whole new wave of people who are going to come in. Get ready, because you will hear of it. It's not time yet, but the time shall come. Because God's not through. There are still people who need to be touched. There are still people who need to be changed.

When we take what's precious to us and we pour it on Jesus, He takes what's precious and pours it on us. It's the sweet fragrance of Heaven. He binds up broken hearts, He heals sick bodies, He sets captives free, and you'll never be the same. He's pouring perfume on you right now as you are reading this. He is setting captives free and chains are falling off of you. Hallelujah! He's pouring it out and you'll never be the same.

WHEN WE TAKE WHAT'S PRECIOUS TO US AND WE POUR IT ON JESUS, HE TAKES WHAT'S PRECIOUS AND POURS IT ON US.

5

EVANGELIST OR REVIVALIST?

Wearing the Coat Your Father Gave You

A prayer of Habakkuk the prophet upon Shigionoth.

O Lord, I have heard thy speech, and was afraid: O Lord, revive thy work in the midst of the years, in the midst of the years make known; in wrath remember mercy. God came from Teman, and the Holy One from mount Paran. Selah. His glory covered the heavens, and the earth was full of his praise. And his brightness was as the light; he had horns coming out of his hand: and there was the hiding of his power.

HABAKKUK 3:1-4

In other words, if you ask God for revival, it is more than likely that He is going to show up with lightning coming out of His hands. Do you want God to show up with lightning coming out of His hands?

Romans 10:14–15 says,

> How then shall they call on him in whom they have not believed? and how shall they believe in him of whom they have not heard? and how shall they hear without a preacher? And how shall they preach, except they be sent? as it is written, How beautiful are the feet of them that preach the gospel of peace, and bring glad tidings of good things!

There are some people who are called, some people who are sent, and others who just bought a microphone and went! Notice what the Gospel entails: the Gospel entails glad tidings of good things, and the power of God is linked to glad tidings of good things. The power of God is never linked to sad tidings of bad things.

So the first thing that you have to decide is, are you going to be a bad news preacher or a good news preacher? Because the more good news you preach, the greater the anointing will be. I have never found a bad news preacher who carried much of an anointing. I have never found a bad news preacher who carried much of any demonstration of the power of God. The whole message of salvation is always about the goodness of God, the glory of God, joy—the message that was announced at the birth of Jesus, "Joy to the world, the Lord is come" (Luke 2). And that message never changes.

It is not just for the Christmas season that we should sing, "Joy to the World." "Joy to the World" should become our theme song every day. I know there are some people who want to preach more of the judgment of God, but really, what we're supposed to do is preach more of the joy, the glory of God, the goodness of God, the mercy of God, and the grace of God. For God so *loved* the world, not God so *hated* the world. "For God so loved the world, that he gave his only begotten Son, that whosoever believeth in him should not perish, but have everlasting life" (John 3:16). And John 3:17 says, "For God sent not his Son into the world to condemn the world; but that the world through him might be saved." So our message must be one of glad tidings, good news, and joy.

EVANGELIST OR EXHORTER?

> YOU DON'T NEED TO GO LOOKING FOR A MIRACLE BECAUSE THE SIGNS WILL FOLLOW YOU. IF YOU ARE LOOKING FOR THE MIRACLE, THEN THE SIGNS ARE NOT FOLLOWING; YOU ARE FOLLOWING THE SIGNS. WHEN YOU DO WHAT GOD'S CALLED YOU TO DO, THEN THE SIGNS WILL TAKE PLACE.

There are people who fulfill a ministry of what we call "exhorters," but they are not really evangelists. Exhorters go around and sing and exhort a little bit, and some people get saved and blessed. In fact, you can go very far on the ministry of an exhorter. You can have a worldwide ministry and just be an exhorter. You might not know that, but you don't have to be an evangelist to have a worldwide ministry. You can just be an exhorter. You exhort people to get saved, and they get saved, but you will find very little demonstration of the power of God in operation.

The true ministry of an evangelist has sign gifts attached to that ministry. Somebody says, "Well, I'm a pastor. What's it got to do with me?" You had better know about this, because the Bible says to every pastor that he is to do the work of an evangelist (2 Timothy 4:5). True evangelism is connected with signs: "These signs shall follow them that believe" (Mark 16:17).

When the evangelist comes into town, there are going to be signs—a notable miracle, a creative miracle, something that will get somebody's attention. In 1991, we had a revival in Juneau, Alaska. The first Sunday night, a woman came out of a wheelchair. At that time, Juneau had a population of thirty thousand people, and everyone knew this woman. Because of this notable miracle, we had about three thousand people come through the church in the following ten or fifteen days. That's ten percent of the population of Juneau, Alaska that came through the building. You could go to the restaurant, you could go to the airport, the hotel, go anywhere, and they would talk about the revival happening down at the church because of the woman who came out the wheelchair.

That started the revival where hundreds upon hundreds were touched. People were flying in from the outlying areas on the inside passage of Alaska, and just one miracle did it. But you don't need to go looking for a miracle—the signs will follow you. If you are looking for the miracle, then the signs are not following; you are following the signs. When you do what God's called you to do, then the signs will take place.

THERE IS A KEY TO UNLOCK EVERY SERVICE

All you need is one breakthrough, and with every meeting there is a key that unlocks the door for that service. If you are called by God to minister, then you should look for the key to unlock the door of that service.

There are a lot of services that remain shut and locked and no one ever enters in. If that service were like a Boeing 747, it would be loaded up at the gateway, the door would close, attendants would serve some drinks, you'd taxi to the end of the runway, and at the end of the night, the pilot would taxi back to the gate and people would get off. It didn't go anywhere. People fastened their seatbelts; they had some peanuts and something to drink, but they never took off. They never went anywhere because they didn't know that there was anywhere that they could go.

WEAR THE COAT YOUR FATHER GAVE YOU

YOU CAN'T WEAR SOMEBODY ELSE'S ANOINTING, BUT YOU CAN WEAR YOURS. FIND OUT WHAT YOUR ANOINTING IS, AND THEN STAY WITH IT.

Now the evangelist gift operates with several sign gifts. Some evangelists might have the gift of knowledge, or the gift of healings, or the working of miracles. It is so diverse. Just as the faces of the evangelists differ, so the gifts differ. The anointings are different and there's a uniqueness about it. A person who is truly used of God will be very unique. You can't put them in a box; they might even be a little strange!

And when the power of God touches you, don't ever expect to be normal. Rather, expect to be strange, or let me find a better word for it: expect to be *peculiar*. You will be peculiar, but it's the peculiarity of the anointing on you that will make you stand out. It's like a coat of many colors. You have the choice to wear the religious plain-issue coat that is just one color—grey—that buttons up right around the neck with a little white collar or, you can wear the coat of many colors of the anointing that God places upon your life.

But I guarantee you right now, when you put on *your* coat and you wear *your* anointings, you're going to get criticized. Because you're going to stick out and folks will say, "Why can't you just be conservative?" They'll mock you and say, "Did you bring batteries for that bright coat?" And you'll be intimidated to put your coat away. But you have to make a decision to wear the coat that your Father has given you (Genesis 37), because it's a special, designer-made coat. It's limited-edition and tailor-made for you.

You don't want to go wearing somebody else's coat when God has already got one for you. That's why you really want to press in and find *your* coat. You need to wear *your* coat.

That's why you need never be jealous of somebody else's coat. You can't wear somebody else's coat; it's not made for you and won't fit. If I put on someone else's coat, I'll walk around with a coat that doesn't fit me: it's too big, or too small. So don't try to wear somebody else's coat. God has got one specially made for you.

I would have a hard time going anywhere with someone else's coat. It's the same with the anointing: you can't wear somebody else's anointing, but you can wear yours. Find out what your anointing is, and then stay with it.

THE MINISTRY OF THE EVANGELIST IS MARKED BY A PASSION FOR SOULS

Ephesians 4:7–12:

> But unto every one of us is given grace according to the measure of the gift of Christ. Wherefore he saith, When he ascended up on high, he led captivity captive, and gave gifts unto men. (Now that he ascended, what is it but that he also descended first into the lower parts of the earth? He that descended is the same also that ascended up far above all heavens, that he might fill all things.) And he gave some, apostles; and some, prophets; and some, evangelists; and some, pastors and teachers; for the perfecting of the saints, for the work of the ministry, for the edifying of the body of Christ.

So, the evangelist is there for the perfecting of the saints. But it's very hard to function in the true office of an evangelist in a local church setting because there are a limited number of lost people.

For an evangelist, the number one thing that marks his ministry is the passion for the lost, for souls and for the harvest. And that's why an evangelist is always going to be coming up with new ways to reach the harvest. We come up with many different, new, and innovative ways to reach the harvest, and we catch fish on all different levels. We use a fly rod, we use a net, we use a dragnet, and we even use sticks of dynamite in the water if necessary, because fish will come floating to the top! We will take them any which way we can. We take them, we bring them in, we process them, and we make them disciples. They belong to the King.

THE HEARTBEAT OF JESUS IS FOR SOULS

But evangelism must be an integral part of every local church. Everyone must be stirred up with a passion for the lost whether or not you are an evangelist per se. "The Son of man has come to seek and to save that which was lost" (Luke 19:10), that is the heartbeat of the Lord Jesus Christ. If that is the heartbeat of the Lord Jesus Christ, and we want His heart, then our heart will be His heart when we have a heart for the lost. Period! So, if somebody says to you, "I don't really have a heart for the lost," then they need to get saved. They need to fall in love with Jesus.

Don't let people off the hook! Some people say, "Well, we are more into teaching," or, "We are more into discipling." Rubbish! You've got to get people saved to make them disciples. How can you take old religious deadheads and try to make disciples out of them? No wonder you've got so many problems in your church! Go catch some new fish. Some people are very hard to make disciples of; they won't submit to anything. They won't submit to the Word, they do what they want to and they are a part of "Do-Your-Own-Things Ministries International!"

You can't make disciples out of that! Disciples are followers, and you can't make a disciple of somebody who is always running off here, there, and everywhere. So don't even try to make disciples of goats, because it is sheep that follow. Goats *butt*! No matter what you say, they reply, "Well, we know that, Pastor, *but* . . . ," and that's a manifestation of a goat right there! And don't turn your back, because you're going to get butted. You might be able to get a little milk from the goat, make some cheese, and if it's an Angora goat, you can get some wool, but that's about it.

You are really looking for people who will follow, submit themselves to the Word of God, and you are looking for people whom you can actually make disciples of. Some people don't want to follow the plan of God for their lives. They already have their own plans, and they flounder out in no-man's-land for years.

A TRUE EVANGELIST HAS THE FIRE OF GOD

YOU HAVE TO HAVE THE FIRE AND THE FIRE HAS TO HAVE YOU.

I believe that an evangelist must possess the fire of God to be a true evangelist. An evangelist with no fire is like a horse with no legs! It's still a horse, but it's *still*! An evangelist with no fire is like a shark with no teeth or a lion with no roar. He's a lion, but there's no roar. You have to have the fire, and the fire has to have you.

So, if you feel that God is leading you into that arena, then above all, seek the fire of God. Get the fire of God and don't leave home without it! Don't go to some place to preach with some cute little message, three points, and a poem. Don't go to some place to preach just to get invited back and say the politically correct things. Jesus said that He didn't do anything but what He first saw His Father do (John 5:19). You had better be obeying Him and doing what He says do, and if you do it, you are probably going to create some controversy. Any evangelist that is worth anything is going to be controversial. So don't think that you are going to have a noncontroversial ministry. If you do that, then basically, you are not going to have a ministry!

It always amuses me when someone reports that an individual's ministry is "somewhat controversial." Do you think the ministry of Jesus wasn't controversial? Jesus led the way in controversy!

Do you think that Paul's ministry wasn't controversial? So, if Jesus' ministry was controversial and Paul's ministry was controversial, why would you want to have a ministry that was different from them? You should rejoice. I'm not saying you should look for controversy, but you should rejoice when it comes. The anointing will bring it anyway. The closer you get to the power of God, the more the controversy.

It doesn't matter what you are doing. It was controversial at The River when we gave away a yellow Hummer. What's so funny is that the businessman who gave us the yellow Hummer actually drove a hybrid because he wanted to save on gas. But he said, "I didn't give the Hummer because it was good on fuel; I gave it because it will stick out." And it's true, you pull into the projects in the inner city of Tampa in a hybrid vehicle and you won't get anybody's attention. But you come in with a big yellow Hummer to preach the Gospel, and it will attract a crowd. And that is what that vehicle was used to do.

And it's the same way with the anointing. That's why God will drop a sign gift. He doesn't come with some hybrid thing, some hybrid anointing that nobody is really interested in. That's the problem. There are too many hybrids in the church—very conservative on fuel! But the evangelist is part of perfecting the saints, and you need an evangelist to come in and shake the place up with a passion for the harvest. If you had brought Reinhard Bonnke anywhere near a church, people would have been stirred up for the harvest.

> THE CLOSER YOU GET TO THE POWER OF GOD, THE MORE THE CONTROVERSY.

EVANGELISM AND TEACHING ARE DIFFERENT

Don't expect an evangelist to be a teacher of the Word of God, because there are many of them that can't teach a lick. In fact, some of them when they teach, just need to be quiet! As far as doctrine is concerned, as far as "line upon line, precept upon precept" is concerned (Isaiah 28:10, 13), you might be able to get there, get saved, and get healed, but the last thing you want to do is sit under their teaching ministry.

I've heard some of the weirdest stuff come from evangelists. There was one noted evangelist of years gone by who would get up and preach against women in the ministry. He would rail on it, but then ten minutes later under the anointing, he would call a woman out and prophesy over her that she was called of God to go into the ministry! Under the anointing, he did what God told him to do, but the moment he came out from the anointing, he would preach against it.

Can you imagine a woman trying to receive a word when the guy has just preached for half-an-hour that women shouldn't be in the ministry, and then the same guy is calling her out saying, "Yea, the Lord would say unto thee, thou art called into the ministry!"?

BUILD YOUR MINISTRY ON THE WORD, NOT A GIFT

You cannot build your ministry on a gift. In the early days of the ministry, the Lord really impressed upon me to build the ministry on the Word and not on a gift. It's very hard when you build a ministry on a gift because the Word is the foundation. I'm not saying that some of these evangelists couldn't teach—some of them could, but they haven't even studied the Bible!

I watch some people with the Word of God, and they are like a crazy cowboy with a six-gun. They just pull the thing out and fire everywhere. Bullet number one is so different from bullet number six that you leave the meeting more confused than when you came. You should be able to look at your life and see a pattern in the Word of God, of doctrine in the Word of God, and stability in the Word of God—going all the way back to the origins of your ministry.

That's why I love to get the tapes of when we were starting out and listen to them because it's the same message we are preaching right now, the *exact* same message! And the message doesn't change with the season or the month of the year.

EVANGELISTS MUST GO TO WHERE THE LOST ARE

If an evangelist was just stuck in churches constantly, that would be enough to drive anybody totally insane. I meet evangelists all the time who do the circuit, traveling in churches. They are upset and irritated and they are disgruntled because they are going to this church and that church and from church to church. I say, "What are you looking for?" They say, "We're looking for the lost." And then I say, "Then bless God, get out of the church and go to where the lost are!"

That would be like me trying to catch a marlin in somebody's koi pond. Imagine every week, sitting at the edge of the koi pond with a huge marlin rod and reel and trying to catch a marlin there. You are not going to catch marlin in somebody's koi pond. If you are going to catch a marlin, you have to go out into the deep.

You have got evangelists trying to bring in the great harvest of souls just in the churches. The sinners are not in the church, (well, that depends on which church you go to of course. There are some churches that are full of them!), but for the most part, if you want the harvest, you've got to get out to where the sinners are.

And then the whole ministry must be geared for the harvest. Don't get up there and teach on the "Seven Ways to Better Living." I heard one guy say when he was with a group of sinners, "Tonight we will give an invitation, but it will be nonthreatening." A "nonthreatening invitation" to the lost? Do you think I'm there with a gun stuck in the guy's nostril, threatening, "Confess Jesus right now?" No! And the gun they've taken away is actually the Holy Ghost convicting people. That's what they are talking about when they say "nonthreatening." It means they are not bringing the Holy Spirit into this.

They might be packing, but there are no bullets. But when a person with a true gift, or an evangelist gives an altar call, it's like a vacuum cleaner. If there's a sinner in the house, he is going to get sucked out of his seat and brought forward. Superglue is going to have to hold him to his seat.

AN EVANGELIST IS A SALESMAN

If God has called you to be an evangelist, learn how to give an altar call! Please practice it; learn how to give an altar call, and practice giving it over and over. It shouldn't be, "Well, umm, if you are here and you know you would like to have a deeper walk with the Lord . . . umm, if you meet us in the back, there will be tea and cookies afterwards, and some of our deacons will be glad to introduce you." No, an evangelist is a salesman, and do you know what a salesman does? He sells, and he closes the deal.

What salesman walks away without closing the deal? A salesman comes and says, "Hey, I'm coming to tell you about this great product. I've got it; you need it; you can't live without it; you want one. I'm telling you: you want two. You want two for the price of one." They don't walk away just saying, "Call me when you feel like it." A true salesman will sell refrigerators in the Arctic in the middle of winter; a true salesman will sell deep freezers to the Eskimos. A top salesman will sell a hairpiece to a man with hair!

If someone says, "I'm called to evangelize the world." I say, "Then get up and give an altar call. Convince me." If they stutter and stammer, "Well, I, errr, umm . . . ," then I say, "Sit down and be quiet. You'll be a failure as an evangelist. You persuade almost no one to be a Christian!"

REVIVALISTS REVIVE THE CHURCH

This leads me into the next thing that I want to look at, and this is the call of the *revivalist*. You might ask what the difference is. Somebody says, "Well, we are having a revival here." Is it really a revival, or just a series of meetings? What is revival? Is it a sign on the marquee that says, "Revival?" How can you have a revival where there were no signs and wonders? How can you have a revival that's over by 9:00 p.m.? Someone says, "I'm conducting a series of meetings, and we are having revival. We start at 7:30 p.m. and finish at 9.00 p.m." But you've got to allow the Holy Spirit to move. I went to a meeting one time, got all dressed up, sat there, and I was just getting into the service and they said it was over!

Revival is a place where God moves. Revival is for the Church and this is not for the lost. There is a difference between evangelizing and revival meetings. When we were in Soweto, we went for the harvest of the lost. But then there are meetings that are for revival in the Church. There is a difference between evangelizing the lost and reviving the Church. Some people don't know the difference, but there is a distinct difference between evangelizing the lost and reviving the Church. The Church has to have revival because you can't take dead people to win the lost! Dead people are not going to go where no one has gone before. Dead people are not going to go and tell the glory of God. It takes revived people to go and preach and boldly proclaim and to demonstrate. The result of revival will be that the people will go and win the harvest.

So, the revivalist goes in, gives an altar call, and gives people a chance to get saved. Then once they are saved, he gets them in revival and then takes them to go and get the lost. You can't sit there every night getting everybody that is already saved, saved again! But you can get them revived and keep them in revival, and keep them on fire for God.

A REVIVALIST BRINGS CHANGE

> A REVIVAL IS LIKE A HURRICANE, AND A REVIVALIST IS LIKE A HURRICANE. WHEN A REVIVAL COMES INTO TOWN, THE WHOLE AREA IS GOING TO BE CHANGED.

A revival is like a hurricane, and a revivalist is like a hurricane. When a revival comes into town, the whole area is going to be changed. The river will flow a different way; trees that used to be there won't be there anymore. And the impact will be felt for many years. So you have to make a decision: are you a revivalist? Somebody says, "I'm a revivalist." Okay, then you have got to find dead churches and revive them.

That's why at The River at Tampa Bay Church, I don't have speakers come through to preach on revival. Why would I do that? That's what I do! I'm not saying that there aren't people that come to The River that need reviving, but I bring people in to come and teach and do other things that I don't do.

And that's why as pastors, you need to bring people in who are specialists in their field to come and do what you can't do. But don't bring them in and put restraints on them. Don't bring them in and say, "You can't do this; you can't do that." If you have to say that, then you picked the wrong horse!

You should check them out before and have God witness with you that this is the individual to have in the church. Somebody says, "Well, if they go wrong, I'll get up and stop them." Once you give them the mic, you can't do anything about it. Let me tell you, if you give a speaker the mic and then stop him, then you are out of line. The best thing to do is to let him preach, close the service, and don't say anything about it. Most people won't know about it. There will be a few people who might know something was wrong, they just couldn't put their finger on it, and over the next few weeks you can then teach some principles that will counteract what happened. The worst thing you can do is get up there and say, "Excuse me. I didn't know he was going to do that." Well, you should have found out what he was going to do before you gave him the mic!

I went to one place to preach and the pastor said to me, "If I don't like what's going on. I'll get the mic." I said, "You had better not touch the mic!" He said, "I'll get the mic." I said, "If you do, I'll knock you out!" He said, "You wouldn't do that." I said, "Don't even try! I'll knock you flat on your back, and then I'll cast the devil out of you in front of all your people. Don't give me the mic and then take it away from me! I'm not here so you can check me out and then come and correct me in front of people. If you have a problem with me, we will talk behind the scenes, but don't you get up after you've given me the mic and try and straighten me out. You are not my apostle. I am under your authority here, but we will talk behind the scenes and we will discuss it behind the scenes. Don't mess with my ministry and I won't mess with yours."

A REVIVALIST SHAKES PLACES UP

A revivalist goes into a place and shakes it up. When a revivalist comes to town, the place shakes and there's an upheaval, like a whole herd of swine running down a hill into the sea (and the swine could include deacons!). When a revivalist comes to town, you had better watch out; the roof of the church is going to get ripped up because somebody is coming through the roof. It's not going to be your normal service with people coming through the door—somebody's going to be coming through the roof; that's the unconventional way!

What God is about to do is send fiery, Holy Ghost revivalists to shake towns, cities, villages, and nations, and you are going to see it come forth in the coming months and the next several years. You have got to decide if you are going to be popular, or if you are going to obey God. If you are in this to be popular, you are in the wrong place. If you are in this to obey God, then you're in the right place.

You will cause a stir because when you come into a city, the first thing that will happen is that all the pastors will say, "We've been here for thirty years. Who do you think you are coming here?" It's as if they own the place and when you drove across the county line, there was a sign that said, "This county belongs to the Right Reverend Honorable Dr. So-and-So." Or when you crossed the county line and there was a sign that said, "Gatekeeper," and then had a pastor's name under it.

Gatekeeper? Sounds more like "Crypt Keeper!" If you walk in their church on Sunday morning and it looks like Friday the 13th and Halloween all wrapped in one, with Sister Franken-Monster on the organ! Don't worry, because the deacons will suck your blood by the time they've gotten through the first hymn!

There were several years that we traveled around and had crusades and we put a sign up in the foyer of every church we went to that said, "This service is not recommended for religious people, or Pharisees, Sadducees, Wouldn't-sees or Couldn't-sees!" Just like a ride at Disney World that says that a ride is not recommended for people under a certain height or if you're pregnant or have back problems, so our sign told you in the foyer that this service was not recommended for religious people. And today at The River, we have those signs on our doors.

Test yourself to make sure religion hasn't got a hold of you. And you can always test how religious you are by seeing if you can come to one of my meetings, sit through it, and remain peaceful throughout. You should have an annual checkup by coming to one of my meetings, and checking that you can sit through one service and remain peaceful without getting your feathers ruffled and your fur turned around the wrong way. Then you'll know that you passed the test, and you haven't let religion grab ahold of you!

TRUE REVIVAL HAS A COST

Even before I did an extended revival in any church, I used to tell the pastor, "You have to come sit in a week of my meetings." And when he would ask why, I would say, "Because I want to watch you closely." I would bring the pastor to a meeting two thousand miles away and sit him on the front row. I would preach and do what I do, and then I would stand right in front of him and watch him closely. I'd watch his reactions, because if he winced in the meeting, then what is he going to do when I get to his church? I'd put him through the wringer, and then at the end of the week, I'd ask, "So, do you still want me to come?"

"Yes sir."

"Are you sure? Do you know what you're letting yourself in for? Do you realize that you might not have a church when we finish?"

Now you think that I'm making this up, but Wesley in his writings said that he went to a place where they had one hundred and fifty people. He preached and left them thirty-five strong! Go read history! What does that mean? He cleared out the place. When you go to a place that hasn't had a move of God and has not had revival, and you have got crack dealers there, all kinds of things going on and then you come in there with the power of God, a clean-out will take place!

For some places, revival would be very detrimental to their religion, so you have to count the cost if you want true revival. Over the years, the problem has been that a lot of people in leadership want revival for the church, but they don't really want revival for themselves. I tell them, "You don't understand, it actually starts with you!" They say, "What do you mean, me? I don't need revival." I say, "Oh, yeah, it starts right at the top! You can't expect your people to get what you won't get yourself. And if your people did get revived, what good would that be for you because you're going to turn right around and put them back into tradition!"

We had a four-week revival in Los Angeles, California, back in 1989, and the pastor got up after I left and said to the people, "Okay, the fun's over. Now back to work!" He doesn't even pastor today. He's not even in the ministry today. God was moving in a powerful way during those four weeks. Hundreds were being saved, and he got upset.

I went to another church and when I left, the pastor spoke for six weeks on Martin Luther. I thought, *That will sure kill it! Six weeks of lectures on the life of Martin Luther!* He could have taught on the family, taught one session on Martin Luther, but six weeks on Martin Luther?

A REVIVALIST MAKES AN IMPACT

> GOD IS RAISING UP REVIVALISTS FOR THE TWENTY-FIRST CENTURY. IF YOU ARE GOING TO BE A REVIVALIST, DON'T EXPECT TO BE ON SOMEBODY'S CHRISTMAS CARD LIST!

A revivalist is there to make an impact, to impart something. I don't go to a place to go and have a meeting. When I go to a place, in my spirit I see the place being transformed and changed. I see people's lives being transformed and changed, and I release my faith to that. Many years ago, we were in San Antonio, Texas, for four nights. The Sunday after I left, they had the biggest offering in the history of the church. The pastor told me that the church was only eighteen months old, and on that Sunday morning, the offering was $82,000! Why? Because we released our faith for that. We released our faith for the blessing of God. We released our faith for lives to be changed. We released our faith for the place to be injected, and for there to be a divine deposit in the lives of the people. I don't go just to speak; I go to deposit something. We're not there to speak and for the people to say, "Nice message; I'll get the tapes." We are there to make an impact.

You have to see yourself doing that, and you have to release your faith in that. I say, "When my feet touch the soil of that place, I receive the anointing to minister there and I receive the anointing to meet the needs of the people there."

In my own life and ministry, the Lord has allowed me to plug into whatever has been necessary. If it was just coming for souls, we plugged into that mode. If it was to teach, we plugged into that mode, and that's why you need to get yourself well-rounded in the things of God so that you have all the arrows in your quiver to use. It's hard if all you can do is sing and dance. After a while, your voice gets tired and your legs get tired. It's hard when it's a dog and pony show and the dog is tired and the pony is sick!

God is raising up revivalists for the twenty-first century. If you are going to be a revivalist, don't expect to be on somebody's Christmas card list!

GET RID OF COMPETITIVENESS

> IF YOU GET INTO COMPETITION, YOU'RE ALWAYS GOING TO BE IMITATING WHAT EVERYBODY ELSE IS DOING.

Let me just share a few things now about what I see in the current condition in the world of evangelism. First of all, competition! Back during the healing revival in the 1940s, the competition was so great that it was about whoever had the largest tent, even if it was only a foot bigger than the other guys. "One tent could hold 10,000, but this tent could hold 10,001!"

Nowadays, it's about who has the greatest crowds. I hear people reporting that they are preaching to ten million people in one service. But how many people do you want in a service? Because it'll never be enough: if you have one million, you'll need two; if you have two million, you'll need five.

"I went to America and the whole of America showed up at my meeting!"

"Well, don't worry. I went to Asia and China showed up at my service!"

"We used seven hundred miles of speakers!"

"Well, I'm preaching to a potential audience of so many . . ."

Who cares? Who gives a rip? Where does it end? You get around evangelists and preachers and they are all talking big: "I get hundreds of invitations a month." I think, *Well, that's amazing. I don't!*

I was with a guy one time who said, "Everybody that I touch gets healed." I said, "You know, I had a meeting once in Fort Worth, and a man dropped dead of a heart attack. We never even prayed for him. We just had to stand and wait for twenty-five minutes while the ambulance took his dead body out!" I say stuff like that just to cause confusion. I thought, *Boy, it's like having Jesus Christ with skin on here. I nearly fell at his feet and started worshipping him!* Some preachers say, "My anointing is so powerful; my word of knowledge is so accurate," and I say, "All right. Tell me the color of my underwear, then!"

It's amazing how some people have got a word of knowledge for everybody except themselves. They say, "The Lord just spoke to me in a dream last night," but then they say, "Brother Rodney, I really need you to pray with me for direction." If God's telling you everything for everybody else, why can't you just have some direction for yourself? You ugly thing, you!

Do you know that the greatest ministry on the earth only traveled in a 20- 40-mile radius? Jesus didn't even get on a plane. He used a boat and He walked on water, but He hardly traveled anywhere. And what if God tells you to go preach to the eunuch, just to the one? Philip went and preached to the eunuch. Do you know how many times I've had to go and preach to the "eunuch," to the one? But then, Philip went to Samaria and preached to the whole city. Somebody says, "Well, what are you doing in the ministry?"

"Well, I went over to this city."

"What did you do there?"

"I just saw a man."

"Oh my! Things must be hard in the ministry!"

"No, I went by the direction of the Spirit of God to go speak to a eunuch."

Do you know how many times God takes me out of the way because I went into a place and found a "spiritual eunuch?" No life was being produced there. But we spent time with them and ministered to them, and now they are starting to bring forth life in their ministry. It wasn't a "Good News New York" or a crusade like we did in Soweto, but it was of God just the same.

It is like when we held the revival we had in Ketchikan, Alaska, a town of thirteen thousand people. Somebody hads got to go to Ketchikan. Or, when we went up to Barrow, Alaska with a population of four thousand where we had eight hundred decisions in four days.

They hadn't had a proper whaling season in years, and the Lord gave me a message to tell them, "The whales are coming." I believe that the year before, they had had four or five whales, but that next year, they had twenty-one whales! And there was a lady, 86 years of age, who said that this was the biggest whaling season she could remember since she was a little girl. Somebody had to go.

What about when we went to the aboriginal villages in the outback of Australia? You need to get excited about what God is doing whether it's on the stage at Madison Square Garden, London's Royal Albert Hall, or if it's sleeping in a sleeping bag by a fire in the Outback in Australia, and I've done all of these.

Just be happy and rejoice, get excited about your ministry, and stop worrying about what somebody else is doing. "Well, they are doing this, so I need to being doing it." No, only do what Heaven tells you to do. Trust me. You don't want to be in a place God doesn't want you to be in, so get rid of competitiveness! Get rid of it; just kill it. Chop the thing off at the head.

Pastors, please get rid of it too. Here at The River, we are not in competition with anybody in the city of Tampa. I don't care who has the biggest church. I didn't come to Tampa to build the biggest church. I came to do what God told me to do. Jesus said, "I will build my church" (Matthew 16:18). Not everybody's going to come to our church. I wouldn't allow that. I'd run them off the first Sunday! I don't want everybody in this church. Just like in my family, I know who my kids are and I don't want everybody to be my kids, and so it's the same with your church.

I have pastors say, "Isn't it amazing what the Lord has done in Houston, Texas, with Joel Osteen and the church there?" I say, "Yes, it's phenomenal, but let me tell you, his father built a great work and his father built a big foundation." So, it's great to come in and multiply what your father did, but you can't get rid of all those years in ministry of Brother Osteen, and I'm not taking away from Joel's ministry.

Thank God for what Richard Roberts did with what Brother Oral Roberts built, but it was Brother Oral who built it. Some people are blessed because their father was there to build it. Others don't know what their father built and wouldn't receive what their father built. Others had to build because nobody else built. So just be happy where you are building.

Let me tell you something that will shock you: the buildings of some of the greatest churches in the world don't even seat more than a thousand people. From Argentina to England, some of the great churches in the world are not ten-thousand-seat buildings, and yet you see the impact of that church all over the place. But in America, everything is about buildings.

People used to come into The River and say, "Oh, I see a large, ten-thousand-seat auditorium," and I'd say, "Get away from me, you worker of iniquity!" Now if they had come in and brought a check for $20 million and then had said that they saw a building, I'd have said, "Hey we can talk!" But now of course, under the guidance and leading of the Holy Spirit, we have our outdoor Pavilion of Dreams, that can hold up to 10,000 people and our new sanctuary, seating over 2,800 people—which was finished in five-and-a-half months and everything is paid in full. And we are about to start the next phase of our building project. We are not competing with anyone, we are simply doing what He told us to do, how He told us to do it, and following His timetable and plan. And it's all part of the vision.

If you get into competition, you're always going to be imitating what everybody else is doing. If you do what God tells you, He might tell you to do something that is unique, that has never been done before. I'm just trying to help people so they don't get disillusioned. Just run the race God has for you. If God's using somebody, rejoice and get excited about it, but don't ever get into competition about it.

We've even had pastors in the Tampa area come here to be trained by our team to win souls for their church which is within ten miles of our building! They don't understand it and ask, "What's your angle?" How about the Kingdom of God is our angle? How about souls coming into the Kingdom is our angle? They ask, "Why would you help us?" But why shouldn't we? We help everybody! You have to get rid of competitiveness. Shut it off. Relax in who you are and just chill out.

GET RID OF PRIDE AND JEALOUSY

Then, you must get rid of spiritual jealousy. It's a terrible thing in ministry; it's a terrible thing among people in the music ministry. The competition of, "I sing better than you." You have to deal with that little green monster that tries to raise its head. It's as if when the devil fell, he fell in the choir! Remember this: we are nothing; Jesus is everything, so get rid of pride.

I said earlier that I heard a preacher say that he was one of four people in the world doing anything for God, but let me tell you that when you say that, you are heading for a crash. You are heading for a brick wall. Other people did that just before they crashed; those are the leaves that are dropping from a tree that's about to fall to the ground. There are people all over the world doing things for God, and you have never even heard about them—and they're not on Christian Television!

GET RID OF COVETOUSNESS AND GREED

> THE MINISTRY MUST GROW BY FAITH AND PATIENCE, NOT BY COVETOUSNESS, GREED, AND COMPETITION. THOSE MUST NOT BE THE DRIVING FORCES BEHIND MOTIVATING AN INDIVIDUAL, BECAUSE THEN, THE MOTIVES ARE IMPURE. AND WHEN THE IMPURE MOTIVES THAT ARE DRIVING YOU ARE GREED, COVETOUSNESS, PRIDE, SPIRITUAL JEALOUSY, AND COMPETITION, THEN WHAT FOLLOWS IS FEAR.

You must also get rid of pride and hidden sin. Just get rid of it! Get rid of greed. You don't have to be greedy, and you don't have to be covetous. You just have to learn how to plug into the blessing. Don't covet anybody else's wife. Don't covet anybody else's donkey or ass; (that's what the Bible says—Deuteronomy 5:21). Don't covet anybody else's house or have something just because someone else has one.

A lot of what is achieved is done through covetousness and greed, and what you have to understand is that the ministry must grow by faith and patience, not by covetousness, greed, and competition. Those must not be the driving forces behind motivating an individual because then, the motives are impure. And when the impure motives that are driving you are greed, covetousness, pride, spiritual jealousy, and competition, then what follows is fear. Fear is the next factor that is in that ministry and everything will be done out of fear.

If you are fearful, then the next thing you're going to need is bodyguards. But we cannot operate on the base desires of the carnal, fleshly nature and try to build a ministry that's going to stand and last until Jesus comes. We have to build it on the fruit of the Spirit—love and joy.

Now, you can use what people are doing to inspire you to new heights, but don't ever go somewhere and say, "I want that. I don't know why they've got it. If anybody should have it, I should have it. How dare they have that?" Because that greed will come in you, but the Bible says that "the blessing of the Lord, it maketh rich and he addeth no sorrow with it" (Proverbs 10:22).

I am totally believing God for hundreds of fiery, flaming, Holy Ghost evangelists and revivalists to come forth. My faith is released in that. We went to Soweto for ten days, and we did the best we could. We spent $550,000 and the crowd started at 20,000 and went to 115,000. We had all opposition break out and we had all hell break loose, but we had 177,600 conversions on the field and 28,845 in the schools and on the streets. I realized then that we needed a hundred of these crusades going on at the same time and that one man cannot do it all.

I also learned that we were not ready to do mass crusades at that time. You won't hear preachers telling you that, but we came back to the drawing board. Did we do what God told us do? Yes, you'd better believe it. With all the hell that broke loose, you'd better believe we did what God told us to do! Not only did we have churches saying we had canceled, but they were undermining us and were saying that we had hardly anybody there and that we were lying about the turnout. It went from bad to worse. So we had to ignore everything, and just go for the harvest. We realized that an estimated forty percent of the crowd was

HIV positive, so probably many of them will have already died unless God healed them. But they are in Heaven now. And we learned from this experience!

So get rid of competitiveness, pride, jealousy, covetousness and greed. Thank God we can take the Word and just follow the pattern of the Word. If we build on the Word, we will stand the storm. We will stand the test of time. If we build on the Word, the Word will never fail. Remember, you cannot build on a gift. The gift flows and fluctuates, so you must build on the Word.

COOPERATION BETWEEN A REVIVALIST AND A PASTOR

In order for a revivalist to have a revival in an area, the key is cooperation between one revivalist and one pastor. If the two join together, you have a team that can do a knockout punch in the community.

So, if you are starting out, don't try to bring ten churches together; just find one key pastor in the district who loves God and is desperate for God to move—then just plug in and talk it all out. Spend much time with that pastor, and become that pastor's friend so that he can trust you. Then he won't want to take the microphone away from you, and the two of you can lock in together and knock that city out. Everyplace we've had an awesome move of God has been because of that combination.

IDENTIFY THE MOTIVE FOR WANTING REVIVAL

As a revivalist, you must get through and identify the motives of why a church wants revival. If a church just wants to have a revival because they want church growth, it's the wrong motive. If they want revival because they want their finances to go up, it's the wrong motive. If they genuinely want a move of God because they have a genuine love for people, that's the right motive.

I meet more and more people in the ministry who don't love people, and you cannot be in the ministry if you don't love people. Ministry is about people. Someone says, "I love the ministry; I hate the people!" You can't! Ministry is about people! Ministry is about giving your life for the sheep. I'm not talking about a wolf coming and taking a chunk out of you; that's different. A shepherd doesn't ever sit around and just let a wolf come take a chunk out of him, but a sheep will never bite you. I've never been bitten by a sheep. But with a wolf or a goat, keep your eyes open, and don't turn your back!

Some people want miracles, signs, and wonders, but they don't want the message. We saw that happen at the outbreak of 1993–1994. People said, "Don't listen to what he says; wait till the joy hits." That's why they're not in revival today and why they're not in the move of God today. They didn't want to listen to what I'm teaching right now. Because if they had listened to what I'm teaching, then they would have had to change something, and they didn't want to change. They said, "I'll just wait for the joy," but the move of God comes *because of the message*. Revival always comes with the message.

REVIVAL DRIVES OUT RELIGION

As I've mentioned earlier, revival will be detrimental to religion and even end up closing a church down. Just like the fig tree was cursed because it had no fruit (Matthew 21), so some places need to be shut down and put out of their misery—and that is still revival! Someone says, "What did you do?"

"I went into a place and closed the church down."

"Oh my God! How terrible!"

"No, it was good. It was just a fig tree that needed to be removed!"

I preached for a guy that I've known all my ministry life who was in southern Africa at the time. He had struggled with his church for seventeen years. I talked to him and said, "Listen, you know the time has come when you just probably need to 'get out of Dodge.'" But he wouldn't listen. He was stubborn. He said, "We are out of Egypt and going to the Promised Land. Jesus is Lord; everything's going to be fine. We are going to do great, and we will have a breakthrough one day." I said, "Look, I'm just telling you right now, by the Holy Ghost, it isn't going to happen here! Do you want to sit here until you die? I know you love the people but let somebody else love the people."

In desperation, I paid for the man and his wife to get out of there. I got him to hand over his church, and I took him to another country and put him in a training school for a year. I started helping him to get traveling, and he traveled for three years. Now he pastors a church in England, and he's been made overseer of some churches both there and in the south of France! Later when I spoke to him on the phone, he was like a pig in mud; he was so happy. He said, "I'm fulfilling the call of God. I see it now." But if I had left him where he was, he'd still be there saying, "We're coming out of Egypt. Jesus is Lord!" I could see there wasn't fruit on this tree. It was dead and it was hurting him and his family.

PASTORS MUST FEED THEIR FLOCK

When revival comes to a church, one of the resons that it does not continue in that church is because people try to produce revival in every service. That's why on Sunday mornings here at The River (and if you hang around The River or watch by way of the Internet, you'll know), I bring the Word of the Lord pastorally to the people.

Someone says, "We went to church today, but we didn't have revival." But what is revival? It's a revival message; it is a message that just came from Heaven. If they think that revival is just falling on the ground, flopping like a fish and laughing like a hyena, then I guess that's all they're going to do.

I don't search for a message during the week. I don't go looking around. "What can I preach on? My God! I'd better pull something out of the hat quickly." There are even Saturday nights when I still don't know what God's going to do. I say, "Lord, I know tomorrow morning I will have it." The Lord gives me many of my messages in that moment just as I am waking up. The title of the message will suddenly hit me, and I'll get up, take a shower, go straight into my office, and write my whole message out. Then I walk in with a fresh message from Heaven that God's given me for the church. And it can be on any different thing that God wants to deal with.

When the revival first broke out, I had a pastor call me saying, "I don't know what to do because people are leaving the church." I said, "Why?" He said, "I haven't preached in eight weeks." I said, "I don't blame them for leaving; I'd leave too! What are you doing?" They said, "I get there, and the power of God falls, and I fall out behind the podium." I said, "What do you do then?" He replied, "Oh, I just lie there for an hour-and-a-half!" I said, "No wonder people are leaving the church!" Imagine that every time you go to a restaurant, the chef comes out of the kitchen and goes, "Ha-ha" and falls out. You are sitting there looking at the menu and you want some food, but the chef's rolling on the ground and he's covered in food. He's eating and saying, "Oh, it's so great; it's wonderful." You are there saying, "Can I get some?"

Some people try to duplicate everything in revival in one service, and you can't do it. You don't have to be bopping up and down like a chicken, running around and jumping over pews. There are different kinds of anointings, and often people pull back because of excesses. Then they quench the Spirit in every area. Don't quench the Spirit and don't despise prophesying, hold fast to that which is good.

So pastors, you have to feed the flock of God, and on Sunday mornings, bring a pastoral message. Bring something that will feed the flock and put food in them. This is my number one goal on a Sunday morning, to feed the people. I want them to leave the service feeling that they got fed.

Now, if a "tornado" hits in the middle of the service, that's great. If the power of God flips people over, that's wonderful, but we have got to feed the people. Now on Sunday night services, who knows what's going to happen? I don't even know what's going to happen!

FOLLOW THE HOLY GHOST

As a pastor, you must follow the Holy Ghost. There are different times and different seasons. God might lead you to take your whole church in a season of prayer for a month; just follow Him. It doesn't matter what the church down the road is doing. Not everybody has to have a home cell. I'm not against them, but you don't have to have them. If you do have a home cell, make sure they are under the anointing, everyone is on fire, and they are winning souls. I know I'm messing in somebody's kitty litter box right now! If you want to have a home group, have one, but I've watched some of the biggest churches in the world struggle with these over the years. They have thousands of home groups, and I've seen them build the church up and destroy the church down. Some of them have built the greatest churches that then go down to the smallest churches, then built the greatest churches up again that then go down to the smallest churches again. And they go up and down every five years. They have a brand new church every five years. "We are growing, we are growing!" I tell them, "You were five years ago!"

Only do what God tells you to. What happens in a lot of churches is that they are schizophrenic. For two years, they'll run on *this* and they try *this*, and then two years later, the pastor comes back from another conference, saying, "We are going to do *this*," and he changes everything around. He fires people, moves things around, and then they run on that rabbit trail for three years. Then three years later, he goes to another conference somewhere else, and comes back and changes all that. Eventually, the people don't know where they are or what's happening.

If you come to The River, at least you know what's going on. We're not changing every week!

KEEP YOUR OWN FLAVOR

And don't let your church lose the flavor of what you are. Can you imagine me trying to minister with the flavor of the high church, speaking in Elizabethan English? "Now, as we are gathered in this place, let us bow our heads for a word of prayer, Our most gracious heavenly Father, we thank Thee that Thou in Thy great love and Thy great Mercy dost look down from Heaven and Thou dost look upon us, O God, and Thou dost see our need. Oh, Lord, we pray even this day, as we gather in this place, that Thou wouldst touch Thy people, oh God."

No! that isn't going to happen! And if you think I'm going to stand up at a podium the whole time, it isn't going to happen. If you handcuff me to it, I'll pick that thing up and walk to the front row. Don't let your church lose its flavor.

So, pastors, just relax in what God has called you to do. Just as in a restaurant if you serve Chinese food, then serve it to the best of your ability. Have the best chopsticks you can; have the best egg drop soup you can; the best sweet and sour pork. If you serve Mexican food, don't try to bring out Chinese food!

DON'T LET MONEY BE YOUR MOTIVE

Now moving to look at finances, evangelists and revivalists, don't ever preach with a financial motive. Don't try to give what you don't have. Stay with your anointing and get the full cooperation of the pastor, because he is in charge of the church. Don't bite off more than you can chew, and don't try to get in the pulpit just because it has a famous name. "Oh, I'd love to preach there." No, you idiot! Come here; let me pray for you. You don't want to go there! Why would you want to put yourself through that? Only go where God has opened the door. Don't try to get into some pulpit. It's almost like notches on a belt: people think, *If I can get into that pulpit, it'll be really . . .*

So don't do anything for a money motive. Don't go to preach someplace for money; don't get hired to be a pastor because they give you a great salary. It might be the worst salary you ever received, and they've paid you into a living hell! Do it for nothing if God tells you to, and that's going to bring the increase!

KNOW WHEN TO QUIT A REVIVAL

Lastly, you have to know when to quit a revival. We have walked away from meetings in the height of the meeting with the place packed. I have closed down meetings on a Friday when it was packed with three thousand people in the building and a thousand in the overflow. That's when I ended the meeting and told the pastor, "This is the last meeting today." I left, and in the natural, everything in me was screaming, "Are you crazy?"

But you have to know when you have to leave. There is a saying, "He who fights and runs away lives to fight another day" (Oliver Goldsmith).

Now regarding extended meetings, don't just decide to have an extended meeting for the sake of having one. If you have an extended meeting, the thing should grow and the numbers should increase. If you are having a meeting and the numbers are dropping off, do you know what that means? Shut it down! That means it's over!

Somebody says, "I'm running an extended meeting, it's been running for seventeen weeks."

"How many have you got?"

"Forty people a night."

"That's extended nothing; that's extended purgatory!"

WILL YOU LAY EVERYTHING DOWN FOR JESUS?

THE FACT OF THE MATTER IS THIS: IT MIGHT COST US OUR VERY LIVES. BUT THE BIBLE TELLS US THAT JESUS IS LOOKING FOR THOSE WHO LOVE NOT THEIR LIVES EVEN UNTO DEATH (REVELATION 12:11). THE STRENGTH OF THE EARLY CHURCH WAS THE BLOOD OF THE MARTYRS THAT CRIED OUT.

Do you feel called to carry the fire of revival to shake America? If you are a pastor, are you going to have a church of the fire of God? Are you called to be a fiery, flaming, Holy Ghost evangelist and revivalist? Will you lay everything down for Jesus?

I had a call from one of our associate evangelists who was in a certain city. He said, "The police are here! The rabbis are here. There's major upheaval." I said, "What's the problem?" He said, "I want you to pray for me." I said, "For what? Haven't you been praying for exactly this? Haven't you been crying out for revival? Well, you are having it! Show me another church that has rabbis trying to shut it down and the police outside! Rejoice! Get arrested! The apostles were thrown in prison!" I started laughing, and I don't think he was too excited with me. I said, "What do you want me to pray for you—that it goes away? That you don't have revival? You've been asking for it, and now you've got it buddy. This is wonderful! Hallelujah! This is great. Get arrested! Get thrown into prison! This is it; this is the big one. This is what you've been praying for."

Maybe we should count the trophies we have, not by the crowds or accolades, but by how many bones were broken at the last place we preached, or how many times we were thrown in prison. I'm serious. People wanted to kill Charles Finney; they tried to run him off. We have to choose what we're going to do.

I heard the story of a group that went into the Siberian part of the former Soviet Union for two weeks and handed out, I believe it was, the Gospel of John and the Book of Acts. They came back two years later, and there was a young girl, twenty years old, pastoring a church of a thousand people. She had a black eye and was bleeding, and they said, "What happened?" She said, "I just came out of prison. I got beaten up," and they were all shocked and horrified. She said, "What's your problem?" And she opened the Book of Acts and read where the apostles were beaten. She pointed to the Bible and said, "It's here. It's here. That's how I knew it was all right. It's here." A young girl, twenty years old, pastoring a church of a thousand. All she had was John and Acts, but she knew it was fine to be beaten because she saw it written there.

Just close your eyes right now and raise your hands to Heaven.

> Father, I pray that from those reading this book, there would come an elite group of "Green Berets" and of "Holy Ghost Rambos." That the fire of revival would not only consume them but consume all in their path. I pray that you would use couples to ignite fires from here to the Black Sea, across the plains, to the tip of South America, across Asia and Europe, for the time is so short. You can't do it without somebody set on fire, somebody set ablaze, somebody carrying this fire, somebody who's died to self, somebody who's dead to what other

people think, somebody who's full of, prompted by, stimulated by, and manipulated by the Holy Ghost. Oh, may we become more Holy Ghost possessed!"

This is pretty radical, but what if I gave a call for some martyrs who are willing to give their lives? Who would say, "I'm willing to lay down everything, everything. *Everything*! My reputation, my possessions." Somebody says, "Well, God's not asking us to die for Him." No, He's asking us to live for Him. But if we love our life, we're going to lose it. If we lose our life, we will find it (John 12:25).

What you don't realize is that many of you *are* beaten on a daily basis by the words that are inflicted on you from the mouths of people. They are like stones coming at you. You are already beaten; you are already lashed; it's just a different kind of beating. It's just not the kind of beating where the Gospel is underground and you've been incarcerated in some communist nation.

The fact of the matter is this: it might cost us our very lives. But the Bible tells us that Jesus is looking for those who love not their lives even unto death (Revelation 12:11). The strength of the early Church was the blood of the martyrs that cried out. Yet, do you know what people from other nations say who have come out of China, out of the underground church? They say that what shocks them about America is that people build such big churches without God!

Will you lay everything down? Will you die to self and what others think? Will you become Holy Ghost possessed?

MAYBE WE SHOULD COUNT THE TROPHIES WE HAVE, NOT BY THE CROWDS OR ACCOLADES, BUT BY HOW MANY BONES WERE BROKEN AT THE LAST PLACE WE PREACHED, OR HOW MANY TIMES WE WERE THROWN IN PRISON.

6

THE PURPOSE OF PENTECOSTAL POWER

The Witness of the Resurrection

> Father, we thank You for Your Word. We thank You for utterance in the Holy Ghost. I pray that every heart will be receptive to receive all that Heaven has for each one reading this book and that each one will receive what they need. I pray that special endowments and graces of the Holy Ghost will be made manifest, and Lord, that You would cause Your anointing to destroy every yoke, to set every captive free, to bind up every broken heart, to let all the oppressed go free. Father, we bless You now and we praise You. We thank You for it. And we give You all the glory, the praise, and the honor. Lord, I'm nothing You are everything. Come now and touch Your people. In Jesus' Name I pray. Amen.

I want you to go to probably one of my favorite passages of Scripture, and we will start at Acts 1:8, and then we will go right on to chapter 2. No matter how many times you have read this before, follow this now. Jesus is speaking:

> But ye shall receive power, after that the Holy Ghost is come upon you: and ye shall be witnesses unto me both in Jerusalem, and in all Judæa, and in Samaria, and unto the uttermost part of the earth.
>
> (ACTS 1:8)

> And when the day of Pentecost was fully come, they were all with one accord in one place. And suddenly there came a sound from heaven as of a rushing mighty wind. And it filled all the house where they were sitting.
>
> (ACTS 2:1-2)

"And suddenly." I love that word "suddenly." I love the Amplified Version, Classic Edition, here, which says, "like . . . the rushing of a violent tempest blast" (v. 2a AMPC).

> And there appeared unto them cloven tongues like as of fire, and it sat upon each of them. And they were all filled with the Holy Ghost, and began to speak with other tongues, as the Spirit gave them utterance. And there were dwelling at Jerusalem Jews, devout men, out of every nation under heaven. Now when this was noised abroad, the multitude came together, and were confounded, because that every man heard them speak in his own language. And they were all amazed and marvelled, saying one to another, Behold, are not all these which speak Galilæans? And how hear we every man in our own tongue, wherein we were born? Parthians, and Medes, and Elamites, and the dwellers in Mesopotamia, and in Judæa, and Cappadocia, in Pontus, and Asia, Phrygia, and Pamphylia, in Egypt, and in the parts of Libya about Cyrene, and strangers of Rome, Jews and proselytes, Cretes and Arabians, we do hear them speak in our tongues the wonderful works of God. And they were all amazed, and were in doubt, saying one to another, What meaneth this? Others mocking said, These men are full of new wine. But Peter, standing up with the eleven, lifted up his voice, and said unto them, Ye men of Judæa, and all ye that dwell

> at Jerusalem, be this known unto you, and hearken to my words: for these are not drunken, as ye suppose, seeing it is but the third hour of the day. But this is that which was spoken by the prophet Joel; and it shall come to pass in the last days, saith God, I will pour out of my Spirit upon all flesh: and your sons and your daughters shall prophesy, and your young men shall see visions, and your old men shall dream dreams: and on my servants and on my handmaidens I will pour out in those days of my Spirit; and they shall prophesy: and I will shew wonders in heaven above, and signs in the earth beneath; blood, and fire, and vapour of smoke: the sun shall be turned into darkness, and the moon into blood, before that great and notable day of the Lord come: and it shall come to pass, that whosoever shall call on the name of the Lord shall be saved. Ye men of Israel, hear these words; Jesus of Nazareth, a man approved of God among you by miracles and wonders and signs, which God did by him in the midst of you, as ye yourselves also know:
>
> ACTS 2:3-23

WHAT ABOUT PENTECOST?

One of the men that greatly influenced my life, even as a young boy, was my dad's older brother. He was 18 years older than my father. He went home to be with the Lord when he was 93. But I can remember the family would travel up to the city of Pietermaritzburg to visit him. He had been a moderator of the Church of God of Southern Africa for a number of years, and He founded the Berea Theological Seminary on his front veranda back during the 1930s. He was what I would call a theologian's theologian. He was an amazing man and had such a knowledge of the Scripture. I've traveled all around the world and met many theologians, but you would be hard-pressed to find someone who had studied the Scriptures on the level that he had. I believe that he had studied every one of the Epistles probably a thousand times apiece.

As a young boy of six, seven, eight years of age, we would go over there, and as my parents would pull into the house, the other kids would go and play. But I just couldn't go and play; I wanted to sit and listen to my uncle. He talked for hours on the Word. He would begin to speak from the Book of Ruth and would spend five hours on just the first three verses. I would think, *When is he ever going to end the book?*

He took probably over thirty trips to the Holy Land and really became an irritant to the guides and anyone who took him on tour because they didn't know what they were talking about. He would just raise his hand and they would say, "Yes, sir?" And he would begin to talk about the surroundings and what happened, and everybody would shut up and just listen, and they would hand the tour over to him because he knew more about what was going on than they did.

I was blessed to pick up several of his study Bibles, which I have at home. As I was looking through some things, I found what I'm about to share, just written down in his notes. I don't know where he got it from, it probably comes from way back, because nothing is original. Somebody got it from somebody who got it from somebody else who got it from somebody else who got it from the Holy Ghost! It starts with a question, just three words: "What about Pentecost?" Then it continues as follows:

> What's in the name? Some say that "Pentecost" means fifty; technically they are correct, but to every Spirit-filled child of God, it means vastly more than a mere technical definition. There are words in our language that mean more to us than mere technicalities. For instance, the word "sterling" stands for certain quality of silverware. When we buy sterling silver we know that we are obtaining a certain definite standard of silverware. We are assured of its genuineness and we know that it will stand the test of time; we know it has value. We also know that there are cheap imitations on the market, and if we are looking for quality, we know enough to let spurious articles alone. Pentecost, what does it mean?
>
> What does it mean? What does Pentecost mean? It represents a pattern, a standard; it signifies in its spiritual significance an

empowered church. It represents a Spirit-filled experience. It stands for revival fires. It holds within its inner meaning a burden for the lost, conviction for sin, repentance, and faith towards God.

The early Church walked in the light of Pentecostal fires and these were the results that followed: not only was the Gospel preached uncompromisingly, but signs and wonders accompanied the preaching of the Word. Pentecost meant something more than a name to the early Church—a Spirit-endued people who aroused opposition from unbelievers—persecution was the result. Pentecost not only meant glory and shouting and great joy, it also meant being despised by the world, hated, stoned, being beaten with stripes, imprisonments, and many other trials. Pentecost, what does it mean today? From a scriptural standpoint, it means as much as it ever did.

It is a proven fact that those who are truly Pentecostal, with a Pentecostal message and a Pentecostal experience, backed up with a Pentecostal life of holiness, will have Pentecostal results in Pentecostal meetings, in a Pentecostal way.

Instead of putting the soft pedal on Pentecost, let us magnify the work of the Lord as manifested in Pentecostal power and glory. Pentecost has meant something wonderful to us. It has meant the mightiest revival the world has ever seen since the days of the apostles. It has meant the conversion of hundreds of thousands; likewise, untold thousands have received the baptism in the Holy Spirit and have been set on fire for God. The sick and the deformed have been miraculously healed; restitution has been made in numerous cases; a life of holiness has been the experience of those who have come up under the blessing of Pentecost. Churches have been revived, a great evangelistic movement in home and foreign fields has been established.

Sadness, sickness, sin and shame, half-heartedness and indifference have given way before the mighty God-sent avalanche of Pentecostal revival!

When I read this to another minister, the power of God hit me and I began to weep uncontrollably.

PENTECOSTAL POWER MUST TRANSLATE TO OUTSIDE THE CHURCH

> THERE'S A PURPOSE TO THIS PENTECOSTAL POWER.

Some would think that the purpose of Pentecostal power is just to come and "hoot and holler" and jump over the pew and run around the building. Growing up in Pentecost the way I did, people did that often. There would be great moments of heavenly ecstasy where people would burst out in other tongues. In the church that I grew up in, we had three people who would just burst out at any time. You never knew what was going to happen! Brother "Rubababanda" would start, then Sister "Hekikicoola," then Sister "Rukoondu." At any one service they might all three take off. The power of God would fall, people would come under the influence of the anointing of the Spirit of God, and they didn't really know what to do other than what they had done last time. It didn't matter what was happening; they would just interrupt everything, "Rub-ba-ba-ban-da," "He-ki-ki-cool-a," "Ru-koon-du," and off they would go in their own little realm.

I'm not saying this is wrong, but they were not taught how to translate that to outside the four walls of the Church. People came in with marriages in a mess, home in a mess, business in a mess—everything a mess and upside down. In the church you'd think all Heaven was breaking loose, but they would go right outside and all hell was breaking loose, because they could only connect the display of the power of God to when it was in manifestation in a meeting.

The power of God is present now, and the fire God can touch you in a very special way and impact your life. It's not just about coming to a meeting and hooting and hollering and running around the building. There's a purpose to this Pentecostal power.

PENTECOSTAL POWER IS EXPLOSIVE POWER

> YOU ARE WHAT YOU ARE. YOU WILL NEVER FIT INTO ORGANIZED RELIGION. YOU WILL NEVER FIT INTO THE STATUS QUO.

What good is it if you buy a sports car that has 400 - 675 hp (horsepower) on paper, but you just sit and look at it? You know that it has all that power, but you never get to drive it. There's nothing like punching the accelerator and feeling the power when you need it! But there's nothing worse than punching the accelerator, and you get stuck in the slow lane. God has not designed for you to live in the slow lane, because He's given you the power necessary to pass and overtake every obstacle that stands in your path.

This power is more than just an experience when we gather together in His Name. This power is to be applied when you walk out of the door, when you face life's problems. This power is like dynamite; it is explosive power! Did you know that you are a walking stick of Holy Ghost dynamite? Some of you just haven't had your fuse lit!

It's explosive power. It comes from the Greek word *dunamis*, which means "explosive power." "Ye shall receive [explosive] power, after that the Holy Ghost is come upon you" (Acts 1:8).

Have you ever lit a firecracker? Have you lit one and the fuse fizzled? That's how some Christians are! When they come, they all they look great and they have this long fuse, but you light them and they fizzle.

As kids, we used to take firecrackers and bend them over so they broke and then tap some of the gunpowder out on the ground and light it. We used to call it a *shuri* because that was the sound it made, and I've seen many "shuries" in the Body of Christ!

Somebody says, "What's he doing?" He's a shuri—a dud or a blank—that's what he is. The powder is there and the fuse is there, but somehow there was no connection to cause the explosion, so he is a dud or a blank. But God has not ordained that you be a dud or a blank!

I'm a big-game hunter, and when you are in the African bush, and you have an elephant coming at you, or you have a leopard, a lion, a buffalo, or a rhinoceros coming at you, the last thing you want is a blank in your gun! You can have the best firearm in the business, but the last thing you want is to find that somebody swapped your gun for a starter pistol! I have met many believers out in the field, and a "buffalo" is charging them, an "elephant" is charging them, and they are sitting there with a blank, a starter pistol, or a little cap gun!

I like what I heard one preacher say; he said, "If all the power in their life combined with dynamite exploded, it wouldn't be enough to blow their nose!" You don't want to get rid of the gunpowder. You were made to "explode" for God. Some of you are waiting for a breakthrough in the ministry, but you need to explode for God! God is sitting there thinking, *I put everything in him. We lit that fuse*. He turns to the angel. "We lit that fuse, didn't we?" And the angel sighs and says, "Lord, I know: he's a dud, a blank!"

You can't stand and sing in your church, "I'll be a dud or a blank for Jesus." Maybe that mentality comes from "you in your small corner and I mine," and "like a little candle burning in the night." You are not a candle. You are a light but you are not a candle with wax it all over the place. No, this is explosive power! You cannot get away from that, so stop trying to apologize for it. Stop trying to water it down. You are what you are. You will never fit into organized religion. You will never fit into the status quo. You are filled with explosive power.

DO NOT BE OFFENDED BY PENTECOSTAL POWER

If you go over to Disney World and go to any of the firework displays that they have every night, they don't use any duds! And if they had a batch of fireworks that came in that didn't explode, they would contact the company and say, "Listen, the stuff you are sending us is a dud. People are coming here to see things being blown up." And if you are someone who names themselves as one who has had this Pentecostal experience, then shame on you if you are a dud! If you are trying to get accepted, trying to tone down your ministry, you need to come forward and put your credentials on the platform and promise that you'll never say that you had this Pentecostal experience. "Well, Brother Rodney, I embarrassed myself. I went preaching somewhere, and the fire of God got on me and I embarrassed myself." You think I'm kidding, but I heard a national minister tear his own ministry to pieces for this for about three hours. You know that you must be really offended when you tear your own ministry apart! That's like "Shoot-Yourself-in-the-Foot Ministries International."

How can you get offended at what God has placed on the inside of you, just because some sinner out there doesn't like what you do? So suddenly, does that mean you're going to change to become acceptable to that sinner? Don't you realize that the world is never going to understand what we do. We are not here to be understood!

Someone says, "Oh, you are that ministry that goes around and all those people get joy and fall on the ground and they have to be carried out." Yes! That's what we do. We carry around with us explosive joy. People don't just sit and smile in the meetings. They get ahold of what's called "joy unspeakable." I see a watering down taking place, where everybody is trying to stray away from what is Pentecostal power, but I have decided we will just crank it up a notch. Someone says, "But people will leave the church." Well, I just tell people what they are letting themselves in for when they come. I tell people what to expect—that anything can happen and probably will! There will be walking and leaping and praising God (Acts 3:8). There will be cups running over (Psalm 23:5). There will be rivers flowing out of your belly (John 7:38).

DO NOT BACK DOWN FROM PENTECOSTAL POWER

"Rivers," Jesus said. "*Rivers*!" The devil doesn't want that river to flow because he wants to stop the explosive power. Look what happens in the natural with tsunamis. Look at the devastation. That's what you will have on the devil's kingdom when the river of God begins to flow. The devil can't stop it, he doesn't know what to do with it. So he comes with persecution; he comes with intimidation because he wants to stop the flow. He wants you to just be a "dud for Jesus."

You have to make a decision that you are not going to back down. It's not about being loud for loudness' sake; it's not about making a noise; it's not about jumping a pew. But it's not about having a funeral service each week either, "Ashes to ashes, dust to dust. The Lord giveth and may He taketh it all away soon!"

Many times people talk to me and say: "Well, Jesus didn't walk around and jump up and down and make a noise." But that's not true! The Bible talks about him spinning around (Zephaniah 3:17, "....He will joy over thee." The Hebrew primitive root for 'joy' means, "to spin round [under the influence of any violent emotion]" Strong's Exhaustive Concordance). He whirled around. Did you think that He was dead, walking around barefoot with a lamb under His arm, speaking Elizabethan English?

When the woman with the issue of blood touched the hem of His garment, what happened? Virtue flowed out? Do know that word *virtue* is the same Greek word as "power," *dunamis*? When she touched the hem of His garment, boom! Power flowed into her body (Matthew 9:20-22).

If you, as children of God, full of the Holy Ghost, are embarrassed by your own explosions, there's something seriously wrong with you. You asked God for power: "Oh God, give me power. Give me your fire." But then when the Lord puts it in you you say, "Oh! I'll control myself! Last time I went to the meeting, my God! The fire of God hit me, and I took off and cleared three pews!" Your head might have said, *You are crazy and you are making a fool of yourself,*" but oh, didn't it feel so good? Don't be offended by Pentecostal power.

PENTECOSTAL POWER CHARGES YOU UP

> THE PURPOSE OF THE POWER IN A MEETING IS FOR THE EDIFICATION OF THE BODY OF CHRIST, TO CHARGE PEOPLE UP, LIKE A HOLY GHOST GENERATOR.

The purpose of the power in a meeting is for the edification of the Body of Christ, to charge people up like a Holy Ghost generator. You might not realize it, but an angel comes and connects the terminals while you sit, and the Lord's charges you up, getting you ready. Because He knows that you need to be charged up and ready for what you need to take care of.

The Bible says, "Now when they saw the boldness of Peter and John, and perceived that they were unlearned and ignorant men, they marvelled; and they took knowledge of them, that they had been with Jesus" (Acts 4:13). Why? Because from them came the same power that was on Him. He said, "These works and greater works than these shall you do" (John 14:12, paraphrased).

Someone says, "I'm not going to jump a pew. I'm not going to run down the aisle." But you can't help it! It's fire! It's firepower! It's the power to live right, the power to walk right, the power to talk right, the power to preach right, the power to pray right, the power to do right! If it was necessary for the early Church, then how much more for the latter Church? This power is dynamic in its working. And it's the only thing that will shake Europe. It's the only thing that will shake South America. It's the only thing that will shake North America. It's the only thing that will shake Asia.

All I'm trying to do is get you fired up. That's what my job is, to get you fired up. We used to sing a song when I was a kid, and we would sing it for hours. I remember as a little boy standing Sunday night around the piano and the organ, and singing it:

It's the Holy Ghost and power
That is keeping me alive
Keeping me alive, keeping me alive
It's the Holy Ghost and power
That is keeping me alive
Jesus is keeping me alive.

(EMMA COTTON AND MARVIN V FREY)

As we sang it, the people would start falling out. People would gather round the altar to sing for hours and then just start falling out unde the power of God. Boom! Boom! Boom! You've heard of, "shop until you drop," but they sang until they dropped!

DO NOT BE ASHAMED OF PENTECOSTAL POWER

> NO ONE CAN BE ASHAMED. WE CANNOT BE ASHAMED OF THE BOOK OF ACTS.

We always say there's enough firepower in one meeting to shake the whole of America. Pentecostal power brings Pentecostal noise and, it was a violent tempest blast and a mighty rushing wind on the Day of Pentecost (Acts 2:2). Jesus didn't say some a gentle little breeze and a little spark!

If ever the Church needed the power, they need it today. People are dying like flies! There are more sick people on the planet than there have ever been. There are more demon possessed people on the planet than there's ever been; there are more people bound up. If ever the Church needed power, it needs it today! And it does have the power; it's just not using it because it's afraid what somebody else might think. We *cannot* back down! No one can be ashamed. We cannot be ashamed of the Book of Acts.

When you come to a Holy Ghost meeting, you are going to have an opportunity to have a Pentecostal experience. Why do you think the prophet of old said that it's just like "fire shut up in my bones" (Jeremiah 20:9)? But in many circles of the churchworld, there is a power shortage! That's why God wants to use you like a Holy Ghost power plant for whole areas that have had blackouts, where the power has been down for years. We know what that's like living in Florida with hurricanes and the power outages. Thank God for generators! But right now, God's been using different people to be "generators" to go and take some power to places where there is no power. It is time not just to have some portable generators, but to put up some *permanent* power plants.

YOU ARE A CARRIER OF PENTECOSTAL POWER

> EVERY TIME YOU DEMONSTRATE THE POWER, YOU PROVE TO THE WORLD THAT HE IS ALIVE.

In order to do that however, the Lord Jesus must have faith in you. He must have confidence in you because He chose you to be the carrier of that power. After all, it's not *your* power. So why would you be ashamed when it's not your power? Why would you be embarrassed when it's not your power? If you could not take the glory for the power that's on display, then how can you take the criticism for the power that's on display? All you are is a conduit. If they want to criticize the person who dispenses the power, they have got the wrong person. They have to go to the source, because He said, "I will pour out of my Spirit on all flesh" (Acts 2:17). So it's originating right from the very throne of God. It is coming from the throne of God to the earth, and then hitting the believer who would yield himself or herself, and then being dispensed out of that believer.

You are a distribution point. That's why He said, "Lay hands on the sick" (Mark 16:18), because as you reach out your hands and touch the sick, it's His power that flows through you, but you must be under His command.

The power is dynamic in its working. Do you know why He says that you're going to be a witness? Do you know what you are going to be witnesses of? You are really witnesses of the resurrection! Every time you demonstrate the power, you prove to the world that He is alive.

PENTECOSTAL POWER MOVES YOU

> THIS POWER IS BIRTHED IN THE PASSION OF PRAYER, AND THE POWER MUST THEN BE RELEASED THROUGH THE VESSEL.

This power is going to move you; it is going to move you from Jerusalem to Judea, then to Samaria, and then to the uttermost parts of the earth (Acts 1:8). This power is birthed in the passion of an encounter with God. This power is birthed in the passion of prayer, and the power must then be released through the vessel. Somebody says, "Well, I want God to do it." He's going to do it, but He's waiting for you! That's why this whole thing of, "I don't want it to be me" is false humility, because who's it going to be, then? Somebody else?

That would be like a coffee cup or a teacup arguing and saying, "I don't want to be the one who carries the tea. I don't want to be the one who carries the coffee." Okay, then don't. Stay on the shelf. Give me another cup! All the cup does is stand and be the vessel. That's what the Holy Ghost requires you to do: be the vessel. So stop arguing! Be the vessel. Because He fills you up to pour you out.

PENTECOST POWER IS FREE

THIS IS HEALING POWER. MIRACLE-WORKING POWER, TRANSFORMING POWER; POWER THAT IS DISPLAYED EVEN IN THE VERY FACE OF DEATH.

This is power that money can't buy. In the Book of Acts, Simon the sorcerer wanted to buy the power of God (Acts 8:9–24). But you don't have enough money to buy one ounce of this! You can't buy it and it's not for sale!

This power is free! This is overcoming power to overcome every obstacle the devil puts in your path. This is delivering power to bring you out of a sticky situation, to bring you out of prison, to bring you out of captivity, to bring you out of bondage. This is healing power, miracle-working power, transforming power; power that is displayed even in the very face of death.

If we this day be examined of the good deed done to the impotent man, by what means he is made whole; be it known unto you all, and to all the people of Israel, that by the name of Jesus Christ of Nazareth, whom ye crucified, whom God raised from the dead, even by him doth this man stand here before you whole. This is the stone which was set at nought of you builders, which is become the head of the corner. Neither is there salvation in any other: for there is none other name under heaven given among men, whereby we must be saved.

Now when they saw the boldness of Peter and John, and perceived that they were unlearned and ignorant men, they marvelled; and they took knowledge of them, that they had been with Jesus.

ACTS 4:9-13:

And by the hands of the apostles were many signs and wonders wrought among the people; (and they were all with one accord in Solomon's porch. And of the rest durst no man join himself to them: but the people magnified them. And believers were the more added to the Lord, multitudes both of men and women.) Insomuch that they brought forth the sick into the streets, and laid them on beds and couches, that at the least the shadow of Peter passing by might overshadow some of them. There came also a multitude out of the cities round about unto Jerusalem, bringing sick folks, and them which were vexed with unclean spirits: and they were healed every one. Then the high priest rose up, and all they that were with him, (which is the sect of the Sadducees,) and were filled with indignation, and laid their hands on the apostles, and put them in the common prison. But the angel of the Lord by night opened the prison doors, and brought them forth, and said, Go, stand and speak in the temple to the people all the words of this life. And when they heard that, they entered into the temple early in the morning, and taught. But the high priest came, and they that were with him, and called the council together, and all the senate of the children of Israel, and sent to the prison to have them brought. But when the officers came, and found

> them not in the prison, they returned, and told, saying, The prison truly found we shut with all safety, and the keepers standing without before the doors: but when we had opened, we found no man within.
>
> ACTS 5:12-23:

Talk about a surprise! The soldiers were outside the doors and the doors were still locked, but when they opened the doors, there was nobody in there!

> Now when the high priest and the captain of the temple and the chief priests heard these things, they doubted of them whereunto this would grow. Then came one and told them, saying, Behold, the men whom ye put in prison are standing in the temple, and teaching the people (VV. 24-25).

They realized, "We can't stop these people!"

PENTECOSTAL POWER IS UNSTOPPABLE

> THIS POWER OF GOD CAN'T EVEN BE PURCHASED. YOU CAN'T RUN YOUR CREDIT CARD ON IT, AND IT CANNOT BE STOPPED.

This is unstoppable power! Look at Acts 8: "Then Philip went down to the city of Samaria, and preached Christ unto them. And the people with one accord gave heed unto those things which Philip spake, hearing and seeing the miracles which he did" (vv. 5–6). Now, the Church in modern-day America loves the hearing part, but it doesn't just say "hearing;" it says, "hearing and seeing." Verses 6b–8: ". . . hearing and seeing the miracles which he did. For unclean spirits, crying with loud voice, came out of many that were possessed with them: and many taken with palsies, and that were lame, were healed. And there was great joy in that city." And I love this—"There was *great joy* in the city!"

> But there was a certain man, called Simon, which beforetime in the same city used sorcery, and bewitched the people of Samaria, giving out that himself was some great one: to whom they all gave heed, from the least to the greatest, saying, This man is the great power of God. And to him they had regard, because that of long time he had bewitched them with sorceries. But when they believed Philip preaching the things concerning the kingdom of God, and the name of Jesus Christ, they were baptized, both men and women. Then Simon himself believed also: and when he was baptized, he continued with Philip, and wondered, beholding the miracles and signs which were done.
>
> Now when the apostles which were at Jerusalem heard that Samaria had received the word of God, they sent unto them Peter and John: who, when they were come down, prayed for them, that they might receive the Holy Ghost: (for as yet he was fallen upon none of them: only they were baptized in the name of the Lord Jesus.) Then laid they their hands on them, and they received the Holy Ghost. And when Simon saw that through laying on of the apostles' hands the Holy Ghost was given, he offered them money, saying, Give me also this power, that on whomsoever I lay hands, he may receive the Holy Ghost. But Peter said unto him, Thy money perish with thee, because thou hast thought that the gift of God may be purchased with money. Thou hast neither part nor lot in this matter: for thy heart is not right in the sight of God. Repent therefore of this thy wickedness, and pray God, if perhaps the thought of thine heart may be forgiven thee. For I perceive that thou art in the gall of bitterness, and in the bond of iniquity.
>
> ACTS 8:8–23

This power of God can't be purchased. You can't run your credit card on it, and it cannot be stopped. Revelation 12:11 says, "And they overcame him [the devil] by the blood of the Lamb, and by the word of their testimony; and they loved not their lives unto the death." What do you think happened when they testified? There was a display of the power. That's why the devil wants to keep your testimony quiet. He tells you, "Don't talk about it!" But you just want to talk about what happened to you; you can't help it. That's your testimony. You sure don't want to spend the rest of your life being told about what happened to somebody else. But as you testify about what happened to you, there's a display of the power of God.

PENTECOSTAL POWER IS REAL

When I hear preachers say that people need to calm down and not get emotional, I think, *What are they trying to do? Do you think the world is going to accept us because we're nice?* This power embarrasses religion. Let me tell you how the religious deal with it. They say that I stand and hypnotize the people with hand signals and embedded commands, through mass hysteria and methods of crowd control. They say that through music, I whip the people into altered states of consciousness as an intoxicating spell! That's how they see it, and they cannot see it any different. They say that about us, but then they said that about Jesus!

For anyone who watches the services by way of television, and people who the view recordings of my meetings, I'll just say, "If we were hypnotizing people, don't you think we'd have David Copperfield and many of the other magicians and people involved in that sphere, coming to sit on the front row to learn what I'm doing because of the unbelievable control we have over the masses?" Magicians have to take people in the back room to work on them first, but we just come out and total strangers get hit and fall under the power of God!

Don't you think they would be coming to ask, "Can we learn from you? Who taught you this?" That's what Simon the Sorcerer did! He came and saw and said, "I also want this." Because when the apostles laid hands on the people, something must have happened.

I know exactly what they would say about Pentecost—"On the day of Pentecost, they created a wind tunnel and set fire to the people's wigs!" So just settle it once and for all: you are not going to explain this to the rest of the world, and you are not here to explain this to the rest of the world. You are here to display the power of God, and it's not to be explained! It's not to be watered down. It's not to be a sugarcoated pill. The power of God in its raw form is the best, so just let it flow. Let the chips fall where they may; just let it all hang out. And if it means we get arrested and thrown in prison, beaten, bones broken, and punched in the head, then let's get on with it! Thank God for Pentecostal power!

PENTECOSTAL POWER IS ALWAYS IN THE NOW

> THESE ARE OUR DAYS! THESE ARE DAYS OF THE HOLY GHOST! THESE ARE DAYS OF HIS POWER.

Pentecostal power is not a denomination, because at certain denominational headquarters, I'm not welcome. So it is not a denomination. But I believe that if you make a firm commitment before God that you will not back down, you will not compromise what God has placed on the inside of you, that you'll never be a dud, then cities and towns and villages and nations will be shaken.

You won't just be reading the history books about Smith Wigglesworth and John G. Lake and saying, "Oh, the days of Maria Woodworth-Etter," and "Oh, the days of Aimee Semple McPherson, the days of Kathryn Kuhlman." It will be *your* days! You won't be singing about the days of Elijah! You'll be singing, "These are my days. These are days of the Holy Ghost! These are days of His power."

But you have to yield. I have watched people hit by the power of God, and then they get up and they refuse to yield to the Spirit of God. The same anointing is coming on them, but they refuse to yield because they don't want to make a fool of themselves. Then they grieve the Holy Ghost, and the anointing lifts and it never stays with them. Please understand, if you are ashamed of Him, He's ashamed of you, and He'll go somewhere else.

Someone says, "I'm not going to make a fool of myself in that way." Well, that's fine; you'll make a fool of yourself another way then, but you *will* make a fool of yourself!

There is a pastor from Africa that God is using and he is filling tents of five thousand people, and miracles are taking place under his ministry. But when he came to one of my meetings in a place called Stilfontein, he was about to quit the ministry. The fire of God fell on him that night and shook him and he has never been the same since that fire grabbed him and shook him like a rag doll. And after this encounter, he didn't quit the ministry. Now everywhere he goes, there are miracles, signs, and wonders. He's had many motor vehicles given to him, and he has experienced greath wealth and prosperity. He is walking in a realm that many don't even know and don't even understand, but he grabbed ahold of the anointing and the anointing grabbed ahold of him.

He said that after the encounter there was such an anointing that was released upon his life, and God began to do new things in his life. People were healed and got out of wheelchairs, blind eyes opened deaf ears opened, and people started coming to Jesus in thousands. He had been frustrated and had decided to resign the ministry because of the financial situation in South Africa. But he learned the principles of how finances are released. It taught him to change his focus from the material, to God. Because when you look unto God, God moves the materials to you.

He has traveled the whole of the Eastern Cape, where I was born, and has even had mayors of the towns attending his crusades because they see what God is doing.

He told me about the impact that our crusade in Soweto had on him. He was challenged because he saw something happening there that had never happened before in the history of Soweto. He said that as he drove to Soweto, there was no room on the roads to drive. The roads were so congested with people walking and running to the crusade that even the police could not control them. He could hear and feel the anointing in the Spirit of that crusade twenty kilometers away.

He was so moved and challenged that he launched out in crusades himself, following the standard that he said that our crusade in Soweto had set. He was going to order a tent that seated ten thousand but canceled the order, and he now holds open-air crusades. When I think about all that we went through for the crusade in Soweto, hearing this testimony makes it worthwhile!

This Pentecostal power that I'm talking about is passed on and transferred, to all those who grab ahold of it. It is explosive power, but you cannot be offended by it. You cannot back down from it, and you cannot be ashamed of it.

THIS POWER THAT I'M TALKING ABOUT IS PASSED ON AND TRANSFERRED, TO ALL THOSE WHO GRAB AHOLD OF IT.

7

THE PRICE OF REVIVAL: PART ONE

Counting the Cost

Go to Luke 14 and I'm reading from verse 16: "Then said he unto him, A certain man made a great supper, and bade many." Now, let's just stop right there. I really see revival as a banquet table. The psalmist said, "Thou preparest a table before me in the presence of mine enemies" (Psalm 23:5).

How many have ever prepared a banquet or gone out of your way to make everything just right, and then the people you invited didn't show up? They said they were coming, but they didn't show, or you laid out this banquet for a whole evening event and they came, but they only spent an hour!

We come from a South African culture, where you don't need an invitation to come to somebody's house. You just show up at anybody's house, anytime of the day or night. South Africans are very hospitable. They invite you in and you might be there for lunch, but you end up having supper and you leave at midnight.

In America, it's not that way. You never show up to somebody's house or you'll die! And even if it was an invitation of, "Y'all come back," you know that they don't really mean it! I found that out when

I first came to America. People said to me, "Y'all come back, now," and so I went back and they said, "What are you doing here?" I found that that "Y'all come back, now," didn't mean "Y'all come back." It meant, "Don't come back too soon!"

So, it was a shock to me when one time, we had a whole evening deal going on and we invited people, but then we looked again and they had all left. It's partly because in the American culture, you are told to go but not to overstay your welcome. So you go in, you bring a gift, you kind of nibble at the food, and then you leave. But that really devastated me. I thought, *I invited them for the evening and they've already left, and it's only nine o'clock!*

REVIVAL IS A BANQUETING TABLE

But I found out that it's the same way with the Church. No matter what banquet has been set out on the table, people are going to come in, and they'll snack here and grab something there, and then they'll go. They'll get up in the middle of the service! Now it could be for several reasons. But when you've gone to the trouble to prepare a meal or banquet and you haven't finished feeding people, it's shocking they would leave.

What if the dessert was just unbelievable, but you left before the dessert? A dessert in the southern African culture is something you hang around for because we have steam-baked puddings with hot custard and just some of the finest desserts. It is good stuff.

But I see revival in the exact same way. There are delights that God has set out for us, yet I see people leaving because they come with a preconceived idea that the meeting will be over by 9:00 p.m., and then they can leave. When they leave, I'm thinking, *Man, do you know what we've got cooking here? We've actually been spending hours in preparation for this!* Then I almost want to run and chase after them and try and give them a serving! But they have left, and they didn't get to eat anything.

DON'T LET BUSYNESS STEAL YOUR HUNGER

YOU CANNOT WAIT FOR ALL THE CONDITIONS TO BE FAVORABLE. THERE'S A SACRIFICE; THERE'S A PRICE TO PAY TO HAVE REVIVAL.

In Luke 14, we read about this whole supper that is being prepared. Verses 17–18: "And sent his servant at supper time to say to them that were bidden, Come; for all things are now ready. And they all with one consent began to make excuse." I've heard so many excuses about why pastors can't have revival—"Well, we really have the year planned out. We've got all these meetings booked."

One pastor said to me, "I canceled thirty-five events this week to have you here." I nearly fell on my face and said, "Thirty-five events! Oh my God! Let me kiss your feet!" Basically he was saying, "Do you know what I've had to do to have you here? I've had to cancel thirty-five events, men's groups, women's groups, youth groups, businessmen's fellowships, I've had to cancel all these events to have you here this week!"

Pastors say, "We'd like to have revival, but we have got this event." I went to one church and we were there four nights. We had 2,200 people saved, and the power of God fell. They went right out of that into a Christmas pageant and program for fourteen days and killed whatever was there. I came back in April, and I knew the Spirit of God was grieved.

The place previously was packed with three-and-a-half thousand people a night, and the air was electrified. But I came back in that April, and they were too busy working on the Easter pageant! The crowds were only half of what they were, and then they wanted me to come back and try to get the revival going again. But I just couldn't because you can't tell God when He can serve food.

Pastors, you cannot wait for all the conditions to be favorable. There's a sacrifice and there's a price to pay to have revival. That's why some of the revivals have happened where the church is about to close; they are about to lose their property; they are about to go bankrupt. The pastor is so desperate he says, "Look, please just take it. Have it. Do whatever you want," and then God comes and moves. But the rest of the churches have money in the bank, their properties are paid for, they have everything, and they are not desperate. They are not hungry. They have built up this work, and it is successful, so they don't want to ruffle any feathers.

Adonica went to speak in a place, and the pastor said to her, "Listen, now. I want the service over by 12:00 noon." The problem was that it started at 10:30 a.m., so the service was only an hour-and-a-half. He gave her the service at 11:20 a.m. and said to her, "Now be careful because we have a lot of people that are not used to revival." So she said, "Would you like me to get rid of them?" She was just being honest—"Do you want me to run them off?" He said, "No! No, I want them here."

She had thought that he would be glad that she would be the one to get rid of those people, but he said, "I want to finish by 12:00 noon." So, she did, and she handed him back the service, but she was upset because she could have been back here at The River with us.

THE HUNGRY WILL COME AND DINE

> GOD ALWAYS MOVES IN SOME OF THE WAY-OUT PLACES, WHERE PEOPLE SAY, "REVIVAL HAS NEVER HAPPENED HERE."

So, for the supper in Luke 14, people made excuses. Verses 18–21:

> The first said unto him, I have bought a piece of ground, and I must needs go and see it: I pray thee have me excused. And another said, I have bought five yoke of oxen, and I go to prove them: I pray thee have me excused. And another said, I have married a wife, and therefore I cannot come. So that servant came, and shewed his lord these things. Then the master of the house being angry said to his servant, Go out quickly into the streets and lanes of the city, and bring in hither the poor, and the maimed, and the halt, and the blind.

That's why you find that when revival breaks out, people come in from the hedges, they come in from the highways, the byways, the "hi-yous," and the bayous. It's the whole thing of, "To the hungry calleth now, Come and dine" (Charles B. Widmeyer, "Come and Dine"). Those who are full have already been fed, so they have no desire for more. But the hungry and the thirsty people, call them in from the highways and the byways, just call them in. It wasn't really their place at the table, because we had somebody else's name there, but that person didn't show up. They didn't come, so the hungry and thirsty can dine instead.

That's why God always moves in some of the way-out places, where people say, "Revival has never happened here." You might think, *Well, I come from a way-out place*, but you are probably one of the greatest candidates for the move of God! You can have revival anywhere, anyplace. All it takes is hungry people who want to come and eat.

Now again, I'm going to refer back to the South African culture. The true South African housewife (not the ones today who don't cook—they just eat out—but the ones who spend time in the kitchen, like your mama and your grandmama), when you go to her house and you finish a plate, she puts another plate in front of you and you are going to eat it!

You actually have to beg her—"Please! I can't eat any more." That's just the way it is. And if you don't eat more, you are insulting her!

We have some Lebanese South Africans, and if you go to a Lebanese house in South Africa, when they bring the food out, you daren't even argue! The last thing you want to do is argue with a Lebanese woman! Not when she's been spending hours in the kitchen baking and making something! I think we're going to eat Lebanese food when we get to Heaven! That food is unbelievable; it's heavenly food!

I'm relating this in the natural, but the Lord is the One who's preparing this table for us. It's plenteous in goods. There is heavenly bread to eat, there is the living water to drink, there is new wine, your head is anointed with oil, and there are heavenly delights. Will you come and dine?

Why do you think the psalmist said, "O taste and see that the Lord is good" (Psalm 34:8)? It involves eating spiritual food and drinking spiritual drink. We eat spiritual food and we drink spiritual drink for nourishment. But so many in the Body of Christ are malnourished and they are spiritually dehydrated. They haven't drunk living water, and if they have, the water is polluted and they are drinking it out of a gutter somewhere. There's nothing like fresh, pure water coming straight from the river of God.

Luke 14:22–24: "And the servant said, Lord, it is done as thou hast commanded, and yet there is room." There is room, there is always room. There's always room at God's table. "And the lord said unto the servant, Go out into the highways and hedges, and compel them to come in, that my house may be filled. For I say unto you, That none of those men which were bidden shall taste of my supper." Could it be possible that the ones the Lord is inviting will never come in? In other words, the ones the Lord gives an official invitation to won't come and dine? Jesus is standing and saying, "Come and dine." But they are saying, "I'm busy. I'm busy, Pastor. I'm busy, Brother Rodney. I'm busy. I can't come." No! They don't understand; this is an official invitation to "come and dine!"

What if you got a letter from the president of the United States, inviting you come to the White House? Many would make arrangements to separate from everything else to attend, yet we have a higher One calling us to come, and His Name is Jesus.

HUSBANDS AND WIVES MUST WORK TOGETHER

Now I want to look at the price of revival, and I am going to reflect back on over forty years of ministry. Please understand that I'm not playing some violin or looking for sympathy. I'm not even speaking out of hurt or anything. I'm just going to talk to you about the price of revival because a lot of people don't understand that there is a price to pay, that there is a cost. If you don't realize this, then the moment you step out and you start to have to pay something, you'll say, "Do I have to really do this? Do I have to really put up with this?"

First of all, let's get real personal and talk about the family, and start with husbands and wives, because I've seen so many ministries sacrifice their marriages for the ministry. And part of that is because there's no communication between husband and wife. The husband's doing his thing, and the wife is doing her thing, and the ministry is more important to them than their relationship.

That doesn't mean to say that you are not working in the ministry together. Adonica and I work nineteen, twenty hours a day and more, but husbands and wives should be hooked in together, with one aim, one goal, and one vision. I see a lot of couples working against each other—the enemy is in their own house. I can't even imagine that! Ministry is hard enough without waking up every day with the enemy in your bed, working to destroy your ministry. Imagine if you have somebody in your bed against you as well as the devil against you!

I would think that the first thing you have to do is make friends with that person in the bed with you. That would seem like a very wise decision to make!

I'm not trying to cause marital problems, and I'm not trying to stir up any issues, but I tell you that once a couple can get into agreement, they are ten thousand times stronger. "One can put a thousand to flight, and two can put ten thousand to flight" (Deuteronomy 32:30, paraphrased). And whatever the two of you agree on will come to pass (Matthew 18:19, paraphrased).

For those who are married, the best friend in the whole wide world is your spouse. And if they are not your best friend in the whole wide world, why did you marry them? It must be to the point that if you had to choose someone to go to a remote island with you for ten years, they would be your one and only pick. You must learn to communicate and work together.

THE HUSBAND MUST BE THE HEAD OF THE HOUSE

When Adonica and I got married, I was twenty and she was nineteen, and in the early part of the ministry, she was very quiet. Not quiet to me when we were alone; then she was very bold and very vocal, and combative just in our discussion.

We would drive down the road, going to a meeting, and we would have to pull the car to the side and sit there for twenty minutes, with our conversation going backwards and forwards. The moment I could get into that place of repentance, we could go on.

It wasn't that I was just trying to be difficult, but when you are the head of the house and you are taking the family in a certain direction and you have someone pulling in another direction, you have to make a decision: "Okay, which direction are we going to go here?"

A marriage is the coming together of two different worlds, but you can't have two people leading the thing. And it's not really my position to come into the place of submission to my wife, where she makes all the decisions and I just go, "Yes, dear. Yes, dear." A lot of husbands have had to do this because the wife is so strong, and if they don't submit, they'll have a third world war and three mortar attacks on the way from the bed to the bathroom, and you don't want that to happen!

So in the case of husband and wife, the man has to be the head of the house. You can't have the wife as the head of the house. I'm sorry, ladies, but I'm just telling you right now that your security comes in the fact that he is the head of the house.

There's a difference between sitting down and discussing what you are both going to do and her just saying, "We are NOT doing that. We are doing this!" What we decided a long time ago was that I make the final decision after we sit and discuss it. And if I'm wrong, I say, "I'm sorry," and she would never bring it up and say, "You were wrong, so now I'm taking over. I'm taking charge here!" Because you cannot have two heads.

It took us probably the first seven years to work through some major stuff, so it wasn't all plain sailing. We never talked about divorce or thought about it, but there were some "wars and rumours of wars!"

The way I was brought up was that you could have an argument with somebody, but two minutes later talk to them and everything is fine. The way she was brought up was that you don't talk to the person for three or four days, and that drove me insane. I'd say, "Don't ever do that to me. You look me in my face right now; we're going to sort this thing out. We're going to kiss and we can make up, and we're going to go on. This thing is going to be over in the next ten minutes because I've got to get on the platform in half an hour, and I'm not getting on a platform with an attitude. So, we are going to straighten this thing out." She'd say, "Well, I don't want to," but I'd say, "Well, you will, right now! You repent right now and I'll repent right now, and we'll get this thing over and done with."

She'd cry and then we'd pray together, and then I would go out on the platform to preach. You can't minister whilst your wife is sitting there looking at you like she's going to kill you.

I knew one pastor who, if ever they counseled a married couple, his wife would just chip in and say, "Don't listen to him; he's talking rubbish!" She played the organ in the church, and when he'd get up to preach, she would play the wrong songs and do everything to irritate him! And he put up with that for maybe thirty years of his ministry! If he went anywhere, she would steal stuff out of the house they were staying in. If they stayed in a hotel, she would walk off with the bath towels, she was just a crazy woman. It's a wonder he ever had a ministry!

So I say to all the men reading this, "Be the head of the house." And by that, I don't mean that you beat your wife into submission, where she just says, "Yes, sir. Three bags full, sir." You have got to sit down and discuss things and find out what she's feeling about it and what you are feeling about it.

I've learned how to do that, and I've learned never to spring something on Adonica. I drop hints; I share words months before and prepare her in advance, because she has to think it all through. I'm already thinking it through, and when I say it to her, it is already after months of contemplation.

I've learned over the years that when I'm thinking it, I'm already speaking it into her. And I share it with her, and then, when it comes out of her mouth as her idea, then I know we're ready to go ahead and do what needs to be done. And it doesn't matter that it came back as her idea!

SPEND TIME TOGETHER

YOU HAVE TO JUST MAKE TIME FOR THE FAMILY.

I think if you look at a lot of couples in marriage, the husband and wife don't spend enough time together. Then the wife gets resentful toward the ministry because he's always out with people, he is always giving himself to people, and he never gives himself to her and the kids.

So, you have to make time. Making time for us meant sometimes having very little sleep because the only time we had might have been from midnight to 6:00 a.m., or midnight till the start of the next service!

I can remember many Saturday nights that I would fly in from the crusades somewhere, and at 10:00 p.m., I'd land and go to the house and we would have a barbecue and sit down to watch a movie with the kids. At 2:00 a.m., early on Sunday morning, everybody was still running around and we were having fun, and I'd just pretend there was no Sunday morning, because this was the only time I was going to have with the family. And at 3:00 p.m. that afternoon, I would be getting on another plane and flying off somewhere. So, it didn't matter how tired I was—it was going to be family time from 10:00 p.m. Saturday night to 3:00 a.m. Sunday morning. I'd catch three to four hours' sleep, go to church and minister, and then get on the plane to fly out. You say, "I can't do that. I'm too tired," but you *have to* make time! You have to just make time for the family.

I told my wife after we arrived in the United States (we were married in October 1981, and revival broke out in 1989), "I guess I probably would never have said this when we first got married, but if I had to choose between you and the ministry, I'd pick you. As much as I loved you when we first got married, I probably would have picked the ministry, but I've now come to the place where I can tell you with all truthfulness that if I had to choose between you and the ministry, I would pick you." And she looked at me, and that shocked her, because she knew how important the ministry was to me, but it also dawned on me that if I didn't have her, I didn't really have a ministry. So it wasn't a matter of picking. It was a matter of really working out a mutual understanding and a flowing together, because we are two very strong people, very opinionated, and total opposites. Now, after over forty years of marriage, I still try to work out what is going on!

It is a mystery, and for her it is the same. I think that's what keeps us intrigued with each other because we're still trying to work things out. There is never a boring moment and there is never a dull moment!

PROTECT YOUR WIFE AND FAMILY

I say this to all the ministers: "Protect your wife and protect your children." That's why people know around this ministry, "Don't touch my wife and don't touch my kids because they were there when nobody else was. They were with me packing the vans, driving for four days, sleeping in one hotel room, so don't mess with them. Don't even go there! You are touching an area that is going to get you into more trouble than you can even shake a stick at, and it's not negotiable."

If they are out of line, I'll get in the middle of them, but don't anybody else do it! Because I'll get a little "unsaved" and "unsanctified" for a while. Sadly, ministers just allow their families to be abused and then the kids grow up and they don't want to serve God. My daughter Kelly (who is in Heaven) and my other daughter Kirsten, and my son Kenneth, love Jesus with all of their hearts. I'm not saying that they are angels with wings and a halo, but they love Jesus with all their hearts, and they are serving the Lord.

Protect your family; watch them; spend time with them; get into their stuff. Don't allow what hurts you in the ministry to come on them and don't go running the ministry down in front of them. Don't criticize the people in the church in front of them. Don't pull people apart or they'll see what's going on and they'll turn away from God. Protect them; keep them in the things of God; keep them in the love of God; keep them *in* the anointing of God. Keep them *under* the anointing of God.

Keep your wife under the anointing of God. At one time, my wife was getting emotionally involved in everything, and I shut it off and said, "You're not getting into that situation. You're not even going there!"

Protect your families! Your family is your greatest treasure, not the ministry, not your church, not your new building, not anything that you've done. Your greatest possessions and treasures are your wife and your children, so thank God for what He's given you and rejoice.

In the early days, I nearly sacrificed my family. If people even gave me an offering that was for me personally, I would stick it in the ministry. My wife would be believing God for something and somebody would come and bless me, but I would turn around and give it right away again. The Lord began to speak to me and said, "You are giving to everybody else. Charity begins at home!" I just couldn't receive it. "No, put it in the ministry; the ministry needs it." The ministry did need it, but we needed it too! And then I'd go back to praying, "Oh God, I need a miracle." The Lord said, "I just gave you a miracle, but you gave it away again!" Protect your wife and your children.

YOUR SPOUSE IS YOUR MOST PRECIOUS POSSESSION

> REALIZE THAT OUTSIDE OF YOUR SALVATION IN THE LORD JESUS CHRIST, YOUR HUSBAND OR YOUR WIFE IS THE MOST PRECIOUS POSSESSION THAT YOU HAVE ON THE EARTH.

You have to realize that outside of your salvation in the Lord Jesus Christ, your husband or your wife is the most precious possession that you have on the earth. And I say this because I know of ministers who really don't even care about their spouses.

There's one international minister who told his wife, "You will live a very lonely life being married to me. That's the price you have to pay for this ministry." And when they travel, she doesn't even travel with him. When they stay at a hotel, she has her own hotel room on another floor, because he's "under the anointing!"

I don't believe that that's the kind of price that needs to be paid. If you were married to somebody and they didn't want to serve God and they walked away from the marriage, then that would be a price that you paid.

Somebody says, "I was married; I love the Lord and my wife loved the Lord, but she didn't want to be in the ministry." Now, if she doesn't want to be in the ministry, what are you going to do? She doesn't want to serve God! What are you going to do if your wife wants to go to the nightclubs? She wants to party. There are some pastors' wives who are in clubs every weekend. Pastors of great churches, and their wives are in the clubs. The wives don't really want to be in the ministry. That is a big problem, and those are things that you should have sorted out before you even tied the knot.

But that's where love comes in, because when I told my wife and made this commitment to her (that if I had to choose between her and the ministry, I'd choose her), I knew after that, I'd never have to choose because she locked in. She locked in!

THE HUSBAND CASTS THE VISION FOR THE MINISTRY

You need to get rid of any war in your own house. That is the last thing you want. And then let me just say this to husband and wives: you cannot have your wife coming up with the vision for the ministry. She cannot be the driving force behind the ministry. If you are not motivated and she's the one with the motivation for the ministry, then she's going to end up being the head of the house, and you just can't do that.

I know I'm scratching in some areas, and some people might not like it, but Adonica and I spend hours and hours talking about everything and discussing things—not making a decision, just talking, and then praying. If we don't have a solution to something and we don't have answer, we just keep praying about it. We don't have to make a decision just for the sake of making a decision. We just keep praying and keeping it before the Lord.

SPEND TIME WITH YOUR CHILDREN

> THE PRICE THAT GOD EXPECTS YOU TO PAY IS NOT ONE WHERE YOU SACRIFICE YOUR WIFE AND YOUR KIDS, AND THEY GO TO HELL, AND YOU END UP GOING TO HELL! THAT'S NOT THE PRICE YOU ARE EXPECTED TO PAY.

And then, the second thing after your wife, of course, is your children, and you can't put your children ahead of your marriage because they are going to grow up and leave. It has to be your marriage first and then your children. As much as you love your kids and sacrifice for them, they are going to desert you, and that's just natural. But you have also got to spend time with your children as they grow up.

As hard as I worked, especially during that fourteen-year period of two meetings a day and sometimes three meetings a day, I always tried to spend time with the kids. Just having them with me on the road was unbelievable, and in fact, when they quit traveling on the road for about eighteen months, I almost quit the ministry! Because no matter what the opposition was, no matter what the circumstances were, I could always go back to the hotel room and hug them, and just holding them was like new life to me.

So I tell every minister, if you're traveling, take your wife and kids with you, homeschool your kids on the road, and be together as a family. Don't travel for extended periods of time separated from your family; take them with you.

Someone says, "Well, if you do that, they won't grow up normal." What's normal? Explain to me, what is normal? Is snorting crack normal? Is drinking bottles of vodka normal? Is pornography on the internet normal? No! Loving God is normal. Serving God is normal.

The price that God expects you to pay is not one where you sacrifice your wife and your kids, and they go to hell, and you end up going to hell! That's not the price you are expected to pay. The price that you pay is on your flesh because you're going to have to sit down and work it out.

CORRECT YOUR FAMILY

My kids know, Kenneth especially, that I want to look at them. And if I didn't see him for day or two when they were younger, I'd say, "Kenneth, please present yourself in front of your father," and he would come and stand in front of me, and I wouldn't say anything. I'd just look at him. "Let me look at you for a while, son. Let me just see what's going on here." Because as a parent, you can know immediately if there's an attitude, and you are responsible to make sure that the heart of your child is pure. If there was any little bit of rebellion or an attitude, then it had to be dealt with.

Don't tell me that you don't know when your wife's got an attitude! And don't allow that attitude to run on for two or three weeks. Sort it out! "Honey, we need to talk. Sit down here. I noticed you're mad, so if we have to have a nuclear war, let's have it, but we're going to get this thing out of the way!" This business of just letting stuff go is not allowed, and I don't care if it's the time of "the monthly!"

In fact, in our house that was not even an excuse. It didn't matter what was going on; you have no excuse. You have to walk in the fruit of the Spirit. So don't go throwing that around: "Hey, it's that time of the month again!" "It is? Oh great! So this is a time that we have just got to put up with your rubbish until everything blows over? No, this time you're going to walk in the fruit of the Spirit and in the joy of the Lord and you can get your hormones under control!"

So, let's not sacrifice our families on the altar of religion and tradition. Love your wife, love your husband, love your kids, and grab them to yourself when everybody is gone. And that's why I said earlier that if you ever want to get in trouble with me, touch my family! If they are out of line, I'll straighten them out. But don't you get in the middle of that, because I'll get unsanctified for a while!

But you must keep your children in line. Just get in their faces. I don't care if you have a war in your house, but you have to get in their faces. Don't allow your kids to get out of hand.

Kenneth, at the time of writing, is now thirty-four years old, married, with three children, and is the administrator here at the ministry. But growing up, he knew that I would get right in the middle of him; I would take him down in the house because he is going to go to Heaven!

More preachers' kids cause trouble for their parents than you can ever imagine. No matter what the daddy built, the kids are going to destroy it in later years. And that's another story and another message, but we don't want to be like Eli with his two sons, where we don't take care of them or straighten them out (1 Samuel 3:13).

Be in prayer, and pray over your children. I've probably prayed more over my kids than anything else. Pray over them; pray over your wife or husband, because that's the first line of attack that the enemy will try to come against. The first thing he is going to try to do is come on your family. So, you need to cover them.

PROTECT YOUR DAUGHTERS

Also, you must protect your daughters. You don't know how many ministers I've spoken to who have told me that young men came around to marry their daughters with ulterior motives. And the moment they married the daughters, they went totally nuts.

I can mention top names in America where their daughters have been through the most traumatic time because young men came around and just misrepresented themselves. Some of the stuff they have sat down and shared with me, you won't believe what they went through!

So, I tell you right now, "Protect your daughters!" Protect them and put those young men through the wringer. Send them to me, and I'll straighten them out. Here's a little key: if they don't respect the mother and father, don't let them marry the daughter!

It's the only thing that will work. If they don't respect the mother and father, if they don't respect the ministry, then why should they come and marry the daughter?

TAKE CARE OF YOURSELF

Then, the next thing I want to talk about is not paying the price of your health, and I say this not because I'm some health nut who lives in an oxygen tank, swallowing handfuls of vitamins and eating weeds and plant shoots! We eat healthy and we try to do what we can, but I nearly killed myself. I pushed myself almost to the limit, to where, if God hadn't come to my rescue, I probably would have dropped dead. So, I really want to encourage you to look after yourself in that area. Take a rest. There's nothing wrong with taking a rest. Ministers say, "Well, I can't, the ministry is too busy right now." But sometimes in the busiest time, you just have to say, "We are going away. And if there's no ministry when we get back, we'll just close it down, but we are going away."

Put everything on hold. Go away for ten days. Drop off the edge of the earth, shut off the cell phone and the computer, and be inaccessible. In the early days, I could never shut anything off. If we went on vacation, it was always to go and try to help some pastor or try to encourage some pastor. My wife and kids wanted to spend time with me, and I would be caught up with the pastor in town. The pastor was hurting, and then I'd take our vacation money and spend it on the pastor, buying his family food and clothing and looking after them, and meanwhile, my family had no money for a vacation because I'd spent it on this pastor. The pastor was encouraged, but we left even more tired than when we came because we had been dealing with all their stuff.

We would go somewhere and I'd remember a certain pastor who lived there, I'd phone him and say, "How are you doing?"

"Not good. We are out of groceries."

"All right. Well then, let's go shopping and buy groceries." And he'd show up and his suit was falling to pieces, so I'd say, "Come; let me take you shopping," and I'd buy him a suit. The wife looked all dejected, so I'd get her hair done and send her to the beauty shop. But *you* need to take time for *yourself!*

And my wife eventually said to me one day, "When are we just going to have a vacation? Do you always have to help every hurting pastor? You are hurting, and I'm hurting—let's help *us*! Take *us* shopping. Spend money on *us*."

But if it hadn't anything to do with the ministry, I thought I was backsliding. So I just had ministry, ministry, ministry on my mind all the time, morning, noon, and night, and during vacations. Now, if I'm in an area and somebody says, "Are you coming to church?" I say, "No. I'm on vacation."

Another thing that we have done over the years, is find couples that need a vacation, and we've sent them away and paid for them, looked after them for a whole week, and just rolled out the red carpet to try to get God's people to rest. But even though I was doing that for others at that time, I wasn't resting myself!

THE IMPORTANCE OF REST

You need to rest. I thought that I could just keep going but around the end of 2001, I found myself in a place physically, mentally, and emotionally, that I have never been before. I was so horrified to even find myself in that place where I was so tired. I was strung out but I couldn't get out of it, and I didn't know how to get out of it. I didn't know that it would take almost seven months of long sleeping to get back to feeling normal.

Because over those fourteen years of two meetings a day and sometimes three meetings a day, I had spent myself physically, mentally and emotionally, and I was running on a huge overdraft. Really, it was New York and Shreveport that did it. Those two crusades took me out for the whole of 2001. We moved into the property for the church that year, but we were traveling to I believe it was, sixty cities that year.

I was still pastoring the church, traveling in and out, and I thought, *Is there any way I can get out of it? Can I just go fishing? Can I go?* I actually thought maybe the only way out of the ministry was if I robbed a bank or something and got arrested! I didn't know what to do. I didn't know how to stop it, because you get to the next place and everybody's waiting for you to minister, and they all want you to lay hands on them.

But the Lord was so gracious to me. I was in the bush in Africa on a hunting trip and God spoke to me and said, "Go home and command the harvest to come in."

The Lord began to speak to me about rest, and I canceled the whole of 2002, and I came home. Then we went on satellite and we beamed up from The River to a hundred million homes. And we just stayed home and I started sleeping and resting. I played some golf, and I saw birds again for the first time in fourteen years. I saw the sun, I saw the grass, the trees, and the flowers. I'd stand outside and breathe and sigh and say, "I don't remember all of this."

All I'd seen for fourteen years was airports, hotels, churches, and sick, sad, depressed, religious people, and I didn't realize what had happened. I'd be out on a golf course and I'd just look at the sky (and I love blue skies), and I'd look at the sun, and the trees, and the birds, and say, "Oh man, this is beautiful. This is awesome. Where did this go for all these years?"

And then the power of God would fall on me. The anointing of God would fall on me stronger than in any service. Sometimes, I could hardly finish the round of golf because I was drunk. And I would think, *I'm getting anointed just playing golf. This is unbelievable!*

Then I realized the importance of what I am now sharing with you. Even though I had spoken about these things, even though I knew these things to be the truth, I realized the importance of them. Because there will always be something in the ministry that needs your attention next. And there comes a time when you just have to say, "Let the dead bury the dead" (Luke 9:60). You cannot sacrifice your health.

YOU MUST HAVE A BALANCE

It's not that you don't love people; it's not that at all. But you have to take care of yourself. I know a pastor who died at fifty-nine years of age because he overworked. He worked until 1:00 a.m. every morning and then he started a 5:42 a.m. prayer meeting. He was at every hospital visitation, pastoring a large church, and he worked himself into a frazzle.

Now obviously, it is the opposite with the people who do nothing.

There are lazy bums who do absolutely nothing. They are always on vacation, always resting, and if they preach Sunday morning, they are tired till Wednesday!

So there is a balance. Some people are always going to be on vacation, and there is nothing you can do about it. It's the never-ending American dream of less work, more rest, more leisure, and more vacation! But you'll never have a successful ministry that way. When I work, I'll put in eighteen hours a day. I crank it in, but when I start feeling myself losing strength, I'll just pull back and start resting.

There's nothing like good, hard work, so I've got to be careful as I share this, because people don't know how to keep a balance. And do you know what will crush you more than anything? The needs of the world!

There's a world dying and going to a lost eternity and you think, *How can I sit here in Hawaii on the beach, how can I be on this golf course, when there are millions of people dying and going to a lost eternity?* Well, okay fine. Go reach them, but you'll drop dead sooner and ultimately, you'll reach fewer people!

Even Jesus said, "Come ye . . . apart . . . and rest a while" (Mark 6:31). The burden of the ministry will drive you like it was driving me: "We've got to reach the harvest; we *have* to reach the harvest." But you're not Superman. Your body needs to rest; your body needs to go the restroom.

There were days I didn't eat breakfast, didn't eat lunch, and the first meeting I had was 4:00 p.m. Because it was just run, run, run, and in the latter days of that time period, where I was exhausted, every day it became an effort to even get out of bed!

I would pray that God would just energize me and give me enough strength to get to the shower. And I would actually use the shower as a point of contact and say, "Lord, when I put the shower on and it rains on me, I'm receiving fresh anointing for today, strength for today. Only for today. I can't believe for tomorrow; tomorrow seems too far away."

YOU MUST PACE YOURSELF

> WHEN THE FIRE OF GOD COMES ON YOU, YOU WANT TO OBEY GOD AND YOU WANT TO GO TO THE NATIONS OF THE WORLD, BUT THERE MUST BE A BALANCE.

In 2001, I was fighting for Kelly's life, and when she went on oxygen, it almost took me out. Here we were, still at that time doing two meetings a day, and I was fighting for my daughter's life.

In the moment I said to my wife, "This is the year that I'm going to get that miracle. I don't care what it takes. I'm pressing in for that complete miracle." It wasn't three or four days later that I came under the severe physical attack that I fought for seven months, and by that time it was too late; she went on oxygen. Because I was just hoping that I would live. I was under the worst physical attack you could ever imagine.

I would come out of a morning meeting, and I would go back to the hotel room. I would close the curtain, switch the lights off, and lie on the bed in the dark for hours, just to try to get enough energy for the night meeting. And then I would get to the service, and the power of God would come down, and I'd preach my heart out and then get home.

And then the next morning I had to pray again to get out of bed. "God, just please help me; help me one more day just to help them. Just help me one more day." People don't understand that it's a war; it is a war. We've had many victories, but there have been battles!

And if you think you're going to go after souls and revival, and the devil's going to give you a free run up the side, forget about it! In 2002–3, I really began to come back into place of restoration as far as physically and mentally. Then in 2004 I thought, *Hey, I'm fine. I can run again*, and I started putting the pressure on just like I did those years before. But then I got on a plane to go to Germany to have a crusade there. We flew from Tampa to New York City, and as I sat on the Lufthansa plane, I had an anxiety attack like I'd never had before! Now, I am not an anxious person and that's what freaked me out. I thought, *How can I be anxious?* I thought I was going to die on the plane. My heart was racing, I had heart palpitations, and I thought, *Oh my God. I'm going to die on this plane. They're going to pull a dead body off in Germany.*

It took me everything I knew to just get my head into gear to where I could focus on the fact that I wasn't going to die. My heart was racing, and I was in a state.

We landed in Frankfurt, Germany and a businessman came and wanted to treat me to a ride down the Autobahn, and he pulled up in this Maserati Quattroporte four seater. I jump in the front seat, and we took off down the Autobahn, 150 miles an hour, and my heart raced and I thought, *I'm going to die. I'm going to die on the Autobahn!*

I love speed, so it wasn't the speed, but for some reason, that anxiety hit me again, and I thought, *My God, this is terrible.* Fortunately, he had some praise and worship on, and I turned it up and I put the air conditioning on, and I lay back and fell asleep on the Autobahn at 150 miles an hour!

We got to the hotel room and I said to Pastors Eric and Jennifer Gonyon, "You're going to have to do the morning services. I can't. I don't even know how I'm going to function."

Then I said, "For the night services, you're going to do the praise and worship and do the offering and have them pick me up from the hotel at 8:45 p.m. I'll be there at the church at 9:00 p.m., and I'll preach and go back." I stayed in bed for three days. I was grabbing my wife's hand and putting it on me for her to pray. I was dying! I know it's crazy what I'm telling you, but I was telling her what to do in the event of my departure from the earth. I thought maybe I was too late, maybe I had just pushed myself to the limit. I thought I was not going to recover out of it.

I remember getting up and going to the shower and as I started the shower I began to pray and talk to the Lord. I said, "Now Lord, come on. Let's talk about this quickly. I'm still young, I know I've worked hard and probably have overworked, and I apologize and repent for it.

And if I have done any physical damage to my body, then please forgive me, and I would come home now in a heartbeat, but first of all, please, can You answer me this question: What are You going to do with me up there? What would You do with me up there at this time? Now, as far as everything else is concerned, You can take it all. I want You to have everything, but I'm asking You for one thing now." And you know what's important to you when you find yourself on the bargaining table and the chips are coming out. I said, "I'm asking You, please, whatever this is, to help me come through it. I ask You for one thing and one thing alone, I ask You for souls. Take everything else, but please give me one hundred million souls and then I can come home."

So, when I came back to Tampa, I went to a doctor that we had at that time over in Orlando. I told him what happened, and he said that it all started with a stunt flight that a pastor took me on when I was up in Minneapolis, Minnesota. He was a jet fighter pilot, and he took me on a stunt plane. He strapped me in, and at 8,600 feet up off the deck, he flipped me upside-down and cut the engines and took it into a spiral, and that's what started the whole process! The stunt pilot had told me that no pastor would ever come with him because they were chicken. Well, I'm not chicken, so I said, "I'll go with you." But I wish I had been a chicken!

The doctor said what I had done was to wear down the serotonin level in my body to where adrenaline kicks in and takes over, and that's why my heart was racing. He said the only way that I could stop it was just to rest. I thought, *Oh great! Rest again. I've got to go rest again. I'm wanting to go and get the harvest of souls!*

So, there's a whole balance you must have. I want to just encourage you with what I'm sharing with you. When the fire of God comes on you, you want to obey God and you want to go to the nations of the world, but there must be a balance.

You're going to have to find the balance for yourself, and you're going to have to ask the Holy Spirit to restrain you when you feel that you're pushing the envelope too much. It's like a juggling act or spinning plates. Have you ever seen the guy spinning the plates on poles? If he spins too many, some of them start wobbling, and he has to run to spin them again. There have been times when I've had eleven plates and they have been wobbling and about to fall off, and only by the grace of God have they begun to spin again.

The problem is that there are people on the outside who think they know what you should be doing. "Well, if you just spin the plate like this," and you look, and they only have one little plate, and they are standing there spinning it, and it all looks easy. I think, *Great! Now you try spinning eleven of them and keep them going at the same time! If you want the job, take over, buddy!*

DON'T BE TAKEN OUT BEFORE YOUR TIME

IF YOU DIE, YOU WANT TO DIE FOR THE CAUSE; YOU DON'T WANT TO DIE FOR SOMETHING STUPID.

Allow the Lord to help you pace yourself in the Kingdom so that you can make giant strides for the King. Severely impact the kingdom of darkness and severely make strides for the Kingdom of Heaven, but still be around to tell the tale. Now, you may get beaten, stoned, shipwrecked, and left for dead; all those things can happen.

If I get shot as a martyr, then, great. I don't mind dying that way. I don't mind getting a bullet. I'm not welcoming one, but I'm not afraid of dying. If I got captured in some country and they tortured me for my faith, that's fine. That would be pretty interesting, but I don't want to die uselessly. If you die, you want to die for the cause; you don't want to die for something stupid.

The great revivalist Jonathan Edwards, died because he volunteered to have an injection for smallpox, and he died at fifty-four. They were looking for somebody to be tested, so he volunteered. I don't want to die that way, but I don't mind dying in the service of the King.

THE COST IN FRIENDSHIPS

Now you will find that there's a price to pay for revival in relationship to friends. And you just have to get used to it. Because I thought, *Okay, I don't want to sacrifice my wife and my children, but what about friends?* You will find out that you're going to pay a price there. When you have friends, you hang out because there's a mutual friendship based around you all having the same set of circumstances or interests. But what happens when your ministry explodes? Now, suddenly, you've gone to another level.

Imagine that a group of you all start in the ministry together. You are all in vans, traveling around the country, and you are all in churches that have 50 to 200 people. You are friends, and your ministries are all about the same size, but then suddenly, God explodes your ministry, and now you are flying all over the place and speaking in arenas. I can tell you that unless the others can make the change and they can adapt, then they are not coming with you.

They are not going to come with you because first of all, they will expect you to give them the microphone, and that's not how it works. You can help people, but you can't help pushy people just because somebody is around and you've known them for a long time.

I had one minister who wanted to commit suicide because I never bought him a car. He sat with a gun on his table and wanted to blow his brains out because when ministry broke through for me, I didn't buy him a motorcar. But I didn't know he wanted one! I thought that the last time I saw him he was driving one but in his mind he thought, *Rodney will buy me a car; he'll give me a car.* I wish I had, but I didn't even think of it.

So sometimes friends won't let you go on because you rattled their comfort zone and they don't want you to change. "No, don't do that. Come. Let's be like it was," but it's not like it was and it *can't* be like it was. It's painful, and you realize that the price for the ministry is that many times, you will walk alone. I told my wife, "If ever I didn't have you and the kids, I don't know what I'd do, because people are here today and gone tomorrow."

Then you suddenly find out that some people are only around to get what they can get. What about Jesus when He was in the Garden of Gethsemane and He took three of His closest friends with Him? They fell asleep! I don't believe they were bad people, they just didn't see what He saw.

So when God births something on the inside of you, sometimes it's difficult for friends and even some of your other family (not immediate family, your wife and kids), but brothers and sisters, to accept it. It can cause a lot of sibling rivalry. "Why does this brother get blessed and that one doesn't get blessed?" Well, I'm older," or "I'm younger," but God doesn't operate that way.

THE COST IN EXTENDED FAMILY RELATIONSHIPS

> THE THING THAT'S MORE IMPORTANT THAN ANYTHING ELSE IS THE ANOINTING AND RESPECT FOR THE THINGS OF GOD.

There is also a cost in wider family relationships. We've had to walk through a lot of stuff with family that I'm not going to get into, but it's heartbreaking because people have expectations. They think that just because they carry the same name or they are related, they should have a path in, and it doesn't work that way. I don't care who people are. I don't care who their family is. If they don't have a heart that's right and they won't pay the price and walk in the anointing, then I'm not interested.

The thing that's more important than anything else is the anointing and respect for the things of God.

THE FINANCIAL SACRIFICE

> NOTHING THAT IS DONE FOR CHRIST IS LOST.

There is also a sacrifice financially. People say, "How much is this going to cost?" It's everything when it comes to the ministry. It doesn't matter if you sell your house and put the money in the ministry. It doesn't matter what you do, all that will never be lost. So as far as personal financial sacrifice goes, sacrifice it all! I can't tell you any different because I don't know any different.

I pay to go preach. It costs to go and have a crusade, but if you believe in your message and you believe in the call, then whatever the cost, whatever you have to sacrifice, whatever you have to sell, whatever you have to give away, you'll do it!

And every one of us has to pay a price in that regard. The only time we took a salary was in 1992, living in one hotel room with three kids. I thought, *God, these are difficult circumstances to live under, but I'll do whatever I have to do.*

I know for Evangelist Debbie Rich it was being in some Alaskan village, lying on the floor, drinking moose head soup with extra nostrils! And sometimes she wondered about the nostrils! But that kind of sacrifice is not lost, and never will be lost. Because God has great things for you and you are laying up treasure in Heaven, where moth and rust cannot corrupt, where thieves cannot break through and steal (Matthew 6:19). And where your treasure is, that's where your heart is going to be also (v. 21).

Can you say that whatever you've done for the Lord has cost you financially? If so, you have never lost it. It's an investment and it's gaining eternal dividends. It's better than investing in Wall Street, it's gaining eternal dividends, and it's increasing. If you could see the rate of your investment increasing, you'd dump everything in. You'd get so excited that you'd run around telling everybody to invest. If you get a revelation of it, your whole life will change. Nothing that is done for Christ is lost.

YOU SHOULD GET PAID

As I said before, in the early days, people gave me some money and said, "This is for you personally," but I took it straight and stuck it in the ministry. My wife was praying for something, and somebody came and gave us an offering, but I put in the ministry. So there were a lot of 'not-happy moments!'

You should get paid from your ministry. "A workman is worthy of his hire" (1 Timothy 5:18, paraphrased). If you don't get paid, then you are muzzling the ox that is treading out the corn. You can't expect God to bless you when the ox is being muzzled. The Bible says that those who labor in the Word and doctrine are worthy of double honor (v. 17), so you should get paid.

Those who are in the ministry right now need to take the time to take themselves out and bless themselves. Say, "Today, I'm going to sow into my ministry and take myself out and bless myself! Today, I'm just going to buy myself something. I have been so blessed by my ministry. I'm just going to bless myself."

There's a lot more I could say in this realm, but God will take care of you. He will provide for you; He will make a way where there is no way (Isaiah 43). If you made mistakes and made some unwise decisions financially, then repent and ask for mercy, and He'll bail you out. He'll come through for you.

DO NOT TOUCH THE OFFERINGS!

> AT THE END OF THE DAY, IT'S SO MUCH EASIER TO SIT WITH EVERYTHING THAT THE LORD BLESSED YOU WITH, THAN WHAT YOU GAVE YOURSELF.

Whilst touching on finances, I feel led of the Lord to deal with another aspect now. As a ministry, if you are a pastor of a church, do not touch the offerings! Don't go digging in the offering looking for cash to buy lunch. I tell you, do not do it!

I've been with pastors going out for lunch, and they've pulled the offering out of their pockets and paid for lunch! Please! Someone says, "Well, I'm going to do it anyway." No! No, you will get yourself in more trouble than you can shake a stick at. Don't touch the money! If you're an evangelist traveling on the road, and the church hands you the money, don't touch the money. Pay yourself, get paid a salary, and put the money in your ministry and don't touch the money.

Somebody says, "It's all mine." It is not! That's why some ministries are blessed and some ministries are not, because there are no guidelines and there is a blurring between what belongs to the ministry and what belongs to them, and it is all intermingled.

That's why I keep everything separate. I've bought my own car. I pay my own gas. The ministry does not reimburse me for gasoline. I did that so when I want to go and get another car, I can. And I can get whatever I want to get. I buy my own clothes. Don't blur the lines, and don't use the faith that God's giving you for your ministry and turn it on yourself personally.

I don't know if this is making sense to anybody, but if your ministry is running millions of dollars a year, that doesn't mean to say that you turn it on yourself. Always allow God to set the parameters for what you do personally, and pray about things. Pray! Ask God if He wants you to have *this* or *that.* Don't just go do it because you think it would be a good idea. Pray about it. Don't go into a purchase decision for something personally without asking the Lord because at the end of the day, you'll sit with everything that you have got and nothing that God gave you! The Bible says, "The blessing of the Lord makes one rich, and He adds no sorrow with it" (Proverbs 10:22 NKJV).

At the end of the day, it's so much easier to sit with everything that the Lord blessed you with, than what you gave yourself.

SET UP FINANCIAL GUIDELINES

> SET UP VERY STRICT FINANCIAL GUIDELINES FOR YOUR MINISTRY AND DO NOT VIOLATE THEM, AND WATCH WHAT GOD WILL DO.

And this leads me to the next aspect. If you want your ministry to go to another level financially, then set up very strict financial guidelines for your ministry and do not violate them. Then watch what God will do. Don't count the offerings yourself; have nothing to do with them. Have two, three, four, five people count the offerings. Have checks and balances in place. Have everything added up; make sure everything's deposited right and submitted right.

We have a rule that if a check comes in the ministry marked, "Rodney Howard-Browne," it doesn't come to me. If it does not say, "For personal use only," it does not come to me. I don't care if it's $100,000. It goes straight into the ministry. The finance office know not to even call me unless it says, "Personal," "Personal for Rodney Howard-Browne's hands," otherwise, it does not even come near me. I don't want it. I don't believe God can bless you financially if He can't trust you.

LIVE WITHIN YOUR MEANS

Set your salary, have it set by your board independently of you, and then live within your means. Scale back. Cut back. Scale down. Do whatever you have to do to stay within your means. Believe God for increase, and don't touch the money.

You can talk to our administrator, our CPA; you can talk to those in our finance department and they will tell you that we run a very, very clean operation. And that's the reason why the Lord's blessed us over the years and continues to bless us, because we will not violate certain principles.

But if you are the main ministry and you are in a hotel room, removing the cash out of the offering, you can't be blessed. You *cannot* get blessed.

DO NOT SEEK PERSONAL BLESSING

That's why I didn't go around expecting offerings from people personally. I'd rather they blessed the ministry. I don't mind every now and then somebody doing something special, but I don't really like that. I get blessed when the ministry gets blessed. I'm not saying people can't bless you, but you shouldn't be going around looking for someone to give you something personally.

I prefer the ministry get blessed. I get blessed from the ministry being blessed, because I'm doing everything I can to bless the ministry financially. I want to bless the ministry more financially.

There have been times over the last years when something special has been done personally and it's been an unbelievable blessing but that's the exception to the rule. Some ministers expect, "Well, this is pastor appreciation month, and I should be appreciated." But we should not just be in the ministry looking to be appreciated. Somebody says, "You are just shooting yourself in the foot again." No, I don't want anybody's money. I am not here looking for somebody's money. I'm looking for *their* blessing, for *them* to be blessed. I don't need anybody's money.

I went to preach for a guy who kept buying me expensive gifts. Between the services, he'd go out and buy me a watch for $4,000–$5,000; he'd buy me a ring; he'd buy me golf clubs. I said, "Don't do that," but he wouldn't stop doing it. So, every time he bought me a gift, I bought him a gift (except he was buying his with ministry money, and I was buying mine with personal money). It cost me a fortune, but I busted that thing in the head and stopped it.

He said, "I want to bless you." I replied, "Yes, but I don't feel right about this. You did bless me, but you don't have to do it every day, and I don't need a new suit tomorrow, and I don't need a new ring tomorrow, and I don't need a new watch the next day! You are making me feel uncomfortable about it. It's almost like there's something ulterior going on here. If you want to be a blessing, write the ministry a check for $100,000 and I'll be very happy!" It was almost like they were trying to buy me or manipulate me with their gift, and I did not like that.

DO NOT TOUCH THE GOLD

IF YOU WANT THE TRUE RICHES, DON'T TOUCH THE GOLD.

If you want the glory, you cannot touch the gold. That's why I don't like people saying, "For $1,000 I'll give you a prophetic word." It would probably be a pathetic word! But I don't like any of that stuff. If you do that, I think you are touching the gold. If you want the true riches, don't touch the gold.

Don't be greedy, looking for natural riches and things. God will bless you; He take care of you. You'll think you've died and gone to Heaven! But let Him do it.

In fact, if somebody ever comes around in the ministry, and I know they have financial means, the first thing I tell them is, "I don't want a dime from you. I want nothing from you. If God tells you to do something, to get involved in the ministry, that's fine. But I'm just telling you up front, I don't want anything from you." Because that's the first thing they do is to come around and think that I want something from them.

DO NOT ALLOW YOURSELF TO BE BOUGHT

I had a large church of 10,000 members say to me, "You can come here and spend a week, but we don't want you to teach on giving. You name your price and we will give it to you. Do you want $100,000, $200,000, $250,000? You can give away your books, but you can't sell them. Name your price, what you need for the week: $50,000, $100,000?" I said, "Please! What do you think I am? I don't operate that way. I come in and pay my own expense. I receive a love offering."

"Well, we don't do that here."

"Then you don't want me!"

"We're going to bless you anyway."

"No, you are not going to bless me. You can't buy me; you are not going to buy me. You are wanting to buy me, and you are going to hold me in handcuffs and chains while I minister!"

"But what if you come and the offerings are only $20,000, and you only sell $5,000 worth of books?"

I said, "If God wants me there, I'll come for nothing, but you're not going to dictate to me and pull strings and tell me that you'll pay me this and you'll pay me that. No, I'm not for sale, and there's no price big enough. You can't pay me."

Another pastor said to me, "I'll give you so much for a weekend. If you'll preach and look after the church. I'll give you this amount and we'll put you up in a certain hotel." I said, "Why are you so hesitant about it? Why aren't you excited about what I'm going to do for you?" And then they said, "Well, we're not even going to do this for the ministry; we will do this for you personally," and that's even worse. I said, "Why? Do you hate my ministry? Why don't you want to bless my ministry?"

Another time I had one man come to me who said, "Brother Rodney, we're not going to give you any money for the ministry; we would like to give it to you personally," because he didn't like some of the staff I had. He said, "We don't like some of the people in your ministry, so we will bless just you." I said, "You can keep your money. I like my staff. So if you don't want to bless my ministry because of some of my staff, you don't like me, because I have them here for a reason. I have them here to keep people like you away!"

So in this chapter, I have tried to give you some practical things concerning the price of revival. It will cost you friendships, wider family relationships and it will cost you financially. But it should not cost you your wife, your children or your health, you must protect those. I don't have all the answers, but I have given you some!

8

THE PRICE OF REVIVAL: PART TWO

Persecution

I want to continue on the subject of the price of revival because we have talked about the great moves of God in the past, but many don't know what took place. For example, when revival broke out in the nation of Wales, 150,000 people were saved during that one revival under Evan Roberts. But within a year, the devil had used writer Jessie Penn-Lewis to put restraints on Roberts. He was only twenty-six years old and Penn-Lewis was used by hell to stop him.[1]

There's no telling what Evan Roberts would have done in the United Kingdom, because the revival would have gone from Wales, to England, and all up through Scotland and Ireland; only Heaven will know and be able to tell. Instead, Evan Roberts pulled himself back and lived almost like a recluse.

Then you think of Jonathan Edwards, how he was mightily used of God in that revival, and yet was kicked out of his church and spent the last seven years pastoring a little church in a frontier town. And the list goes on and on.

1 Penn-Lewis, Jessie with Roberts, Evans. *War on the Saints*, Thomas E. Lowe Lts; 9th Edition (June 1, 1973)

THE PRICE OF RELIGION

IF YOU WANT THE MOVE OF GOD, THERE IS A PRICE TO PAY. BUT IF YOU WANT RELIGION, YOU PAY ANOTHER PRICE, AND IT'S AN ETERNAL PRICE.

If you want the move of God, there is a price to pay. But if you want religion, you pay another price, and it's an eternal price. If you want the move of God, and you want the things of the Spirit of God, that price will only be this side. Religion will cost you on the other side, especially when it comes to the move of the Spirit of God. Jesus Himself said that which is said against the Father will be forgiven, and that which is against the Son will be forgiven, but that which is said against the Holy Ghost will never be forgiven, not in this world or the world to come (Matthew 12:32). So it would seem that what we do on this earth, in relationship to the Holy Spirit, can have eternal repercussions in our life.

I'm not saying for one moment that everyone who rejects the move of the Spirit of God is going to hell, but I do not want to be walking around Heaven a few degrees below the rung of what I should have had because down on the earth, I had sought the acceptance of man and was ashamed of the Spirit of God, and I watered down and compromised everything.

It is one thing if you don't know because everything is in ignorance, but even then you stand in danger. But it is another thing when you know and you've tasted, and you've walked in that realm, and then you walk away from it. That is just not acceptable. I shudder to think what the consequences will be like for an individual who knows the ways of God, knows the ways of the Spirit of God, but then walks away. It's too horrific to even think about. The belly of a fish would be more inviting than the repercussions and the fallout from that kind of a decision.

BE A GOD PLEASER NOT A MAN PLEASER

> THERE'S A PRICE FOR THE SUPERNATURAL POWER OF GOD FOR ANYONE WHO WOULD WALK IN THE SUPERNATURAL.

We made our decision a long time ago that we are not backing off. Any one of you who have been around this ministry know. Anyone who has been with me for a long time, not just in the meetings but on a personal basis, will tell you we are not backing down one little bit. We are stuck in, we stick to, and follow, the course and the plan and the purpose of God.

Whatever happens, happens, but we are not backing down. I talked about the price in the previous chapter. But in this chapter, I want to talk to you now a little bit about some of the things that I believe will help you in paying the price, because there are other prices that have to be paid. There's a price for the supernatural power of God for anyone who would walk in the supernatural.

You can have a normal, traditional ministry delivering the Word (not that I would even call that normal). But if you teach and nothing really happens, and you do not want to ruffle feathers and you don't say anything that would cause people to either get sad, mad, or glad, then that's religion.

You know, every time I get up to speak, people are going to get either sad, mad, or glad. I do not choose my words. I'm just going to speak what Heaven tells me to speak. And I know during the course of that meeting that some things are going to be shaken up, especially when you start addressing and start shooting religious cows!

You always know when you get a religious cow because you can hear the thing bellowing in the background as it dies! You just need to kill the thing! And I wouldn't even make jerky out of the meat lying on the ground! I wouldn't even take the hide and tan it. I wouldn't even try to take the leg of the cow and have some steak back home. It's a religious cow. The steak is not good to eat anyway. I wouldn't even get the horn so you can put it on the front grille of your Chevrolet. I'd just leave it. Just leave the religious cow where it lies.

IF YOU ARE NOT BEING PERSECUTED, THEN YOU ARE COMPROMISING

> IF YOU WANT A SUPERNATURAL MINISTRY, THEN THE SUPERNATURAL MINISTRY WILL BE ACCOMPANIED BY SUPERNATURAL PERSECUTION.

There is a price to the supernatural, and that price is persecution. Somebody says, "I'm being persecuted." Well, that's a sign that you are heading on the right road. In fact, you can gauge your temperature by the amount of persecution you are receiving. If you're not receiving persecution, then your temperature must have cooled off.

I'm serious! I've been doing this a long time—this is not my first rodeo. If you're not being persecuted, then you are compromising, and God hasn't called you to compromise. He's called you to stand up and be bold. Jesus was preaching and everyone left. Now you tell that to pastors, and they can't even begin to comprehend. "You mean I could get up one Sunday morning and preach and the whole place walk out?"

They don't teach you that in church growth seminars. Successful church-growth workshops will tell you to not ever get up and do anything that will cause your whole congregation to leave, yet Jesus had His congregation leave.

Everybody says they want to be like Jesus, but they don't want to be like Jesus, because there's a price to pay!

People are afraid that if they say something, Brother or Sister Big Bucks will get up, go out in their BMW, and head off down the road. I think every choir needs to learn the Percy Mayfield song:

Hit the road Jack, and don't ya come back
No more, no more, no more, no more
Hit the road Jack, and don't ya come back no more
(ABC-PARAMOUNT, 1961, PRODUCED BY SID FELLER)

Hit the road Jack—it will do wonders, not every Sunday, but every now and then, just when you need to do it. In fact, you could always have a bus parked outside your church so you can take people to other churches because some people don't belong in your church. They are not flowing with the vision; they are not hooked up with the vision; they don't believe in the vision. And if they don't believe in the vision, and are not hooked up with the vision and in the flow, then what are they doing in your church? They are nothing more than spiritual constipation!

And that's why we have revival so we can have a good "bowel movement" and clean out all the blockages. I've already mentioned Wesley, who preached in a church of one hundred and fifty people and when he left there were only thirty-five! What was he saying? The rest weren't even saved; that's why they took off and "hit the road Jack," and they didn't "come back no more, no more, no more."

I've gone to churches and ministered, watched people on the staff and in the leadership. Then I've called somebody out and laid hands on them, and I've watched their response to the anointing. I could tell that person was going to cause trouble. Sure enough within a month, they were already causing trouble. I could tell just by putting my hands on them, that person was not open to the move of the Spirit of God, and was actually not in the vision of the house.

I knew that by watching how they responded under the anointing of the Spirit of God. If you don't have the anointing of God and the Spirit of God in your staff, you don't know what they are!

The price of persecution is one of the prices that you pay for the supernatural power of God. If you want a supernatural ministry, then the supernatural ministry will be accompanied by supernatural persecution.

PEOPLE WHO DON'T KNOW YOU WILL HATE YOU

Do you still want a supernatural ministry? You don't know what you're asking for. Are you crazy or something? Because along with persecution, you'll have to deal with rejection, and rejection is the hardest thing to deal with.

Nobody wants to be rejected. Who wants to be considered an oddball? When I start in the ministry over forty-three years ago on January 1, 1980, I just wanted to help people. I didn't want to be rejected. I thought that everybody was going to get excited about my vision and that they would want to reach the nations and bring in the harvest of souls.

But I had no sooner opened my mouth and I got a slap right up the side of my head and was told, "Get back in your box," and, "Who do you think you are?" So, who wants to be rejected? It is one thing if the world rejects you because they don't know, but the hardest place to deal with rejection is within the Body of Christ.

It is just so painful. I thought, *But we are all washed in the Blood. What did I do?* It's got nothing to do with what I did. The Lord had to show me that it had nothing to do with my name being Rodney Howard-Browne. Even if it was Rodney Howard-Purple or Rodney Howard-Orange, it had nothing to do with my name. It just had to do with what *He* was doing.

Somebody says, "Well, how did you deal with it?" I'm not saying that I dealt with all of it the way that it should have been dealt with, but I did learn over the years to get the victory over it. Rejection comes because of the criticism that comes. The supernatural manifestation of the power of God brings supernatural persecution and supernatural rejection. Most amazingly, people who don't even know you, hate you!

It is one thing to be hated by people who know you; it is another thing to be hated by people who don't even know you! You think, *What did I do to them?* You did nothing! It's got nothing to do with what you did to them, they just don't like what the Lord is doing.

PEOPLE WILL MAKE UP LIES

So supernatural persecution comes, supernatural rejection comes, and it is because of the supernatural criticism that comes from people just stirring up and making up all kinds of lies!

They will attack you in your doctrine; they will attack you in your morals; they will make up stories. I've heard preachers make up stories about me and you really have to come to the place where you say, "Father, forgive them, because they don't know what they are doing" (Luke 23:34). Because if you to try to defend yourself, you will be sidetracked from what God has called you to do. Here at our ministry, we would have to hire a staff of a thousand people just to deal with problems around the world from all the lies and stuff that's been said.

Because every time I go into a country for a crusade, they are ready. They are making up stories again, and it ends up being on a global scale, as I found out. However, thankfully, I can't always read it because it's in Japanese, Chinese, French or Dutch! The Lord shields me because of the language barriers. So, you will get supernatural persecution and criticism, and you will feel that rejection.

YOU MUST NOT TAKE THE GLORY AND YOU MUST NOT TAKE THE CRITICISM

REJECTION IS GOING TO COME. CRITICISM IS GOING TO COME. PERSECUTION IS GOING TO COME. JUST PREPARE YOURSELF BECAUSE IT IS PART OF THE COURSE.

The Lord said this to me: "It's got nothing to do with what you know, what your name is, and who you are. You represent something." And then He said to me, "You can't take the glory for what I do." I said, "Lord, I know that." He said, "Then you can't take the criticism for what I do!"

Because how fair is it to take the criticism when you are not allowed to take the glory? If I can't touch the glory for what God's doing, then how in the world can I take the criticism?

So I have to say, "All glory unto His Name," and I have to say, "All criticism unto His Name" as well. Somebody says, "Oh, that's terrible. How can you say that?" Well, Jesus is doing it. He said, "It's not I that do the work, but My Father within Me, He doeth the work" (John 14:10, paraphrased).

You just have to point everything toward Heaven. God's shoulders are very broad, and He can handle all the criticism. God gets blamed for everything. God got attacked for the tsunami that happened a while ago. God gets criticized every single day.

"God, why did You do this?"

"God, how could You do this to my family?"

"How could You do this?"

Criticism doesn't bother Him; it doesn't faze Him one little bit. I know people said, "God shed a tear when the tsunami came." Give me a break! Do they think God was sitting there and everything was fine, but then the tsunami came and suddenly God started weeping? What a bunch of garbage! What a bunch of religious trash!

God sent His only Son to die on the Cross; that's what He did. God is not sitting in Heaven, crying His eyes out about what is going on in the earth. That sounds all religious and cute, but that's not the truth. Do you think that God didn't know about the tsunami? Do you think that God didn't know about a wave that was going to sweep through Asia?

Somebody says, "Well, all the little children died." Yes, but they went straight to Heaven! Those who died were in countries that hated God, but a hundred thousand kids went to Heaven! Some people are just smoking some bad weed. Religion is a terrible thing. It fries your brain and you talk rubbish.

But if you get criticized, think about how God gets criticized every single day, and all He's ever done is bless people. All He's ever done is help people, yet He gets criticized.

You'll go out of your way and you'll find that the people you helped the most, whom you spent the most time on, will be the ones that criticize you. So just brace yourself because sometimes, you'll want to say, "Hit me again. I'm still conscious!" Just prepare yourself. Rejection is going to come. Criticism is going to come. Persecution is going to come. Just prepare yourself because it is par for the course.

PERSECUTION *WILL* COME WITH REVIVAL

I told the story earlier of a young evangelist who has come out of our ministry and God is using him in an awesome way. But he called me from a city where they had just got a building, but it didn't have the right permit, and people were trying to shut him down. A group of rabbis came outside and the police were there, so he called me and asked me to pray. But I told him that I wasn't going to pray because he had been preaching revival, and now he was having it! I told him to get excited and to not worry about being arrested! Because people think revival is easy. If it were that easy, everybody would be doing it. How would you like to be the Apostle Paul? Shipwrecked, stoned, and then stoned again? (And that's not stoned in the way some people think!)

I heard from a friend of mine about a church where the pastor had been pastoring for about five years. He had a church of around three hundred, and one week he got up and said, "I don't feel like ministering today. I'm real tired, so I'm going to rest, and my wife will come minister." Then the wife got up and she said, "Church, I'm sick of it! I can't take this anymore. My husband has been addicted to crack cocaine for five years, and I'm just not taking any more!"

But that's what the ministry will do to you if you don't have the Holy Ghost. If you don't have the freedom and the Spirit of God, you'll have to snort something! Some people snort crack cocaine; others snort "relig-aine." But I've got the real thing. Hallelujah!

I hate religion. That poor pastor, he is probably a good guy; he just got in the ministry and couldn't handle the pressure, so he started snorting, and he's not going to get help from his denomination.

YOU HAVE TO DIE TO THE PERSECUTION

I mentioned this before, that you have to die to persecution. It's almost like every day you have to die. You die, and when people attack you, you die again. I'm nothing. Jesus is everything. I know this is not a popular subject right now, and not everybody's jumping up and running around excited. "Oh, great! He's talking about persecution and criticism and rejection! This is just phenomenal!" But there is a price to pay.

I remember walking off the platform one night—I can't remember what city I was in—and a man walked up and he said, "I have a real problem with your ministry." I said, "Yeah, I guess it is *your* problem, isn't it?"

He looked at me and said, "Yeah, I guess it is mine." I said, "You know, I don't have a problem with my ministry. I actually enjoy my ministry, and I'm one of the biggest supporters in my ministry. And just because you said that, I'm writing out a bigger offering check to my ministry now. Amen!"

YOU MIGHT HAVE TO RUN SOME PEOPLE OFF

Have you been criticized? God can only use you to the place or the point of the criticism that you can handle. God cannot use you past the point or the place of criticism. Because otherwise, you are not going to obey God, and you will only do what you feel will get you by—and not ruffle too many feathers, and won't make too many people upset with you. And guess what you become? A man pleaser, not a God pleaser! Then how can you have revival? Because revival doesn't come according to man's patterns or standards. Sometimes in order to have revival, you need to run some people off.

I remember when we went into Manila, Philippines, and at that time, I had a brother who traveled with me who was anointed to play the saxophone. I walked out there, saw all the Filipinos were hungry for God, but the American missionaries were sitting there resistant. I wasn't going to preach under that condition, so I made him play his saxophone right in front of the missionaries and blast it. I needed them to get up and leave.

I pointed to where the missionaries were and said, "There's a pocket of resistance over there, so stand over there and blast that thing." It took me about twenty minutes, and I cleared out about twenty missionaries. And then, I could bless the natives! The worst thing is getting to a foreign field and seeing a sad American there. It's like, it didn't work in America, so they exported it!

SUCCESS CAN BE YOUR ENEMY

Another price of revival is handling the success. What happens if God drops a miracle ministry on you where people are healed and creative miracles take place? You wouldn't be able to move. If you went to the restroom, a hand would come over the stall. "Pray for me, pray for me." You wouldn't be able to go anywhere; people would stop you in shopping malls. You might say, "Well, I can handle that. Bring it on," but there are not many who can handle the power of God and last, because one of the things that comes with revival and the move of God is success, and success will probably be your greatest enemy.

When you were struggling financially and could hardly make it, you had to believe God for just your lunch, and you were on your knees, crying out to the Lord, just believing God that maybe somewhere, someway, somehow, He'd open the next door for you. But when God gives you a breakthrough and success comes, people stop pressing in.

That's why you'll see that revival, and the move of God, go in cycles. You'll see a church come up from obscurity, explode and hit the city. Ten years later, whatever took them there isn't there anymore. They are a nice, nominal religious institution, and you hear the reports back of what took place years ago.

RELIGION WILL RISE TO FIGHT REVIVAL

When revival hits, you can also expect religion to rise up. Just because there is revival now, it doesn't mean that it is going to stay a revival. As great as revivals have been in recent history, it's not in those churches now. One pastor of a church in revival, felt led to go and travel around the world. He wanted to use the church as his base and put in another pastor. But the leadership did not want that. The pastor, and everyone who was involved in the revival ended up leaving.

That's a sad thing, but you can have revival for a period of time, and then people can change and turn. People can get mean. Anybody who had anything to do with that revival is not there anymore. They got rid of everybody! So, if anyone goes down there to find out, what happened, they can't find it because they got rid of it. But that is just one of the prices of revival.

I could've told everybody it was going to happen. I knew when revivals broke out in certain churches, that the denominational headquarters would cut them off and that's exactly what happened. In one revival, the moment their Bible school got up to 1,000 students, it became a threat so they got the chop. You have got to understand what is going on behind the scenes!

People don't even know this, but there were some leading denominations that got together to form alliances and legions against us. They said, "At all costs, we have to stop that Howard-Browne character!"

Somebody says, "How do you know?" Because I know people in the higher-ups of these denominations, and they called me up and said, "Brother Rodney, you won't believe it. We just sat in an executive meeting, and they said that they'll do anything to stop you." I thought, *This is the Body of Christ. How do I even deal with this?* Because in the natural, you want to get in the car, go down there, and take them out!

And don't look like you are so holy, and that you have never had anything like that as a thought come your way!

DENOMINATIONS AND RELIGIOUS INSTITUTIONS FIGHT REVIVAL

> THE WHOLE OF AMERICA DEPENDS ON AMERICA HAVING REVIVAL.

Denominations will rise up and fight revival too. The whole of America depends on America having revival, and there are places that used to be fountainheads of the move of God, but now they are all blocked up and bound up by religion and tradition. Whole denominations that are locked up in politics and fear, and they manipulate and control. That's one of the reasons why they keep circulating in the preachers every two, three, four years, so that the preachers can never get a strong footing in the ground and have a breakthrough in the city.

They are afraid the preacher might take off if he becomes a powerhouse and then they won't know what to do. Some of the things that took place in the 1980s were not just about a preacher's moral failure. There were a lot of behind-the-scenes denominations trying to take this one, or that one, out. Preachers were jealous of each other, and no matter how pure your heart is, you can go in with the purest of motives and come out looking like a dog.

Let me give you an example: we were invited to go to Columbus, Georgia. I didn't know that the man who invited me was not the pastor of the church, but rather the administrator of the church. The church was part of a huge denomination, and we were there for three nights.

Evangelist Debbie Rich came in, then Evangelist Richard Moore, and I came up to do the last two nights. I met the guy in the back room, and I said, "So, you are the pastor?" He said, "Well really, I'm the administrator. We don't have a pastor. We are believing for a pastor." Now, when I heard that, I freaked out. I thought, *I never go to a place where there is not a pastor; that's how you get yourself into trouble.* If a pastor says, "I want you to come, but I won't be there," I won't go to that church.

We walked out into the church, and there were probably about eight hundred people there that night, and the Lord spoke to me about the guy and said, "They are looking for a pastor, but *he's* the pastor; *he* is the pastor." So why have people come in and stand in the pulpit trying to see if this is the right one to be the pastor when the Lord just spoke to me and said, "He is the pastor!"

I called the couple out, and the power of God was just all over them, and I gave him the word that he was the pastor. I had just met him and his wife, but then probably over the next thirty minutes, as though directed by an unseen hand, I went across the congregation and pulled out his mother, his father, his children, his brothers, his sister, and I picked out his whole family. They were spread over three different sections, and I didn't pick out anybody who was not his family.

Some of them were sitting on one side and some of them on the other side. Some of them were three rows back, but it was like I'd go around and a spotlight was on them, and I would say, "Okay, you come here," and then I'd go to another section and say, "You, come here," and then he said, "That's all of my family!"

That was confirmation of what God was saying to pray for him and the family. Well all hell broke loose, because the church didn't want him because he hadn't been to "headquarters," and didn't have the denomination or insignia tattooed on his underwear! So the Lord took him out of that church, and brought him a whole group of people. They have their own church now, and they are going on with the move of God. But how sad.

YOU NEED A NEW, GODLY CHARACTER TO SUSTAIN YOU

> DO YOU REALLY WANT TO HAVE REVIVAL, OR DO YOU JUST WANT TO HAVE A NICE MINISTRY?

Someone says, "Well, you probably angered some people within the denomination." Listen, I'm a reasonable person, but I'm not an idiot. You have to decide, do you want revival or do you want a nice ministry? You have to count the cost. Are you ready for revival?

I'm here for the move of God, I don't care what the church is, but I'm not going to play games. I was in a Catholic church in Philadelphia and all the nuns were under the power of God and the priest was under the power of God. I've been in Methodist churches; I've been in Baptist churches. It's just about having a move of God.

The only way to deal with the persecution is you really have to die completely. Ministers get upset because people say all kinds of things. People publish rubbish in newspapers or publish stuff on the internet, but you just have to laugh at it. You have to become as though they're speaking about somebody else. Totally detach yourself from it. And you have to allow the fire of God to burn on the inside of you and burn out everything of yourself. As John said, "He must increase, but I must decrease" (John 3:30). But what you have to understand is that when the fire of God comes and burns, it burns out all the dross. It purifies your vessel, making you a vessel sanctified, meet for the Master's use (2 Timothy 2:21). And what God really wants to do is form a new, godly character in you.

Godly character is the thing that's greatly lacking, especially in American churches, where people are promoted based on the gifts rather than on character. So it doesn't matter what the person has done or what their character is. Their own personal life could look like a bomb hit it, but because they have a great word of knowledge, they get promoted. But if you don't have the character, you might get a gift, but your character will be the thing that causes the vessel to blow apart! Then you end up as a vessel put in the kitchen or the garage, and I don't want to be in the kitchen or the garage!

YOU NEED TO CULTIVATE THE NINE FRUITS OF THE SPIRIT

And as well as godly character, the nine fruits of the Spirit need to be cultivated, no matter who you are and where you're from. You might say, "Well, Brother Rodney, I'm not really a loving person. I don't really love that easily." What does that mean? Is that the excuse? "Are you telling me that I have just got to brace myself?"

No! That means you have to work on walking in love and cultivate walking in love. Someone says, "I'm not really a joyful person." So, are you asking me for some Prozac and Zoloft? "I'm not really a very peaceful person." Well, you have got to cultivate all these fruits. Whatever you are lacking in, work on it! Get over yourself and work on it!

You must establish godly character and cultivate the nine fruits of the Spirit, and that's very easy when you are drunk on the new wine of the Holy Ghost. When you are drunk on the new wine, it is so easy to love, it is easy to forgive, it is easy to have joy, and it is easy to have peace. In the world, people will tell you that their only temporary relief was when they were totally stoned. Now they get saved and they think they have no alternative. But we do! There's no high like the Most High!

YOU NEED TO STAY DRUNK ON THE NEW WINE

When you're drunk in the Spirit, you'll find that you will be able to handle all the stuff much better and much easier. Wigglesworth lived like that—he lived drunk on the Holy Ghost.

There is nothing like a drink of the Spirit of God in the middle of the worst persecution. Someone says, "But you are talking about me getting beside myself." That's the point! Some of you need to get beside yourself. You might not like what you see, but nonetheless, you need to get beside yourself.

Someone says, "Well, I don't believe in this being 'drunk in the Spirit' and all that." Then you don't believe in Pentecost, because Peter said, "These are not drunk, as you suppose" (Acts 2:15 NKJV). He didn't say they weren't drunk. He said, "They are not drunk *as you suppose*."

Some people just need to be hooked up to the "Holy Ghost vat" intravenously. Someone says, "How are you going to deal with this crisis?"

"I'm going to get drunk! I'm going to church, and I'm going to get drunk!"

"Brother Rodney, they are attacking you; they are criticizing you. How are you going to deal with it?"

"I'm going to get drunk. I'm going to get a couple of drinking friends together, and I'm going to go hang out around The River. We're just going to get drunk. I'm going to drink all night."

TEACH YOUR FAMILY TO DRINK THE NEW WINE

Let me tell you about my mom and dad. As a child growing up, I saw them get "trashed" many times. You never knew when my dad was going to get drunk. He'd sit at the dinner table, pray over the food, get drunk in the Spirit, and then start prophesying!

My brother and I always knew. My dad would start praying over the food, and he'd say, "Father," and then there would be a long pause and we'd say, "Boy, we are not going to be eating right now." So, if you want to know where I learned to drink, my parents taught me how to drink. I walked in the living room when I was only seven years old, and my mother was sitting laughing and she continued for three-and-a-half hours. She was beside herself, just laughing. I said to my dad, "What's happening to Mommy?" He said, "Jesus is blessing Mommy." I said, "Oh, okay."

It's good for kids to see their parents drunk . . . in the right way. My parents never did drink alcohol, we never even had it near our house. Why would you want to drink alcohol when you have the real stuff?

I thank my dad and mom for getting drunk on the New Wine. We might have been in the middle of a crisis, but the whole family would join hands together and start to pray, and then the power of God would hit. Everyone was drunk and everything was fine, and my dad would look up and say, "It's going to be okay. Everything will be okay. It's all going to be okay." I'd think, *Man, how did he know that?* Well, he'd just taken a swig. He'd just had a drink and knew that everything was going to be okay.

HAVING A CUP THAT OVERFLOWS

WHEN YOU DON'T KNOW WHAT TO DO, HAVE A DRINK. WHEN YOU FEEL LIKE LIFE'S PROBLEMS ARE GETTING YOU DOWN, HAVE A DRINK. WHEN YOU DON'T KNOW WHICH WAY TO GO, HAVE A DRINK. WHEN YOUR PROBLEMS SEEM SO BIG, HAVE A DRINK.

When you don't know what to do, have a drink. When you feel like life's problems are getting you down, have a drink. When you don't know which way to go, have a drink. When your problems seem so big, have a drink. You can live like this. It's not just when you get to a service—you can live like this. You can live in that place. Somebody says, "The world is not going to understand it." It doesn't matter, just have a drink!

I know people say that all I talk about is getting drunk, but when you were in the world, that's all you talked about! But we are not talking about getting drunk in the natural; we are talking about getting drunk in the supernatural.

The drunker you are, the easier it is to handle every one of the problems that come your way. People come to you and say, "The house burned down," and you laugh. Somebody says, "They stole the car." You say, "They what?" And you laugh. Somebody says, "They left the church." You laugh. "They what?" Somebody says, "They don't want you anymore. They canceled your meeting." You laugh! It's the only way to deal with it.

So, you have to establish godly character and cultivate the nine fruits of the Spirit, but you must yield to the Holy Spirit. Desire to become more like Jesus. Be a worshiper, be a person of prayer, be a giver, and live a life based on the Word of God, which is your firm foundation.

It is the only way to live. There is no other way to live for a child of God. Any other way is carnal, or the flesh, and in eternity, it will have repercussions.

I believe that the Lord is filling you up to handle the task that lies ahead, and He fills you to overflowing to where your "cup runneth over." The psalmist said, "You anointest my head with oil and my cup runneth over" (Psalm 23:5). It's pouring on you, the oil of joy for mourning—and you can live like this!

9

THE RISING OF THE NEW BREED

Set Aside, Marked, and Preserved for This Time

The Lord reminded me of something that He spoke to me in April, 1987. I'd come over to the United States from southern Africa on a short trip. I made two what I called "missionary journeys." If you look at the back of the Bible, many times it maps out the missionary journeys of Paul. Well in 1987, I mapped out two missionary journeys that I made from Africa to the United States.

April, 1987, was right after the collapse of a major ministry. I remember I was sitting in Charlotte, North Carolina, watching a golf tournament on television. I believe it was the Masters Golf Tournament. I was minding my own business, and who would believe that God is going to speak to you watching a game of golf on television?

But I've learned something about the Lord: He will speak to you in the strangest places. The commentator was talking, and he was referring to some of the greats who were playing back then, like Arnold Palmer, Jack Nicklaus, and Gary Player, and He said, "There have been the greats that have dominated the sport, but there's coming a new breed of golfer."

And as he said that, the power of God hit me flat in my seat. It was just like somebody hit me up the side of the head with a brick bat. And

I heard the Lord say, "I'm raising up a new breed of preacher," just like that, and I preached a message called "The Rise of the New Breed."

THE NEW BREED HAVE BEEN RESERVED FOR THIS TIME

AS WE CROSSED OVER THE TWENTY-FIRST CENTURY, I BELIEVE WE STEPPED OVER INTO THE GREATEST MOVE OF GOD THAT THIS WORLD HAS EVER SEEN. AND IT'S NOT COMING; IT IS NOW!

I want to talk to you about this new breed in revival of what God is doing in the earth today, because this new breed are on the earth, and you haven't seen anything yet because it has only just begun. The best of what God is about to do He has reserved for the twenty-first century.

Everything that we've seen up to now has been a preparation. It's been preparatory for what is about to come—this new breed. Now, somebody says, "But we are all new creatures in Christ Jesus." That's true, but I'm not talking about being born-again and being a new creature in Christ Jesus; old things are passed away; behold, all things have become new (2 Corinthians 5:17). I'm talking about a group of people whom God is raising up, and has raised up, for this great end-time revival, this great end-time move of God—which I believe we are in the beginnings of right now. As we crossed over the twenty-first century, I believe we stepped over into the greatest move of God that this world has ever seen. And it's not coming—it is NOW!

THE NEW BREED DO NOT FIT INTO A MOLD

YOU KNOW THAT YOU ARE PART OF THE NEW BREED WHEN YOU JUST DON'T FIT IN, WHEN YOU TRY TO MAKE YOURSELF FIT IN, BUT YOU CAN'T.

Remember this: God is looking for people who are sold out, He's looking for a man, a woman, who is totally sold out. But you have to make a decision on what you're going to be, because there are so many outside influences coming at us all of the time, trying to conform us to fit into the mold. But this new breed does not fit a mold. They do not fit the status quo.

One thing is for certain: they are not religious, and they wreak havoc on tradition. You know that you are part of the new breed when you just don't fit in, even when you try to make yourself fit in, you can't.

THE NEW BREED DO NOT CONFORM

PEOPLE WILL TRY TO PUT YOU IN A BOX, AND THEY WILL TRY TO GET YOU TO CONFORM TO A RELIGIOUS PATTERN OR RELIGIOUS STANDARD. THEY SAY, "DON'T ROCK THE BOAT." BUT THIS NEW BREED DIDN'T COME HERE TO ROCK THE BOAT; WE CAME HERE TO TURN IT OVER!

For years, I tried to make myself be a normal, conventional preacher. I really tried, and I worked hard on it. I said to myself, "You're going to change. You're going to adapt; you're going to fit in. You're going to choose your words correctly. You're going to be politically correct. You can't ruffle feathers the way you do. You are going to go and preach with the number one purpose of getting invited back." And I'd get myself all ready and prepare myself and walk out there and just blow it in the first five minutes! And then I'd take myself back after the service and beat myself up in the in the green room. I'd think, *Lord have mercy. I told myself to behave.*

But you just can't fit in. People will try to put you in a box, and they will try to get you to conform to a religious pattern or religious standard. They'll say, "Don't rock the boat." But this new breed didn't come here to rock the boat; we came here to turn it over!

THE NEW BREED DISPLAY GOD'S GLORY

THIS NEW BREED, THEY STICK OUT. WHEN ALL THE OTHERS ARE HEADING DOWNSTREAM, THEY GO UPSTREAM.

The Lord said to me that day in April, 1987, "I'm raising up a new breed of preacher. Those who do not love money and are not covetous. Those who desire to walk in my anointing and my power and see my Spirit poured out. I'm going to raise them up from obscurity. And I'm going to raise them up for My glory. They will not share My glory, but they'll display it."

This new breed stick out. When all the others are heading downstream, they go upstream. I have found out over the years that it takes a real, live salmon to go upstream. Any old, dead fish can float downstream. This new breed display His glory.

THE NEW BREED ARE FULL OF THE HOLY GHOST

The new breed are not just the normal, run-of-the-mill people. These are people who have got the fire of revival burning in their bones. These are people who, just by their presence as they walk in the room, cause the very atmosphere to change. These are people who, when you look at them, you scratch your head, and you think, *There's something different about them. I'm not really sure what it is. But there's something different about them.*

It's got nothing to do with the exterior. It's got nothing to do with the way they wear their hair, or which suit they wear, or the color of their tie, or if they have a moustache or a ponytail. It has nothing to do with whether they wear designer shoes. It is what is on the inside of this new breed—the Holy Ghost!

They are "Holy Ghost Green Berets," "Holy Ghost Rambos." They won't take no for an answer. And if you tell them that no one has ever had a revival in a certain city, that's the place they are going to pick to have a revival! And if you tell them, "This is a real hard place," that's the place they'll pick! It's the new breed! They are unstoppable.

THE NEW BREED ARE VOICES, NOT ECHOES

> THERE'S A NEW BREED IN THE LAND. THERE'S A NEW BREED IN THE EARTH TODAY: THOSE WHO ARE FULL OF THE HOLY GHOST, FULL OF THE FIRE OF GOD. THEY ARE NOT ECHOES; THERE ARE TOO MANY ECHOES IN THE LAND. THEY ARE VOICES!

There's a new breed in the land. There's a new breed in the earth today. Those who are full of the Holy Ghost, full of the fire of God. They are not echoes, there are too many echoes in the land. They are voices! There is a big difference between an echo and a voice. Do you want to be a voice or an echo? This new breed are originals, they are not carbon copies.

So if you're wondering why you never fitted in and why you could never conform, it is because you were just made for another day and another time and another place! I used to go to conferences and sit there like the odd one out. I would go to ministers' conferences with thousands of ministers, and I would stand there all alone, by myself.

I would think, *My God. What am I even doing here?* Have you ever felt like that? I'd spend all this money to go to a conference and I didn't fit in. I'd sit through the morning sessions, the afternoon sessions; I'd go to the workshops. I had never seen so many things broken; that's why they had all the workshops! And the longer the conference went, the more frustrated I would get, just sitting there thinking, *Boy, something must be wrong with me. I just don't seem to fit in.*

And some people won't realize this, but I left some of those meetings and cried my way back for ten hours, driving down the highway.

I told the Lord, "If that's all about You, then I'm in the wrong place. Lord, they said it was a Holy Ghost conference, and I waited all week, and it cost me a fortune to get there. I paid the money and I flew in. I went out of my way. I didn't even have the money to go there, but they promised that the Holy Spirit would be there, and I waited all night. Then He did show for about two minutes, and they shut that up. God, I wasted a whole week!" And I'd drive away just crying my eyes out. I'd drive down the highway with tears running down my cheeks.

I said, "Lord, I know those people know You, and I'm not disputing that they are all born-again and love You, but I just don't fit in there. Lord, I know it's not that hard for You to move." Hanging out with those people was like fishing all night and catching no fish. I know when Jesus gets in the boat, He's going to say, "Cast your net on the other side" (John 21:6, paraphrased), so I said, "Lord Jesus, why can't we just have You get in the boat?"

And the Lord spoke to me and said, "Son, I was in all those meetings; I just wasn't allowed much operating room!" The moment the power of God started falling, they shut that meeting down. They called everybody to the front and the power of God started falling, people started to fall out under the power, there was a little outbreak of revival, but the ushers were there, stopping them!

And then the organizers said, "All right. Come back tomorrow." I thought, *Come back tomorrow? The Holy Ghost just got here!* Going to a Holy Ghost conference with no Holy Ghost is like going to butcher shop with no meat!

Then the worst thing with meetings like this is that you get ready, have a shower, shave and get dressed, get to the meeting, and at 8:30/9:00 p.m. they are finished. You look at your watch and think, *My God! What a ruination of a good evening!* Yet when you were out in the world, serving the devil, you went out on the town all night!

THE NEW BREED ARE NOT RELIGIOUS

> SO, IF YOU'RE WONDERING WHY YOU NEVER FITTED IN AND WHY YOU COULD NEVER CONFORM, IT IS BECAUSE YOU WERE JUST MADE FOR ANOTHER DAY AND ANOTHER TIME AND ANOTHER PLACE!

The new breed expect God to show up. One time I called up some pastors and said, "When we come in, we will need to stay an extended period of time." They said, "Well, we'll have you Sunday morning, and if God shows up, you can stay longer."

I said, "You mean God might not come? If God's not coming, I'm not even coming there!" It horrified me that somebody would think that God wasn't going to show up!

"Well, come over and speak for me Sunday. I'll giving the microphone and you will have forty-five–fifty minutes. I want you to do my church offering first before you preach. And you have to be over by 12:00 noon because there's a buffet line." I thought, *Well, at least that's scriptural, Paul said, "I buffet my body daily!"*

There were some Sundays that I got up and just said, "Hi. My name is Rodney Howard-Browne. I'm a missionary from Africa to America. I just want to tell you that Jesus loves you. Amen." And I sat down.

What else can you do? They had already taken three offerings; the choir had sung. (I could have done a better job with a cat under my arm, squeezing its neck!) But they said they wanted to have revival? "You have got thirty-one minutes, brother. If God shows up, you can stay."

I went to this one church, and this pastor—bless his heart—worked too hard. I told him, "You are working too hard. It's not that hard!" I thought, *He's going to take a knife and start cutting himself! He was just working too hard.* I said, "God is not dead; He is alive."

Before the service, he had prayed, "Lord, we pray for Brother Rodney, Lord, that you will anoint him today. Lord, use him today. Bring great revival, oh God, we pray." I just kept saying, "Amen," hoping he would shut up. I thought, *With a prayer like that, I'm finished before I even get started!* And the worst is when you are called in the back room and all the deacons come and surround you, praying dead prayers!

THE NEW BREED ARE FULL OF THE FIRE OF GOD

THE NEW BREED–IT'S NOT SO MUCH ABOUT WHAT THEY ARE DOING; IT IS ABOUT WHAT HE'S DOING.

The new breed—it's not so much about what *they* are doing; it is about what *He's* doing. There have been times when I've been preaching and people are getting touched, and I've had preachers walk up on the platform while I'm speaking to look at my notes! They are puzzled and they can't understand. *How is he talking in one place, but people are getting hit by the power of God at the back of the room. How is that possible?* They are trying to listen to hear something profound.

But I love to make it even more simple, just totally uncomplicated, and then the power of God starts smacking the place and they get so confused! They are all sitting there, trying to work out what I'm doing; meanwhile, I am doing nothing. All I'm doing is observing what God's doing! It's about what *He's* doing.

CHARACTERISTICS OF THE NEW BREED

Let me give you some of the characteristics of this new breed:

They are not covetous. In other words, they don't want anything that anybody else has, because whatever they get, they get from God. Their eyes are on Jesus, not on anything else or on what anybody else has. Jesus is the number one source in their life for everything.

They are people of faith. When you hang around them and when you leave their presence, you are lifted up. You are encouraged; you feel like you just had a shot in the arm, an injection of faith. They are people full of faith, and you begin to believe for impossible things by just hanging around them.

They are people of prayer. They talk to God and He talks to them. It's two-way communication; it's not one-sided.

They are people of integrity. They have honest hearts. They speak the truth—they don't speak with a forked tongue.

They have a passion for the lost, and they are people of compassion and they are merciful.

They are bold! They are people who operate in the fruit of the Spirit. And if you want to operate in more of the fruits of the Spirit, then you need to drink more of the Spirit. There's nothing wrong with you that a little bit more drink wouldn't cure. God is raising this new breed up from obscurity.

They are heavenly minded. 1 John 2:15–17:

> Love not the world, neither the things that are in the world. If any man love the world, the love of the Father is not in him. For all that is in the world, the lust of the flesh, and the lust of the eyes, and the pride of life, is not of the Father, but is of the world. And the world passeth away, and the lust thereof: but he that doeth the will of God abideth for ever.

2 Corinthians 6:14–18:

> Be ye not unequally yoked together with unbelievers: for what fellowship hath righteousness with unrighteousness? and what communion hath light with darkness? and what concord hath Christ with Belial? or what part hath he that believeth with an infidel? and what agreement hath the temple of God with idols? for ye are the temple of the living God; as God hath said, I will dwell in them, and walk in them; and I will be their God, and they shall be my people. Wherefore come out from among them, and be ye separate, saith the Lord, and touch not the unclean thing; and I will receive you, and will be a Father unto you, and ye shall be my sons and daughters, saith the Lord Almighty.

I'm not talking about worldly people here now. I'm talking about people who when you see them, you know they are just passing through. This has got nothing to do with age. People think the new breed is just young people. But it's got nothing to do with age; it has got to do with something that takes place by the Holy Ghost on the inside of you.

They have been transformed by the Holy Ghost. This new breed are individuals who have allowed the Spirit of God to do a transforming work on the inside of them. That's why they don't fit in. Light cannot mix with darkness. They don't succumb to peer pressure. It doesn't matter what the rest of the world is doing. In fact, the Lord said to me, "Find out what everybody else is doing and then do the opposite, and it will be Me!"

BECOMING A PART OF THIS NEW BREED:

Now, if you are saying, "Well, I don't really feel like I'm a part of this new breed." I'm going to tell you exactly how to become part of the new breed.

Separate from the world. The first thing I mentioned a little earlier is separation from the world. This new breed are not part of the world. They don't fit in to the world; they are just passing through.

The new breed are like Abraham looking for a city whose builder and maker is God (Hebrews 11:10). They set out at God's command, and they are marching to the beat of a different drum. They are in the world, but they're not of it. They are set apart and they know it.

Consecrate to the call. The second thing is that they are consecrated to the call. They know exactly what God has called them to do, and nothing can distract them. They are on a mission.

Dedicate to the task. Thirdly, they are dedicated to the task. You find the new breed now, and you find them five years from now, and they are going to be doing the same thing. You find them ten years from now, and God will have added new dimensions to them, but they will not stray. They are just locked in to what Heaven has.

Yield to the Holy Ghost. They have made a decision to be a vessel, sanctified, meet for the Master's use (2 Timothy 2:21), because other people depend on them. As one of this new breed, there are people depending on you having a breakthrough. There are nations depending on you having a breakthrough. There are cities depending on you having a breakthrough. It's not about a breakthrough just for your comfort; it's a breakthrough for all those who will come on after you, who will be touched through your life.

Obey the call. You must obey the call to be one of the new breed; you must obey the heavenly vision. You must do what Heaven has planned for you to do.

This is not the time to give up. This is not the time to throw in the towel. This is time to run the race because He gives you the grace to run the race and to cross the finish line. And you've got a great cloud of witnesses who have gone on before you, who are watching from the banisters of Heaven, shouting out, "Come on! You can do it. Come on! You can do it!" (Hebrews 12:1).

It's time to lay aside the weight and the sin. The last thing that God has planned for the new breed is to carry a weight of sin on them. You cannot run and do what God's called you to do and carry a weight of sin. You have got to lay it aside (Hebrews 12:1).

Jesus said, "My yoke is easy and My burden is light" (Matthew 11:30 NKJV). From the grandstands of Heaven, those who have gone before us cheer us on and say, "Come on. It won't be long. You can do what God has called you to do."

THE NEW BREED ARE SET APART AND MARKED

> THIS IS YOUR DAY. THIS IS YOUR HOUR. THIS IS YOUR YEAR. THIS IS YOUR DECADE. IT IS NOW! YOU ARE THE NEW BREED!

A new breed! There's a new breed in the land, and no matter what it takes, you want to be part of this new breed for this end-time move of God, of what God's about to do. You're not going to fit in, so don't try. You didn't fit in then, and you don't fit in now. People might call you weird or whatever they want to call you, but you've been set apart. You've been marked. You've been brought into the Kingdom of God for such a time as this (Esther 4:14). God chose you to be living in this day and this hour. God didn't want you to be living a hundred years ago. He put you here right now.

This is your day. This is your hour. This is your year. This is your decade. It is now! You are the new breed!

THE NEW BREED ARE HOLY

One of the greatest characteristics of this new breed is holiness. I'm not talking about the religious kind—hair in a bun, no makeup, walking around looking like a day ghost doing a night service! I'm talking about holiness. I'm talking about purity. Like when Wigglesworth got on a train one day and two priests fell down and said, "Pray for us. You convict us of our sin." He hadn't said one word; he'd just walked on the train and they fell down.

I'm not talking about walking around with a holier-than-thou attitude. I'm not talking about you walking around putting condemnation on people. There is a purity about this new breed, there is a humility about this new breed, and there is a holiness about this new breed.

The Bible says that friendship with the world is enmity against God (James 4:4). This new breed are not people who are afraid to sin because they will get caught. Getting caught doesn't even come into their vocabulary because sinning doesn't even come in their vocabulary. Do you understand what I'm talking about? They are not even planning to do something in secret.

When they refer to "holy men," they are going to really mean it. I'm not talking about somebody dressed up in some kind of a robe, living in a monastery. I'm talking about somebody who is holy and pure.

Do you want to be holy? Do you want to be pure? Just say this out loud right now: "Jesus, keep me holy and keep me pure."

Several years ago, I was invited to appear on a national television talk show on one of the main networks in America. The host and his wife were there, and they were questioning about me about the joy. They were really intrigued and wanted to know about the joy. So they said,

"We're going to talk further with Brother Rodney Howard-Browne, a missionary from Africa, whom God's using in this way with the joy. We'll be right back after the break." So they went to the break. Then he leaned over to me and he said, "When we come back after the break, would you tell everybody watching where this joy is leading to? Can you sum it up in one word?" and I looked at him and said, "Oh yes, it is very easy. I can sum it up in one word." He said, "What's that?" I said, "Holiness."

I'm telling you, when we came back after the break, I was off the air and they got rid of me quicker than you can ever imagine. They excused me from the program and started to talk about their dogs. I was gone, I was off their program, and it was so sudden that I walked off the set wondering what had happened. But obviously, they didn't want to go there. "You mean the joy is going to lead to holiness? Brother Rodney, if you preach this, people will leave the church." I can't believe that everybody would leave. I have to believe that there's a bunch of people who want to be pure and want to be holy. Somebody says, "Who are they?" They are a new breed.

I love my wife so much, and do you know why I love her? Because she's a pure lady. It's nice to be around pure people. I just sense the Lord doing a deep work right now in the hearts of people. There are things being broken right now. As I'm speaking this word, there are things being broken off of people. I'm not trying to put a guilt trip on anybody, but I'm trying to tell you the past is past at last. From this moment, there shall come a greater holiness in your life.

From this moment, there shall come a greater hunger for the pure, and for the things of God in your life. For even now, the Spirit of God strips away the desires of the flesh, the lust of the flesh, the lust of the mind. Even now, the Spirit of God is brooding and moving, working in the hearts of men and women, young and old.

For you shall be pure. You shall be holy, and you shall walk in that which Heaven has destined you to walk in. It shall be said of you, as it was said of men of old that, "Truly, God is with them; truly, the hand of the Lord is upon them." For you are marked, and you are set apart, sanctified for the Master's use. A greater holiness, a greater consecration, and a greater purity.

As I mentioned earlier, I'm talking about when you walk into the room, the very atmosphere of the room changes. When people get around you, they sense the presence of Jesus. You might not say anything. I'm not talking about carrying a Bible big enough to choke a moose and walking around saying, "Hallelujah; amen," all the time. I mean that you just walk into a place and the atmosphere changes.

If you go to somebody's kitchen, you will find some utensils that stay in the kitchen. At one time, they were good enough to bring out when the guests were there. At one time, there were good enough to put on display at the banquet, but now, they cannot make it out of the kitchen. They must just stay in the kitchen.

But the Bible says in 2 Timothy 2:21, "If a man therefore purge himself from these, he shall be a vessel unto honour, sanctified, and meet for the master's use, and prepared unto every good work." Let me tell you again that I'm not pushing condemnation here, but so many people have had setbacks in their life.

God used Kathryn Kuhlman. She married a man who had divorced his wife, and after several years, she knew that what had happened was wrong, and she left him. Do you know that for fourteen years she was in the desert place? But Kathryn was on her face, hour after hour, day after day, and God came and did a work in her, and the ministry of Kathryn Kuhlman was born. That's why she could get up and say, "I died a thousand deaths."

So, what does that tell me? Can somebody come back from a setback? Oh, yes. But you have to press in; you have to cut the past out; you have to erase it. Between you and God, you have to get in there and come to that place of total consecration in yieldedness to the Lord. That's just something that the modern-day Church does not even indulge in.

THE NEW BREED ARE PURE

People don't even want to confess sin anymore; they just call it a "mistake." a "mishap," or something similar. But sin is sin and must be treated as sin. It must be dealt with as sin and then must be walked away from.

There is no one that is beyond hope. For anyone who would hunger and thirst after righteousness, He said you would be filled (Matthew 5:6).

God is moving in such an awesome way, and if the Lord is speaking to you about some things that it is time to let go of, I want you to consecrate yourself and yield to Him. The price to pay is worth it.

Sometimes the pull of the world is so strong, and if you yield to the world once, yield twice, yield three times, then the more you yield, the easier it becomes, and you will give the enemy a foothold in your life. The door must be closed. That must be rooted out. He's wanting to use you as a vessel. He wants to bring you out of the kitchen. He wants to display you at the banquet table. That's His real plan for you. He doesn't want you stuck in the kitchen, or the laundry, or the garage used to put rubbish in. Your desire must be that when the master looks over the vessels, He will say, "Which one should I pick tonight?" And He'll come, and He'll reach in with His Hand, and He'll pick you—a consecrated, chosen vessel, pure and holy. And He'll say, "I will use this vessel. I will fill them up and I will pour them out."

THE NEW BREED ARE YIELDED IN EVERY AREA OF THEIR LIVES

> YOU MUST FIGHT TO KEEP YOUR GARMENTS PURE AND CLEAN.

Oh, to be a vessel in the hand of the Master. You can do it! I tell every one of you, "You can do it!"

Now lift your hands and your voice where you are right now and give Him everything. Hold nothing back. The holiness of God is here. The power of the devil is broken off of your life. Every bondage, every blockage, every hindrance, broken from now on! It's a purging work and a purifying work by the Spirit of God. Chains have been broken and yokes have been destroyed in Jesus' Name!

The fire of God is falling. How can the new breed be the new breed when they are mixed in with the old and they are still contaminated with the things of the world? They can't! We must have clean garments. You must fight to keep your garments pure and clean.

If you were getting dressed, and you spilled coffee on your shirt, you would be embarrassed to even go out. If you spilled fruit juice on your tie, you would go and change it. Likewise, in the Spirit, keep your garments pure and clean.

Parents, bring your kids in close. Bring them closer than you've ever brought them in, and I pray for every preacher's kid, "Devil, you can't touch them. Devil, you can't touch them. They are marked. They are marked for an eternal purpose. In Jesus' Name."

If your kids are with you, take hold of them. Get together as a family and say: "The pure in heart will see God. The pure in heart will see God. 'Who shall ascend into the hill of the Lord? . . . He that hath clean hands, and a pure heart'" (Psalms 24:3–4).

> I pray that every family will be marked and sealed by the Spirit of God. That, Lord, You would be about them as a wall of fire, and that no harm or evil could come nigh unto them. I pray for every single mother and every single person; they are not alone. Be about them as a wall of fire. Seal them by Your Spirit. Do a deep work, Lord. Do a deep work that on that day, not one would be missing. Not one would be missing. Raise them up to be mighty men and women of God who will impact nations and cities and towns and villages.
>
> I pray for every young woman, that she will marry only the one you've chosen for her. I pray for every young man, that he will marry only the one you have chosen for him. Lord, put a guard around them; we put a wall around them—no journeys into the wilderness. No wrong choices. Amen.

The new breed—God is looking for those who are sold out. You have to make the decision on what you're going to be. This is your day. This is your hour. This is your year.

10

BOLDNESS

To Dare to Do

THE GREATEST HINDRANCE THAT STOPS PEOPLE FROM SEEING A BREAKTHROUGH IS THAT THEY ARE TIMID.

I want to now give you one of the key ingredients that you will need to have to carry the fire of God to the nations of the world. Go to Proverbs 28:1, "The wicked flee when no man pursueth: but the righteous are bold as a lion." I want to talk to you about boldness in the move of God.

The greatest hindrance that stops people from seeing a breakthrough is that they are timid. They want to come along and have revival and, like the old song says, "tiptoe through the tulips." They want to walk softly. They want to come in and just tiptoe in and tiptoe out. But in order to have a move of God and have revival, you have to be bold!

BOLDNESS, NOT ARROGANCE

I'm not talking about arrogance. Arrogance always talks about "me, me, I, I, me, me." Boldness, is about "He, He, Him, Him." Boldness points the way to Jesus. "The wicked flee when no man, pursueth" (Proverbs 28:1). Have you watched how some people are always running? I watch some preachers who are that way. They can't sit still; they are always up and down and running around all over the place. They are always "fleeing" from something. "The wicked flee when no man pursueth, but the righteous are bold as a lion" (Proverbs 28:1).

BOLDNESS COMES FROM THE HOLY GHOST

YOU NEED TO BE FILLED WITH THE HOLY GHOST, BECAUSE IT IS THE HOLY GHOST WHO GIVES YOU THE BOLDNESS TO STAND IN THE FACE OF DEATH.

Now I come from Africa, and one of the greatest treats that I have when I go back to Africa is to go to the game park. There's nothing like being in the African bush. Many of you know that I'm a big-game hunter, but I don't always hunt. Probably once every five to ten years, I do a big ten-day hunt in the bush, where it is dangerous and you could get eaten, so you do a lot of praying and you make sure that you are right and ready! There are times when you find yourself going into emergency tongues, especially when you're walking up a dry riverbed and suddenly, there's a big black-mane lion looking at you.

I particularly remember this one trip where we were really on a photography safari and we were traveling in an open Jeep. Now, when a lion looks at a Jeep he doesn't think, *An enemy,* because a Range Rover/ Land Rover or Land Cruiser is open. The lion will walk right by you, and if you put your hand out, you can actually touch him because he does not register that the vehicle is an enemy.

But if the lion saw another deer, another animal, or a human being, you would be in trouble. So, we pulled up on this whole pride of lions, all sitting there chomping on some bones. (I think they had taken down a giraffe and they were chewing on it). There were probably twelve or fifteen lions, and there was one particular big black-mane lion who was getting a big lion's share of everything.

I thought that I needed to get a better photo of him. I had a zoom lens on, but I wanted to get a better angle of him. He was at the back, and there was another lion in front him. So I thought, *I'm going to stand up, and I'll be able to get it a direct angle and get this lion. I'll zoom right in and get it right in the picture.* The lion was eating, and if he looked up at the vehicle, he'd eat again, but I didn't realize that if I stood up and stuck my head up, he would be able to see me as he looked at the vehicle!

I stood up to take the photograph, and as I stood up with the camera lens in my hand to focus, the lion immediately looked up, and he looked through the back of my head. Those eyes were like spears! Those eyes did not show any fear. He looked at me, and when he looked at me, the most amazing thing happened: my knees caved in! The lion didn't make a noise; he didn't make a sound; he didn't get up; he didn't come toward me. He just looked directly at me, and when he looked, it was as if he had looked into me, and my knees went weak and I sat down. He looked again and then he carried on eating, and I breathed a sigh of relief!

When you look at the apostles, what was their greatest characteristic, apart from the fact that they were filled with the Holy Ghost? They were bold! That's why you need to be filled with the Holy Ghost, because it is the Holy Ghost who gives you the boldness to stand in the face of death.

There was a program on TV years ago called *The Brady Bunch*. God is raising up "the Bold Bunch." They are bold in their faith, bold in their walk, bold in their talk, and that boldness comes from confidence in God and His ability and His Word. He said, "I will never leave you nor forsake you" (Hebrews 13:5 NKJV).

BOLDNESS TO DO WHAT HE TELLS YOU TO DO

> GOD WANTS TO PUT THE GIFT OF FAITH INTO EVERY SINGLE PERSON BECAUSE WHEN THE GIFT OF FAITH COMES, IT TAKES OUT ALL DOUBT. IT TAKES OUT ALL FEAR, IT TAKES OUT ALL QUESTIONS, AND YOU GET BOLD.

> Now Peter and John went up together into the temple at the hour of prayer, being the ninth hour. And a certain man lame from his mother's womb was carried, whom they laid daily at the gate of the temple which is called Beautiful, to ask alms of them that entered into the temple; who seeing Peter and John about to go into the temple asked an alms. And Peter, fastening his eyes upon him with John, said, Look on us.
>
> ACTS 3:1-4

You have to have boldness to walk up to a lame man and say, "Look at me." Peter didn't go up to him and say, "Um, are you busy? Could I talk to you? Can I make an appointment?" Boldness! And when boldness is there, then there is the command of faith, "Look on us."

And the Bible says, "And he gave heed unto them, expecting to receive something of them" (v. 5). Remember, people are going to come to you expecting to receive something. "Then Peter said, "Silver and gold have I none; but such as I have give I thee: In the name of Jesus Christ of Nazareth rise up and walk. And he took him by the right hand, and lifted him up" (vv. 6–7). He was a lame man, and Peter took him by the right hand, and the Bible says that they lifted him up. It takes a bold person to lift a lame man up because a timid person would think, *What would happen if he falls?*

Studying the life of the great Smith Wigglesworth, I learned that he followed the Book of Acts so much and he quoted it verbatim. He couldn't read when he started out. He was an illiterate plumber, but he memorized whole chapters of Scripture. He loved this passage of scripture about Peter and John. Smith Wigglesworth was called the "Apostle of Faith," and he's known for his boldness.

He was so bold that when they brought him a man who had cancer and was dying, Wigglesworth punched the man in the stomach! The man fell out on the floor, and the usher said, "He is dead!" And Wigglesworth said, in that northern British accent, "He's 'ealed!" They said, "He's dead!" and Wigglesworth said, "He's 'ealed!" They said, "He's dead!" But Wigglesworth said, "He's 'ealed!"

A few minutes later, the man was 'ealed and running around the place! Now, I'm not telling that you that you have to go around punching people, but Wigglesworth was so bold in what he believed; he was bold in his faith. Whenever he prayed for somebody who had appendicitis, for some reason, he would always punch them! That's the worst thing you can do to somebody who has appendicitis. But he would say, "Ouch!" and punch them right there, and they would get healed of appendicitis. Can you imagine that? They were either 'ealed or they were dead, but in his case, they were 'ealed.

It is reported that he had twenty-seven people raised from the dead. I know one case where someone called him and said a person was dying and Wigglesworth didn't come. They said, "Please come. He's desperate; he's dying," but Wigglesworth didn't show up. Then they called up and said, "Don't worry; he's dead." Wigglesworth said, "I'm coming!" That was Wigglesworth!

He walked right in and took the dead man by the scruff of the neck, and stuck him up against the wall and said, "In the name of Jesus, walk!" and the guy slid to the floor! Now when that happens, that's the time that you and I would be leaving the house. "I'm out of here!"

But Wigglesworth didn't stop. He picked the dead man up and said, "I said, 'In the Name of Jesus, walk!'" And the guy fell to the floor. That's the time you would be thinking, *Brother Wigglesworth, shouldn't we be leaving now?* But Wigglesworth bent down and grabbed the dead man and stuck him up against the wall said, "I told you to walk!" and the guy walked!

Wigglesworth had boldness that comes with the gift of faith. God wants to put the gift of faith into every single person because when the gift of faith comes, it takes out all doubt. It takes out all fear, it takes out all questions, and you get bold.

TO DARE TO GO WHERE HE TELLS YOU TO GO

I DARE YOU TO GO AND SHAKE CITIES, TOWNS, AND VILLAGES. I DARE YOU TO GO AND SHAKE NATIONS, I DOUBLE-DOG DARE YOU. I DARE YOU IN THE NAME OF JESUS. I DARE YOU TO TAKE GOD AT HIS WORD. I DARE YOU TO STEP OUT OF THE BOAT AND WALK ON THE WATER. I DARE YOU.

Vines Expository Dictionary of the New Testament says that to be bold means "to dare to do." Have you ever said, "I dare you to do that?" Some of you might have said, "I double-dog dare you!" To be bold is to dare to do, and God is looking for people who will dare.

I dare you to go and shake cities, towns, and villages. I dare you to go and shake nations, I double-dog dare you. I dare you in the Name of Jesus. I dare you to take God at His Word. I dare you to step out of the boat and walk on the water. I dare you.

The Bible says:

> Immediately his feet and ankle bones received strength. And he leaping up stood, and walked, and entered with them into the temple, walking, and leaping, and praising God. And all the people saw him walking and praising God: and they knew that it was he which sat for alms at the Beautiful gate of the temple: and they were filled with wonder and amazement at that which had happened unto him. And as the lame man which was healed held Peter and John, all the people ran together unto them in the porch that is called Solomon's, greatly wondering.
>
> ACTS 3:7B-11

Listen, that's what you are going to do: go into towns, cities, villages, and nations, and people are going to be greatly wondering.

> And when Peter saw it, he answered unto the people, Ye men of Israel, why marvel ye at this? or why look ye so earnestly on us, as though by our own power or holiness we had made this man to walk? The God of Abraham, and of Isaac, and of Jacob, the God of our fathers, hath glorified his Son Jesus; whom ye delivered up, and denied him in the presence of Pilate, when he was determined to let him go. But ye denied the Holy One and the Just, and desired a murderer to be granted unto you.
>
> VV. 12-14

Is this the same Peter who had denied the Lord? This is fighting talk. He's provoking. Somebody said, "Peter, shut up! You're going to cause a riot. Be quiet!" But when you are bold, you don't even think of the consequences.

> And killed the Prince of life, whom God hath raised from the dead; whereof we are witnesses. And his name through faith in his name hath made this man strong, whom ye see and know: yea, the faith which is by him hath given him this perfect soundness in the presence of you all. And now, brethren, I wot that through ignorance ye did it, as did also your rulers. But those things, which God before had shewed by the mouth of all his prophets, that Christ should suffer, he hath so fulfilled. Repent ye therefore, and be converted, that your sins may be blotted out, when the times of refreshing shall come from the presence of the Lord; and he shall send Jesus Christ, which before was preached unto you: whom the heaven must receive until the times of restitution of all things, which God hath spoken by the mouth of all his holy prophets since the world began. For Moses truly said unto the fathers, A prophet shall the Lord your God raise up unto you of your brethren, like unto me; him shall ye hear in all things whatsoever he

> shall say unto you. And it shall come to pass, that every soul, which will not hear that prophet, shall be destroyed from among the people. Yea, and all the prophets from Samuel and those that follow after, as many as have spoken, have likewise foretold of these days. Ye are the children of the prophets, and of the covenant which God made with our fathers, saying unto Abraham, And in thy seed shall all the kindreds of the earth be blessed. Unto you first God, having raised up his Son Jesus, sent him to bless you, in turning away every one of you from his iniquities. And as they spake unto the people, the priests, and the captain of the temple, and the Sadducees, came upon them, being grieved that they taught the people, and preached through Jesus the resurrection from the dead. And they laid hands on them, and put them in hold unto the next day: for it was now eventide. Howbeit many of them which heard the word believed; and the number of the men was about five thousand.
>
> ACTS 3:15-4:4

You are going to see a great harvest, great signs and wonders, great miracles with great boldness, but there will be great persecution and great attack.

> And it came to pass on the morrow, that their rulers, and elders, and scribes, and Annas the high priest, and Caiaphas, and John, and Alexander, and as many as were of the kindred of the high priest, were gathered together at Jerusalem. And when they had set them in the midst, they asked, By what power, or by what name, have ye done this? Then Peter, filled with the Holy Ghost . . .
>
> ACTS 4:5-8

That's the key right there to getting boldness! The moment you are filled with the Holy Ghost, you just wax bold. You'll be thinking, *My God! What am I going to do? They're going to kill me,* and then suddenly—boom! The power of God hits you and you step into that realm.

BOLDNESS TO LIVE AND BOLDNESS TO DIE

WE HAVE GOT TO BE BOLD TO LIVE AND BOLD TO DIE.

> Then Peter, filled with the Holy Ghost, said unto them, Ye rulers of the people, and elders of Israel, if we this day be examined of the good deed done to the impotent man, by what means he is made whole; be it known unto you all, and to all the people of Israel, that by the name of Jesus Christ of Nazareth, whom ye crucified, whom God raised from the dead, even by him doth this man stand here before you whole. This is the stone which was set at nought of you builders, which is become the head of the corner. Neither is there salvation in any other: for there is none other name under heaven given among men, whereby we must be saved. *Now when they saw the boldness of Peter and John*, and perceived that they were unlearned and ignorant men, they marvelled; and they took knowledge of them, that they had been with Jesus.
>
> ACTS 4:8-13 (EMPHASIS ADDED)

Boldness is something you'll see. The Bible says that perfect love casts out all fear (1 John 4:18). I talk to preachers and ministers who are afraid to fly. They have a great miracle ministry, they cast out devils, but they are afraid to get on a plane and fly. I know preachers who are afraid to go to certain countries, and when they heard I was going to Egypt, they said, "Be careful! If you go to Egypt, you could die." I just said, "Wouldn't that be terrible?"

We have got to be bold to live and bold to die. I'm not afraid to die, and I'm not afraid to live. In fact, if there is something that I have been afraid of, I'm going to put myself in the place where I have to confront it, because I'm not going to live with fear.

I remember when I was a young boy, I was afraid of heights. I knew there was a fifty-story building with glass elevators, so I went there and got on the elevator and I rode that thing for four hours and stood right on the edge. I pressed the button, stood there, and watched all the way to the top to the fiftieth floor. I came down and pressed the button again, all the way to the top. Guess what? Four hours later, I had no fear of heights.

You have to confront your fears; do you realize that? There are some things that you've been afraid of and they have been holding you back. The Holy Ghost gives you the boldness to confront your fears and hit them head-on.

STAYING DRUNK ON THE NEW WINE MAKES YOU BOLD

Remember, the wicked flee when nobody is even chasing them, but the righteous are bold as a lion (Proverbs 28:1). If you are in fear and you are intimidated, that means you have "leaked out." Have a drink; get drunk! Have you seen how drunk people are kind of bold? There'll be a short guy, 4′6″, who drinks the whole night; then he walks out and challenges the whole bar to a fight!

So if you are feeling intimidated or if you are feeling fear, it is because you haven't had a drink.

The best thing I do before a big fight is I get myself drunk in the Holy Ghost. I get myself totally drunk. Holy Ghost meetings at The River are good for that! You just get in and have a drink, then have another one, and another one, until you come out so drunk, and then watch the things you agree to do when you are drunk in the Holy Ghost! Like sign a contract on Madison Square Garden for six weeks, and all kinds of crazy things!

Then when you sober up, you think, *What was I thinking of? Am I crazy?* And then the only way you can handle it is to have a few more drinks, and then it's, "Oh, yeah. We can do it. Not a problem."

If you wake up one morning, and think, *What am I doing?* then you know, it's time for the 'bottle'—and I'm talking about the new wine of the Holy Ghost! I'm not an alcoholic, but I'm a drunk in the Holy Ghost. That is the key. When you are drunk, you are bold and you scare everybody around you. Their knees have fellowship one with the other. It takes bold people to go into a city with all opposition coming against you and to break that thing open. And the only way you can do it is with the ingredients of the Spirit of God on the inside of you. Boldness will come; boldness will come!

I believe that this is the year that you're going to be bolder than ever before.

Let me tell you this about Peter: even though he denied the Lord on three occasions, he still had it in him because he was the one who said, "If that's You, let me come to You on the water" (Matthew 14:28, paraphrased). So boldness was a natural thing to him, even though he found himself sinking. But there are some people who have more boldness than other people, but that does not mean to say that you are boldly deficient, or deficient of boldness. You can ask God, and He can tank you up with the same boldness that the apostles had.

I don't care how quiet and timid you are in the natural; if you get somebody full of the Holy Ghost, like a little grey-haired old granny, you'd better watch out, she's coming after you!

The Bible says in Acts 4:14–22:

> And beholding the man which was healed standing with them, they could say nothing against it. But when they had commanded them to go aside out of the council, they conferred among themselves, saying, What shall we do to these men? for that indeed a notable miracle hath been done by them is manifest to all them that dwell in Jerusalem; and we cannot deny it. But that it spread no further among the people, let us straitly threaten them, that they speak henceforth to no man in this name. And they called them, and commanded them not to speak at all nor teach in the name of Jesus. But Peter and John answered and said unto them, Whether it be right in the sight of God to hearken unto you more than unto God, judge ye. For we cannot but speak the things which we have seen and heard. So when they had further threatened them, they let them go, finding nothing how they might punish them, because of the people: for all men glorified God for that

which was done. For the man was above forty years old, on whom this miracle of healing was shewed.

COME INTO YOUR OWN COMPANY

Now look at verse 23: "And being let go, they went to their own company." There is something about coming to The River for camp-meetings. And I encourage you, no matter where you are in the world, to just come in for a couple of days, even if you can't stay the whole week, because you will come into your own company. Watch online if you are unable to travel. You will come into a company of people who don't think you're crazy, don't think you're nuts, don't think you are a lunatic, and nobody is going to criticize you if you fall out on the floor and spend half the night under the pew.

The Bible says that they went to their own company—so find out where your company is and hang out with them.

> And being let go, they went to their own company, and reported all that the chief priests and elders had said unto them. And when they heard that, they lifted up their voice to God with one accord, and said, Lord, thou art God, which hast made heaven, and earth, and the sea, and all that in them is: who by the mouth of thy servant David hast said, Why did the heathen rage, and the people imagine vain things? The kings of the earth stood up, and the rulers were gathered together against the Lord, and against his Christ. For of a truth against thy holy child Jesus, whom thou hast anointed, both Herod, and Pontius Pilate, with the Gentiles, and the people of Israel, were gathered together, for to do whatsoever thy hand and thy counsel determined before to be done. And now, Lord, behold their threatenings: and grant unto thy servants, that with all boldness they may speak thy Word.
>
> ACTS 4:23–29

They acted boldly and yet, look what they are doing now: "And now, Lord, behold their threatenings." In other words, you can go and act boldly, and then when you go away and sober up, you think, *Oh my God!* Boldness is not something that just comes on you and then you just stay bold, live bold, wake up in the night bold, in the morning you are bold, or you walk around bold all the time.

In fact, there are many moments of fear. Because Peter and John acted boldly, yet when they were in their own company, they suddenly said, "Lord, behold their threatenings." In other words, whilst they were under that anointing they acted boldly, but as they were going away, the anointing kind of waned off. When you start sobering up, you think, *Oh my God. What did I do? What did I say? I said what? I said we were going to what? Why didn't somebody stop me? Why didn't somebody restrain me? I signed what document? I said to go ahead and hire how many buses? What was I thinking of?*

Under the anointing, the boldness is there and you speak the order, and then you sober up and you think, *Oh no! Oh my God!* And then the devil says, "That's it. You're finished now. God helped you every other time, but He's not going to help you now. You're finished; you're through. This is it. You are going to fall flat on your face. People are going to laugh at you."

So you have to do exactly what Peter and John did. They went to their own company, and then they prayed. They prayed! You will feel like you are in your own company when you are at The River. You might be from another church; you might be from another ministry; you might be from another part of the state, but you'll feel like you're in your own company. Why? Because we are a company of people who are of the Holy Ghost.

THE BOLDNESS OF A ONE-EYED SHOEMAKER

I want to share a true story with you. This story is in Marco Polo's writings, the unabridged version. Don't get the versions that have been edited, because they took this out, but in the unabridged writings of Marco Polo, you will find this story.

Marco Polo was an explorer who traveled throughout China. He lived during the twelfth-century time period, and he followed in the footsteps of his father and his uncle, who left Venice when Marco was still in his mother's womb. His mother died during childbirth, and Marco was 19 years old when his father and uncle returned.

That's how long it took to travel in those days. If you read the writings, they said, "It was about fourteen days by camel. And then we went another eighteen days." It's not like they could get on a plane and fly halfway around the world.

Marco picked up this pioneering spirit of his father and his uncle, and he also set sail. You can imagine his father and uncle getting back and telling him all the tales of the great Khan and China as it was back in those days, and it must have sparked something in him. As a young 19 year-old he must have thought, *I must also set out and travel to these distant lands and see the sights. See what is beyond the mountain there, and across this sea, and across this river.*

So he set out, and I believe his journey took him about 28 years. He traveled and came to the town that is known today as Baghdad in Iraq, and there was a certain caliph who was in charge of that whole area. The area was very strong in the Islamic faith, as it is to this day, and they called them Muhammadans.

The caliph kept the Christians under his thumb and kept them intimidated. He used fear to manipulate them and to steal their possessions and their lands. It was a great trade city with silks, carvings, and all kinds of arts and crafts that came in. The caliph had some men in his council, and they would search the Scriptures, and then they would find something and then tell the Christians, "If you can't do this, then we're going to kill you," and he would intimidate the Christians in this way.

This particular time, the caliph called the Christians and quoted to them the scripture, "If you have faith as a grain of mustard seed, you'll say this to mountain, 'Be removed and be cast into the sea' [Matthew 17:20]. He said to them, "Do you believe it?" And they said, "Yes." And he said, "Do you believe that if you command a mountain to be removed, it'll take place? Do you believe that's what the Bible said?" They said, "Yes." He said, "Okay, I'm giving you ten days, and then I want you to meet me in the plain in front of a certain mountain" (and he named the mountain). I'm going to give you an opportunity to move that mountain, and if you move it, you will live and we will serve your God. If you don't, you're going to die, and we will take everything you have."

So, the Christians came under extreme fear, and they fell on their faces and began to cry out to God that He would somehow come and deliver them. It was a group called "The Brethren of the Order of the Holy Ghost." With a name like that, they must have been some of our ancestors!

They were on their faces day and night, imploring God and speaking to God to help them. One of them, a bishop, who was a very pious and holy man, had a dream on the eighth day. In the dream, the Lord told him that they had to go to a certain village and find a shoemaker there. This shoemaker, the Lord said, was the one who could move the mountain.

The Lord told him that the shoemaker had one eye. Apparently, the shoemaker was a very devout man, and one who followed the Scripture to the letter. One day, a young lady came into his shoe store and as she presented her leg so her foot could be measured for the shoes, her skirt fell open and exposed more of the leg than should have occured. The writing says that it awaked in him a momentary concupiscence and immediately realizing that he had lusted after this woman's leg, he dismissed the woman and told her to leave the store, and he did not attend to her anymore. Then remembering the scripture that says, "If thy right eye offend thee, pluck it out" (Matthew 5:29), he reached over and grabbed one of the tools of the trade and gouged out his right eye, because he felt it would be better to enter into the Kingdom of Heaven with one eye than to end up in hell with both eyes!

As I was reading, I thought, *My God! If that was the case in modern-day America, you'd have a lot of blind preachers—a lot of blind preachers!* But that's another story.

The shoemaker was so devout, and he believed God. And obviously he was the one who could move the mountain because the Lord had spoken to the bishop in a dream. The bishop said to him, "You must come and you must move the mountain," but the shoemaker said, "I don't feel like I'm worthy to do this and to have God grant me the special grace to move this mountain"—because that's what it would take, a special grace to move that mountain.

But the bishop said, "You have to. The Lord spoke to me in a dream that you were the one to come, and you must help us. If you don't, we're going to die." So, they begged him, and he agreed to go.

On the morning of the tenth day, all the Christians gathered together and they had a special prayer meeting. They prayed with great fervency and then they set out into the plains to meet at the point that the caliph had determined, right in front of the mountain. They walked out holding a cross on a pole before them.

You can just imagine the caliph there and all his men who were about to kill the Christians, and this one-eyed shoemaker standing there. He knelt down in front of the cross, and he began to pray, "Oh, God, Creator of Heaven and Earth, grant this day the special grace to move this mountain, for several reasons: number one, to protect these Christians who have trusted in Your name, and also to show these that stand by, that there is only one true God. I ask for the special grace." And then he stood up, pointed to the mountain and said, "Oh, mountain, in the Name of the Father, and of the Son, and of the Holy Ghost, be thou removed."

The earth shook and quaked, and the mountain moved, and the caliph and all his men fell into a stupor, and they were stupefied for hours. The mountain moved and many of them converted to the Christian faith, and the caliph secretly embraced Christianity. He did not publicly come out about it, but when he died, they found a cross under his robe. So they did not bury him with his predecessors, but instead, buried him in another grave because they knew that he had secretly embraced Christianity.

This happened in the twelfth century. God has always been moving with miracles, signs, and wonders, and He always finds somebody who is bold enough, even if it is a one-eyed shoemaker. But I just feel something in my spirit about this twenty-first century, that we must be of the ones whom God has raised up in this hour, that we can't reflect back on the twelfth century on the one-eyed shoemaker with the faith to move a mountain. I believe that there are many reading this today and across the land who are bold to stand in the face of death and to do what God tells them to do, and to speak to mountains. You have the ability to move mountains out of your way. Do you know that it would take great boldness to move a mountain?

> And now, Lord, behold their threatenings: and grant unto thy servants, that with all boldness they may speak thy word, by stretching forth thine hand to heal; and that signs and wonders may be done by the name of thy holy child Jesus. And when they had prayed, the place was shaken where they were assembled together; and they were all filled with the Holy Ghost, and they spake the word of God with boldness.
>
> ACTS 4:29-31

BOLDNESS UNDER THE ANOINTING

I watch my wife under the anointing because when we first started out together forty years ago, she was timid and quiet. And she can still be a little quiet, but boy, when the anointing gets on her, she is bold!

It used to be that I would get up and preach and she would cringe on the front row and duck down, and I could see her looking at me, *Oh my God, don't say that; don't do that!* But after the fire of God got onto her, I now sit thinking, *Oh my God, don't do that; don't say that!* To be bold means to dare to do. Daniel was thrown in the lion's den. If you took some Christians today and threw them in a lion's den, they would be yelling! The lions would come over and crunch their bones. But Daniel was just as calm as anything (Daniel 6:16-22).

Shadrach, Meshach, and Abednego were thrown in the burning, fiery furnace (Daniel 3:8-30). If that happened today, some people would go kicking and screaming. Preachers would be begging for their lives. To dare to do, to dare to do.

I know that when I stand up ministering, I'm bold, but it's not always that way. I know some people find it hard to believe that there are times that I really have to pray, "God, You are going to have to help me. I can't do this."

I know there are some preachers who act like they are always like bold. Rubbish! And if you talk to their wives, you'll find out what they're really like. Outside of the anointing, without the power of God, you'll be just weak, like somebody else. But when the Holy Ghost comes on you and the power of God comes on you, then my, my, my! You'll run and you'll take the bear, and you'll rip it to shreds; you'll take the lion and you'll rip him to shreds; you'll take the giant and you'll take him out. Are you getting bold just while you're reading this? Do you feel a holy boldness coming on you?

DON'T LET THE PAST INTIMIDATE YOU

> THE MAN WHO KNEELS BEFORE GOD CAN STAND BEFORE ANY MAN.

I remember years ago, we got a Saint Bernard puppy, and you know how big a Saint Bernard gets. We brought the puppy home, and the cat swatted the puppy up the side of the head, and the puppy ran yelping! Do you know that when that same Saint Bernard was fully grown, if he saw the cat, he was petrified. He never forgot the swat that had come to the side of his head, I kept saying to him, "You can eat that cat for breakfast. That thing is just a fur ball. You can chew it and spit it out!" But every time he saw the cat, he thought of the swat.

There's a lot of "Saint Bernards" walking around, and the enemy swatted you up the side of the head years ago, and you are intimidated and you're afraid. But I tell you, he's just a fur ball. You can take him out right now. Be BOLD! Be BOLD! Be BOLD! Dare to do!

Someone says, "How do I get boldness?" Pray, pray, pray, and drink. Pray and have another drink. The man who kneels before God can stand before any man. This is why we need boldness.

> Now when they saw the boldness of Peter and John, and perceived that they were unlearned and ignorant men, they marvelled; and they took knowledge of them, that they had been with Jesus.
>
> ACTS 4:13

Boldness! You might look at men and women of God who are mightily used of God and think, *Well, they are just the strongest people I've ever met.* But they face the same fears.

DON'T LET FEAR INTIMIDATE YOU

The Bible says that Elijah was a man of like passions as we are (James 5:17). Why do you think that one moment he was taking on the prophets of Baal, and the next minute he was under the juniper tree crying out? Because as human beings, without the Holy Spirit, without the power of God, we will be weak. But sometimes, your weakest moment and your weakest hour will be the time that the greatest strength is manifested and displayed. I can tell you that there have been many times when I felt like I was finished. I didn't know how I was going to do it. And I had to pray and ask God to strengthen me and give me boldness—more times than you'd ever even believe.

The only time I could really step out and act was once I had the assurance from Heaven. In fact, when I started preaching at eighteen years of age, I could not speak publicly because I'd been used to singing with my guitar. As long as I had my guitar, I was fine. But when I put my guitar down and I tried to address somebody, my mouth would go dry and my voice would go squeaky!

I was so nervous! I thought, *Great! This is just great! God's called me to preach and I squeak. I'm not a preacher. I'm a squeaker. I'm going to get out there and mumble and trip over my words.* The problem was I couldn't even say I was drunk on the new wine, or that "I feel the anointing so strong here tonight," because it was just that I was so nervous.

The Lord really had to speak to me about this. He said, "You can't do this in your own strength. You can't do this in your ability. It's not about your ability. It's not about being some great communicator, or being concerned about one syllable pronounced the wrong way." It's happened to the best of them. So if you are worried about how you sound, you have got to forget about it. First of all, you have to forget about how you look, and then you have got to forget about how you sound. If I heard myself on a recording, I used to say, "Ugh! My God! Shut that thing up. Listen to that goofy voice." So, forget about how you look and forget about how you sound. You have to rely on Him.

You can't minister worrying about what people are going to think. Ministers know it's you and Jesus. Remember, He is the one who's going to rise up in you. He's the one who's going to speak out of you. You have to rely on Him. He will put the words in your mouth.

BOLDNESS TO SAY WHAT HE TELLS YOU TO SAY

Evangelist Debbie Rich was telling me about the time when she was being interrogated in Vietnam as she was trying to leave the country. She said she was sitting there and she didn't know what to say, and then suddenly, the boldness, the power of God, hit her, and out of her mouth she began to challenge them. All those armed guards had been interrogating her for three hours, trying to intimidate her because she was a woman. They were trying to frighten her, but she just boldly spoke out. She said, "I didn't know what I was going to do or what I was going to say." But it just came right out of her. You never know what's in you until it has to come out of you—until you are in that place where you have to step up to the plate.

Evangelist Debbie Rich spoke in a service in 2005 and she said:

> When they brought me in the room, there were several soldiers and a big bust of Ho Chi Minh and all the Communist symbols, the hammer, and the sickle above my head. They stared at me and looked at my passport and started running off papers, and they were all speaking Vietnamese. And then they began to say, "Do you wonder why you've been brought in here?" and I said, "Yes, I'm very curious."

They said, "Don't you want to know what laws of ours you broke?" And I said, "I'm sure I have not broken any," and they said, "Well, you have! You need to think back to the day of the thirteenth and the fourteenth and confess before our nation that you broke all of our laws. What did you do on those days? Were you just a tourist?"

And I began to tell them, "No, on those days I went to pray with some of your people," because according to their own laws, you can go in a house and pray; you just can't hold the meeting. I went on to say, "I love your people, and I just wanted to pray for your people."

They said, "You didn't pray; you held a meeting. Tell us what lesson you taught." I said, "I didn't teach a lesson. I grabbed your people and said, 'Let me tell you about what my Jesus has done for me,' and that's not a lesson!" And I began to tell them about the abuse that I lived through, and they were writing all of this down. I said, "But my Jesus intervened and gave me joy unspeakable and full of glory, and you yourself have bragged in your own newspaper that you have religious freedom. I just saw it in the newspaper yesterday, grabbing the hands of a United States congressman, saying, 'We have total religious freedom.'"

Then I looked them square in the eye and said, "This is not religious freedom, and if you come to my nation, you will not have to go through this just to go to a prayer meeting."

And even as I heard it come out of my mouth, my heart was still pounding on the inside, but I felt this anointing just like when you preach and you just step into it.

And after three hours they looked at me and said, "Thank you for your cooperation." And one of the men looked at me and said, "If I give you a postcard, can you mail it to a relative in Texas?" And he actually formed tears in his eyes when I was telling him about some of the things I'd lived through, and how nobody but my Jesus can help me, and I looked at him and said, "He'll help you too!" Right in the middle of a communist headquarters!

> I walked out and almost wanted to faint. I thought, *I can't believe that I just made it through that.* But as I was sitting there, the Holy Ghost just flooded me with the peace of God and with the boldness of a lion, a lion of the tribe of Judah. I felt so honored to even be in a little test like this, where many have given their lives. And if it comes to that, I pray that I'm ready. But thank God for the anointing of the Holy Ghost.

Somebody says, "I'm not sure if I have what it takes." But I believe that every single person, full of the Holy Ghost, has what it takes to step up to the plate and be bold. You were born for this day; you were born for this hour; God raised you up for this moment.

You're not of them who draw back; you are not of the timid ones; you're not the ones who want to hide back in the hideout. You're the ones who shout, "Charge!" And you run with bombs falling all around you, and mortars going all around you. Glory to God!

Let's pray right now. Just lift your hands to Heaven:

> Father, I pray now for holy boldness for every single person, every man, woman, boy, and girl, in the Name of Jesus. I pray that this will be the boldest year of their lives. No more holding back, no more drawing back. To dare to do what Heaven tells them to do, to dare to say what Heaven tells them to say, to dare to go where Heaven tells them to go, to dare to be what Heaven tells them to be. I thank You for it. I thank You that they are sealed with this boldness. Amen.

To all those reading this, I tell you, "Be bold and be strong, for the Lord thy God is with you (Joshua 1:9). He's on your side, and if God be for you, who can be against you (Romans 8:31)" No one! If God is for you, then why should you be afraid of man? I shall not fear man, for God is on my side (Psalm 118:6). The Lord is my strength. He is my help. He is my deliverer with a strong and mighty hand (Psalm 136:12). He will deliver me. So, lift your hands now, you bold bunch, and rejoice. Hallelujah!

11

CONDITIONS FOR REVIVAL

Looking at the "Weather System" for the Storm of God

In the Bible, when you look at places that God dealt with for example, Sodom and Gomorrah, you see that they were totally destroyed, really, without a remedy. But then you see a place like Nineveh, which I'm familiar with, and the whole city was turned around. When I first studied about Jonah and Nineveh, I thought, *That's what I want. I want a whole city to turn like that, but I really don't want to go through the belly of the fish to get that result!*

But I believe that we are living in the days where we are going to see the "Ninevehs" come in. Nineveh was a very large city. Apparently, according to studies of the times, it was sixty miles across—a mass population of the day! Nineveh was huge. It was obviously a very wicked city and God was going to destroy it. And you know that when God wants to destroy something, He can, and He can totally remove it from off the face of the earth just like Sodom and Gomorrah

IT JUST TAKES ONE PERSON

> THAT'S ALL GOD'S LOOKING FOR, ONE PERSON WHO HE CAN USE, ONE PERSON TO BE HIS HANDS, ONE PERSON TO BE HIS MOUTHPIECE, ONE PERSON TO BE HIS FEET. YOU JUST HAVE TO MAKE A DECISION THAT YOU ARE GOING TO BE THAT PERSON.

To turn Nineveh around, God used just *one* person—so all it takes is one person! *One* person can change a city. *One* person can change a nation. That's all God's looking for, *one* person who He can use, *one* person to be His Hands, *one* person to be His Mouthpiece, *one* person to be His Feet. You just have to make a decision that *you* are going to be that person.

As the prophet said, "Here am I; send me" (Isaiah 6:8). You have to sign up for the duty, and I just happened to sign up for the duty and got myself into more trouble than you can ever imagine! But when God is on your side, He's going to back you up and He's going to come through for you every single time.

THE LIGHTNINGS OF GOD

> YOUR JOB IS TO PROCLAIM THE WORD AND THEN TO EXPECT GOD TO MOVE AND TO BACK IT UP WITH SIGNS AND WONDERS FOLLOWING.

> O Lord, I have heard thy speech, and was afraid: O Lord, revive thy work in the midst of the years, in the midst of the years make known; in wrath remember mercy. God came from Teman, and the Holy One from mount Paran. Selah. His glory covered the heavens, and the earth was full of his praise. And his brightness was as the light; he had horns coming out of his hand: and there was the hiding of his power.
>
> HABAKKUK 3:2

As I mentioned before, horns were really bright beams, like lightnings coming out of His Hands. And that's the thing that's going to cause revival. That's the thing that's going to cause the move of God—the bright beams, the lightnings of God. You can't have revival without the lightnings of God. Revival is like a storm in the natural.

If you look on the Doppler weather radar system, you can see the storms coming in. The storm chasers follow the tornados and storms coming in, and I have thought, *Man I'd love to do something like that and try to get as close to a tornado as possible,* but people tell me, "You don't want to!" Nonetheless, you can actually map the storm out and you can see where it's going.

I believe that in the spirit realm, the enemy can see that there's a spiritual storm coming on an area, a region, or a city, and he has no control of that storm. He can try to do everything he can to barricade and block up, but the storm of God will come and the lightnings of God will come. The tornadoes of God will come, the rains of God will come, and the thunders of God will come and bring about a transformation and a change.

I've been in many meetings over the past forty years, and I remember one particular incident. My wife and I were traveling in the north Eastern Cape, southern Africa, in 1983, and we arrived in this little town of about 910 people. It was one of those one-horse towns, and the one horse had died a long time ago! It was the kind of town that if you blinked your eyes, you went right through it. We were in a farmhouse out in the boonies, having a meeting. I had given them about three-months notification that we were coming, so when I showed up, I really expected that there would be a good group of people.

But when I got there, there were eleven people in the farmhouse. I thought, *Well, this is just great! Three months of advertising and all they could do is get eleven people! Boy, we are really going to have a move of God here!*

I was a little tired because I had done twenty-one meetings in nineteen days. I was out there doing what I always do—having a meeting.

And in those days, I did everything—I did the worship, I did the offering (and kept the offering right where I could keep my eye on it so nobody could walk home with it,) then I preached, I prayed, and I would even catch people myself because nobody was there to catch them. I would pray for someone and then run around the back of them and catch them! And I split many a pair of pants doing that! Later on, I realized that it's better to get somebody to help you!

So, I wasn't really excited about the evening to say the least, but I spoke that night on the integrity of the Word of God—how God does what He promises He will do, He always backs up His Word, and He watches over His Word to perform it (Jeremiah 1:12). I thought, *Well, these people all look like they're saved, but I'm going to give an altar call.* But I didn't give a major pull; it was more like a little suggestion, "If you don't know Jesus, just give your life to Him right now." Two people raised their hands, and I found out later that they were brother and sister. I said, "Well, come up here." I had my guitar on, and I took it off and moved it over to the side then walked over to where they were. I raised my hand and as I did, it was as if a lightning bolt came from over my head and smacked both of them and they went flying through the air.

Here I was in a farmhouse with eleven people, and it had looked like they were just dead people sitting there and watching, and I was thinking, *Oh God, what did I get myself in for?* But then I gave this altar call, raised my hand, and my God—it looked like they got slam-dunked! The whole room gasped. The next night, thirty people packed the farmhouse. The next night, sixty people jammed in this farmhouse, and all Heaven broke loose and we had revival.

Now if it hadn't been for the lightnings of God, we would have just stayed for five days with eleven people and maybe gone down to six people and said, "Praise God, we are believing God for a great revival." Without the lightnings of God, all you are going to do is have another little Bible study and a meeting.

The lightnings of God. We even had the Dutch Reformed minister show up. Word went through the town. When you go into a farming community of 910 people and sixty people are smacked in a house, it spreads throughout all the region. And then at that time, they had party-line phones that everybody could listen in to. You would have to pick up the phone, crank it, and then you could hear other people, click-click, all listening on the phone! So, word spread about the revival, like wildfire.

The lightnings of God are very important. If you're going to have revival and carry revival to the nations of the world, you have to expect that God is going to show up with His lightnings and His move. It's not so much what you have to do; it's not something that you are going to do. You don't have to think, *My God, the pressure is on me; I have got to do something. I have got to pull a rabbit out of a hat.* Your job is not to pull rabbits out of a hat. Your job is to proclaim the Word, and then to expect God to move and to back it up with signs and wonders following.

A sign and a wonder are very important because a sign is something that makes you wonder (see Mark 16:17). A sign makes you think, *I wonder what that is? I have never seen that before.* In over forty years now of signs and wonders, walking in the ministry and obeying God, there has never been a day that I have walked out and said, "Oh no. Not that again. I've seen that already!" But the children of Israel were like that when they said, "Oh no! Not another day of manna!" Do you know how supernatural that manna was? But they said, "Water from the rock again? We've already seen that!" or "Quail? Really? Some more quail?" They had a bad attitude.

DO NOT TAKE THE THINGS OF GOD LIGHTLY

It's your attitude toward the supernatural that will cause it to cease. You cannot take the things of God lightly. That's why anybody who knows me or hangs around this ministry any length of time will know that I am very, very serious about the joy. Not only am I serious about the joy; I'm serious about the altar calls, and I'm serious about the laying on of hands.

I'm very intense about what I'm saying because I feel that some have lost the move of God because they've treated it lightly. They think that they know everything about it and what it entails, but really, they don't, because we know in part, we prophesy in part (1 Corinthians 13:9), and we only have a portion of everything we do in the Spirit.

There are so many things to the dimensions of God that the creatures before the throne of God cry, "Holy, holy, holy." They've been doing it for eternity past. Do you know that they are not crying, "Holy, holy, holy" because they are forced to? They cry, "Holy, holy, holy," because that's all they say. We always go to find new praise and worship songs, but the creatures before the throne don't, they have the same song they've been singing for eternity. And it's because God reveals Himself and shows another part of Himself that they have never seen before. So, they don't even have to change the song. They just go, "Holy, holy, holy," because He's so awesome.

The creatures before the Throne of God are not bored. There is not one creature before the Throne of God standing yawning, saying, "Come on. I've been doing this for so long. This is so 'last eternity.'" No! Because God is so awesome, He hasn't revealed everything of Himself to you. And even if you lived a hundred years, and you were in the ministry seventy years, and you preached every day of your life, you wouldn't know anything but the basics. Even if you studied the Bible fifteen hours a day, or if you personally translated the Bible out of the Hebrew and the Greek, you still wouldn't know hardly anything, because He is God.

Because of that, we come around Him with humility; we come around Him with a hunger; we come around Him with a thirst and we come around Him with a total dependency upon Him. But when you go out, He said, "You go in My Name. In My Name you cast out devils, and these signs shall follow them that believe in My Name" (Mark 16:17). So if you believe in His Name, then signs are to follow you. You are to *expect* signs to follow you. It's not you following signs, but you expect signs to follow you, and you never know what God's going to do.

> IT'S YOUR ATTITUDE TOWARD THE SUPERNATURAL THAT WILL CAUSE IT TO CEASE.

THE SUDDENLIES OF GOD CHANGE THE ATMOSPHERE

Then I think of another meeting. I was teaching a third-year class in a Bible school in southern Africa. Sometimes, third-year students are a little harder to deal with because they've been sitting there for three years and some of them have started to fossilize and become petrified! They think they know more than the second-years and they know more than the first-years, so they think they are more "spiritual."

We probably crammed in about a hundred students into the third-year class, and I can tell you that it's those suddenlies and the lightnings of God that will just change the very atmosphere of a room. I looked over and I felt led and prompted by the Spirit of God to call a certain person out, and they came and stood in front of me. What happened next—and God is my witness—did not come from me; it came from Heaven. It was like a lightning bolt, but it was a combination of a lightning bolt and a tornado. I felt it over my shoulder and it picked this person up in the air and their feet came level with my stomach, and then it just threw them on the ground, and several rows of people went out under the power of God. I had to grab hold of the podium to stand up, and I started weeping, because when it hits with that intensity, it is almost like a high-voltage bolt. It totally revolutionizes everything, and the whole room was electrified.

Do you realize that that wasn't just a normal 45 minute class after that? It wasn't, "Ring the bell at 40 minutes and double bell at 45 minutes and we go out of here." People were on their faces before God, and God used that service to touch people and call them into the ministry.

Then I think back to the meetings over the last 40 years of just ordinary individuals sitting in meetings, and suddenly, the power of God hit them and God revolutionized their life. Young kids hit by the power of God, on their faces, and then God called them into the ministry, "You're going to pastor. You're going to be an evangelist"—all those things cannot happen without the lightnings of God.

How can we, the Church of the Lord Jesus Christ, expect to walk in everything that Heaven has promised without the supernatural power of God? And one of the things that you're going to have to realize, is that you're going to have to forget about trying to explain it away or trying to make it acceptable to people. They're not going to accept it if they don't know Jesus and don't have a personal relationship with the Holy Spirit. They're going to look at you like you're crazy. Your job is not to make yourself acceptable to them. Your job is not even to take the move of God and make it acceptable to them. *They* must become acceptable to the move of God.

GOD ALWAYS RAISES UP PEOPLE WITH SIGNS AND WONDERS.

YOU CAN'T HAVE REVIVAL WITHOUT A DISPLAY OF THE POWER OF GOD, AND SOMEBODY HAS TO DISPLAY IT.

Some of the people that the Lord has used in the earth are strange and they have unique methods, but God is in them. Just like when Jesus spat in the ground and made clay and put it on a man's eyes and said, "Go wash." That was God—one hundred percent God!

But that method would not be accepted today. Imagine the headline, "Preacher Spits in Man's Eyes!"

I know people in the religious world got mad because certain preachers were blowing on people, but the Bible says that Jesus "breathed on them" (John 20:22). Well, how can you breathe on somebody without blowing on them? Someone says, "I don't like this blowing on people." It's the winds of God. How are you going to have a wind without breath? Jesus breathed on them. Jesus spat on them and that's a method I have never used intentionally—however, accidentally, a little globule of spit has come out and hit someone on the front row as

I have been speaking, and I've watched it land on them!

You can't have revival without a display of the power of God, and somebody has to display it. Somebody has to be the instrument. Jesus shows up and there are lightnings coming out of His hands, and *you're* going to be His hands, so lightnings are going to have to come out of *your* hands. Someone's going to have to do it.

Someone is going to have to be the point of contact. Someone is going to have to take the brunt of all the accusations and the criticism in order to let the power of God be displayed, because you are called to display the glory of God and show forth the glory of God to a lost and dying world.

DEMONSTRATE, NOT PROTEST, THE POWER OF GOD

You are called to demonstrate, and you are called to be demonstrators of the power of God—demonstrators and not protesters. There are two types of people: demonstrators and protesters. Some people are protesters of the power of God, and they stand up with banners and signs—"Stop! This is of the devil," and that kind of thing. But you are not called to protest the power of God! You are called to demonstrate the power of God.

You never really know what a person, who is full of the power of God, is going to do. They are totally unpredictable. You can try to fathom it all out and you can think that you know exactly what they are going to do, but then they will do something totally different. The only way you're going to find what they're going to do is to get hooked up with the Holy Ghost, and you'll be right there with them every step of the way because that's how the Spirit of God operates.

YOU ARE CALLED TO BE GOD'S STORM SYSTEM

So let me put it this way: you are God's "storm system." If they said, "A storm system is moving in from the West," could you be God's storm system? How strong is your storm? Or are you a tropical depression? There are too many ministers of the Gospel trying to have revival but they are just a tropical depression!

God doesn't want you to be a gentle breeze. The Bible says that the Holy Ghost came as "a rushing mighty wind" (Acts 2:2), and that wind has to be you! Are you a tropical storm? What kind of hurricane are you? That's why the devil wants to slow you down, because he doesn't want you to blow into town.

Psalm 85:6: "Wilt thou not revive us again: that thy people may rejoice in thee?" The revival is to bring people back to a place of rejoicing. There are too many sad and depressed people in the Body of Christ.

You cannot tell me that you are in revival if you are walking around sad and depressed. Now, I'm not saying you can't have a medical condition or be sick, but I'm talking about a normal, healthy individual, walking around sad and depressed. They are a child of God, carrying a Bible big enough to choke a moose, coming to church, saying, "Amen. Hallelujah! Glory to God," but they look like death warmed over.

Something is wrong somewhere! Because when revival comes and the presence of God comes, the Bible says, "in His presence is fullness of joy; at His right hand there are pleasures forevermore" (Psalm 16:11, paraphrased).

KNOWING WHEN THE CONDITIONS ARE RIGHT FOR REVIVAL

WHEN THE WICKED TRIUMPH OVER THE CHURCH AND REVILE IT, WHEN THE WICKED MOCK THE CHURCH, IT'S TIME FOR GREAT REVIVAL.

How do you know when the conditions are right for revival? Well, there are a few things to look out for. You don't want to go to have a revival somewhere when there is already revival—that's like taking ice to the Inuit or bringing sunshine to Florida! You want to go to somewhere that's not in revival.

First, you know that a place is ready for revival when there's a lack of brotherly love and people are fighting one another. That's the time that you rub your hands with glee and say, "I think I just found a place to have a move of God!" You know that a place is ripe for revival when there are dissensions, jealousies, backbiting, and people are slandering each other.

Second, you know that a place is ready for revival when there is a spirit of worldliness in the church. You know that they are ready for revival when they love the things of the world more than the things of God. And when they come to church Sunday, after an hour, they are looking at their watches! They will go and sit and watch a three-hour movie and not budge. But when they come to church, they say, "My God, he's going on past an hour!" Churches can call it an "Hour of Power," but it's not. It might be an hour of being the longest hour you ever sat through, but an "Hour of Power?" I think not!

Third, a church is ripe for revival when it falls into gross sin and people are doing all kinds of crazy stuff, but nobody does anything about it. A lot of times, it starts at the head. Because whatever the head does in moderation, the people will do in excess! People will do what they are around.

Fourth, whenever there's a spirit of controversy in the church or in the land, whenever there's a conflict or turmoil, it's ripe for revival. When it's the hottest, then it's the place for the greatest move of God. When the persecution is the greatest, when the attack is the greatest, when there are death threats against you, that's not the time to run and get on a plane and come back another day, that's the time to get in the middle of the fight. You're going to have a revival! When the wicked triumph over the Church and revile it, when the wicked mock the Church, it's time for great revival.

Fifth, there is a sign of being ready for revival that some people wouldn't even notice, and that's when sinners and careless and stupid people sink into hell unconcerned—people dying and going to hell for no reason. Like the lady who fought for the "no helmet law" for motorcycles in the state of Florida, and the day the law was passed, she got on her bike and rode into a pole and killed herself. How terrible that happened! All she had to do was wear a helmet and she would have been fine. She fought for the "no helmet law" and took off on her bike and plowed into a pole.

That's carelessness. Sinners are carelessly plunging into a lost eternity. That tells me that we have got to have a move of God.

We have got to have a revival. We have got to have an awakening in America. Some people say, "Well, let's just pray, Brother Rodney, let's just pray." You can pray, but *somebody* is going to have to be an igniter.

GOD WANTS TO DISPLAY HIS GLORY THROUGH YOU

Somebody is going to have display the things of God. Think about a graphic on a computer screen used by a sales person to get their point across. People can sit and criticize the computer, criticize the screen, criticize the colors shown, criticize the way it fades in or fades out; it doesn't matter. It's still the display of what you're trying to get across, and likewise, God's going to display His glory through you, and it is going to come forth through you in a very unique way.

We're not all the same. We never will be the same, and we're not supposed to be the same. God wants originals. As I said earlier, God wants His people to be a voice and not an echo. There are too many echoes in the church running around preaching each other's messages and prophesying each other's prophesies.

THE RESULTS OF REVIVAL: REPROACH IS REMOVED

> THE HOLY SPIRIT IS THE RESTRAINING FORCE THAT IS NEEDED, NOT ONLY IN THE CHURCH, BUT ALSO IN THE WORLD.

Now, let's look at what happens when revival comes. It is going to do certain things, and the first thing it will do is remove reproach from the Church.

We went to one church in a certain part of the US and spent six weeks there. We held two meetings a day, and we had a great revival and move of God. Multitudes of people and many ministers were touched. Probably two months later, the pastor called me up and said, "Brother

Rodney, you won't believe what happened. We are one of the largest and leading Pentecostal/Charismatic churches in America, and we have a large home group cell ministry. After your meetings, one by one, I had close to a dozen of the leaders come to me independently of each other, without even talking to each other, and say, 'Please, would you marry us?' I said to them, 'What do you mean, marry you? You've been my leaders here for four or five years.' And they said, 'We have never been married. We have just been living together!'"

When revival is not there, people don't know—they just do what they want. The pastor asked them, "Why now? Why are you doing this now?" They said, "Before the revival, there was nothing telling us what we were doing was wrong, but after the revival, we would get into bed and look at each other think, *Something's wrong.*" Before a revival, anything goes. After revival, there is a fine line and you know the moment you cross that line, because the Spirit of God is there to pull you right back. The Holy Spirit is the restraining force that is needed, not only in the Church, but also in the world.

I know that's a shocking story, and some will say, "How could these things be?" but that's religion. Religion will make you go to church on Sunday, do all the right things, and even get involved in leadership, but behind the scenes, it's so far away from the Word of God and the things of God. And God can't bless that.

THE RESULTS OF REVIVAL: THE LOVE OF GOD

When revival comes, people start falling in love with each other. I love this because I've seen it over the years, but especially since 1989, when the revival broke out. You can have a line of people who don't even like each other, they fall down under the power of God, lie on the ground for an hour-and-a-half, and when they get up, they just love one another. You ask yourself how it could be possible for that to happen when they couldn't stand each other before.

We have seen Methodists, Baptists, Presbyterians, and all these other denominations lying on the ground in one line under the power.

Under the power, all your doctrine is leveled. Under the power of God, all your theories on the end-times, who the Antichrist is, the mark of the beast, pre-trib, mid-trib, or post-trib, are all immaterial. All the differences go. There's nothing like the anointing of the Spirit of God to bring about a leveling.

People tell us this everyplace we go. They say, "When you came to town, there came a unity between pastors and leaders that previously would have never talked to each other." They had never even worked together, yet they were all on the platform together, and people looked and said, "I can't believe he's here. I can't believe he's here. I don't know how this one came." The Holy Spirit has that way of just pulling people together, and then the barriers fall down. The obstacles are moved out of the way, and the love of God takes number one place.

THE RESULTS OF REVIVAL: JUDGMENT IS MANIFESTED

When revival comes, there also comes a separation, and judgment is made manifest. Because if a person continues in the way of sin after there has been a display of the power of God and the knowledge of truth, they are now sinning willfully. So in some cases, revival can be very detrimental to a congregation. If the leadership won't change, if people in the church won't change, then when the fire of God falls, it'll shut that thing down.

Revival is not just about growing the church. "Oh, they came in. They had a meeting. The church grew." Instead, as I mentioned earlier, sometimes it is, "Oh, they came in. They had a meeting. The church shut down. The pastor went out of the ministry!" I know these are the things people don't want to hear. "Well, Brother, Rodney, how can a church shutting down be the plan of God?" Did you ever go there? Did you ever have to put yourself through the misery of sitting in one of those services?

I could think of many places that need to be closed down. I've seen mortuaries with more life! I've been driving down the road and found dead animals lying in the road, run over by a car, with more life than some churches. The only living thing is the ivy growing up the wall on the outside of the building, or the woodworm eating away at the pew!

The only sign and wonder and miracle they have are the stop sign outside of the church, the wonder that people even showed up, and the miracle that they came back the next Sunday!

THE RESULTS OF REVIVAL: HOPE RESTORED

When revival comes, there's a hope to the world that there's an answer, there is a solution, and His name is Jesus! People come out of desperation with no hope, but we have *the* hope. We have *the* solution, and it's not just in a message or a theory, but in the display of the power of God Almighty—you'll see people grow, and you will see people grow in grace.

THE RESULTS OF REVIVAL: CONFESSION OF SIN

You know that you're going to have revival when Christians start confessing their sins one to another. That cannot happen outside of revival because if you started confessing your sin to somebody, they would go and tell everybody else!

Outside of revival, you couldn't really confess your sins to somebody else. Like the story of three great preachers who were out fishing for Canadian pike, sitting on the boat in the middle of some remote lake up in Canada. One of the men said, "Man, I just feel like I need to really confess that I have a real problem with drinking. I have a big church of five thousand members, but I can't stop drinking. I thought I had it beat, but I can't stop. I have got to have a drink. And the problem is that I've gone on to the hard stuff now. But I really just wanted to tell you guys, my friends, as we are here fishing, and I know I can share this with you, and the Bible says to confess your faults one to another. So, I want y'all to pray with me on this fishing trip that God will help me get the victory."

The second man of God said, "Man, you know I've been battling with a problem too. I'm married, I love my wife, but I have real problem with women. I haven't done anything, but I can't keep my eyes off of them. I keep looking at other women, and it's bugging me. I have this great ministry, everybody loves me and respects me, but every time I see a beautiful woman, I can't help looking. I just need you guys to pray with me."

So, the two preachers turned to look at the third guy and said, "Do you have anything to say?" The third man says, "Yes, I do. The problem is that I can never keep my mouth shut. I talk about people all the time. I've tried to get the victory over it, but I just can't. And right now, I can't wait to get back from this fishing trip so I can tell everybody about the two of you!"

Then, I heard the story of a young preacher and an older preacher. The young guy was eighteen years old, starting out in the ministry, and the older preacher was eighty years of age and had pioneered churches. The young guy asked, "Do you have a word of advice for a young man starting out in the ministry?" The older man said, "Yes. Go fly yourself out to the desert; go to Arizona or New Mexico; get out as far as you can and find yourself a jackrabbit. Grab the jackrabbit by the scruff of the neck and confess your sin to the jackrabbit. Then, when you've finished, kill the jackrabbit!" He said, "If you have any hidden sin in your life, that's my advice to you." That's what the old man told the young man to do, and unfortunately, what he said was probably correct.

You can't really trust anybody and go and share something with them, because they'll share it with somebody else "in confidence," who will share with somebody else "in confidence." And then next week, you'll read it in *Charisma* magazine!

However, the Bible does say, "Confess your sin one to another" (James 5:16 NASB), and when people realize the strength of that and they begin to confess their sin, and you have a move of God.

IS REVIVAL SOVEREIGN?

Now, I've had people say to me, "Brother Rodney, revival is sovereign." And then I asked them, "What do you mean that it is sovereign?"

"Well, that's where you would be going along, and then suddenly, God just starts moving."

But I do not agree with that. I don't agree that revival is sovereign in that sense. Revival is sovereign from the standpoint that God moved two thousand years ago. He sovereignly moved two thousand years ago, and He sovereignly moved at Pentecost. So let me say it this way: the sovereign move of God is in the earth today, but you and I by our hunger, thirst, and desire, tap into the sovereign move of God.

Because if we say God sovereignly moves, then people come along and say that God supernaturally picked a city, and because He moved there, there was some sort of window that opened, like a portal in that city. But if so, what about us in other places? Are we chopped liver? Are you saying that God so liked a certain city—maybe He liked a coastal town because of its real estate—that He decided that He was going to open a window over that city and then rain down Heaven's glory? And then everybody must fly in there to get in that atmosphere because there is an open Heaven? What utter rubbish!

Because that means that you couldn't have a move of God anywhere. It would be, "Well, Lord, Thou knowest, yea verily, that it be sovereign. Far be it from us to choose, oh God. We'll just carry on grinding at the wheel here. And if You see fit in some way, some shape or fashion, just come, please. Move, oh God, someway, somehow. Oh, Lord, send revival, but oh, God, we know that is sovereign, Lord. We pray, God in my lifetime. Let me just see it, oh God."

Somebody says, "What are you doing?"

"I'm praying for revival."

You are not praying for revival; you are praying some religious mess!

If it was just a sovereign move of God, then we could take our hands off and say, "Well, we'll just keep going along, and one day, God will come with a sovereign move. We pray He does it in our lifetime, and until then, we'll just carry on." No! No! No! He has already sovereignly moved; you have to plug in and make a decision to plug in to the move of God!

GOD USES AN INSTIGATOR

> IT'S THOSE PEOPLE WITH THAT HUNGER AND THAT INTENSITY AND THAT FERVENCY BEFORE GOD WHO ARE GOING TO BECOME THE ONES WHO ARE THE IGNITERS WHO WILL LIGHT THE FIRE.

Any place that God has moved had nothing to do with the group of people gathering there and some window opening and then it falling. There was somebody who God used as an instigator. God didn't lead the children of Israel out without using someone—He used Moses to get them out.

God didn't turn Nineveh around without Jonah. There is always somebody who has got to be involved in it, and that somebody might as well be you! So, this concept about the sovereign move of God, settle it once and for all that God has sovereignly moved, and then by your hunger, thirst, and desire for the things of God, you press in and you grab ahold of it.

Just like the woman with the issue of blood, when you get so hungry and you say, "If I'm the only one on the face of the earth whose going to grab ahold of this, I'm going to grab ahold of it. I don't care what it takes. I don't care if I have to fast for forty days. I don't care what I have to do, but I'm going to press in. I'm going to grab ahold of the hem of the garment of Jesus" (Luke 8:43-48). It's those people with that hunger and that intensity and that fervency before God who are going to become the ones who are the igniters and who will light the fire.

THE RIVER FLOWS FROM YOUR BELLY AND NOT YOUR HEAD

You must press in. You must hunger and thirst and grab ahold of the things of God. We can say that we are waiting on God, but God is waiting on us. We are not waiting on Him; He's waiting on us. God will move when you move. Some say, "Oh, Lord, move," but He says, "Son, move!" Because He said, "Out of your belly will flow rivers" (John

7:38, paraphrased), but many will try to get a river to flow out of their heads! A river cannot come out of your head; it comes out of your belly.

God does order events. He stacks them up. He moves things in a certain way. You cry for revival and you pray for revival, and God will order all the events and bring things into manifestation.

Revival can come when the sin of the world so grieves and vexes the Church that people rise up and just press in and say, "This is coming to an end! We are going to grab this thing and we are going to shake it and we're not going to let the devil overrun our city. We are not going to allow the devil to overrun our nation." When people grab ahold of that, revival comes. That's why, it's going to take people of faith, people full of boldness.

THE SPIRIT OF PRAYER IGNITES REVIVAL

Revival can also be ignited because the Spirit of prayer fell on people and they just started praying. If you study the revivals of old, you see that people started gathering at lunchtime prayer meetings. I'm not talking about an organized event, where people say, "We're going to pray," and then they get around and they might as well be praying, "Twinkle, twinkle, little star. How I wonder what you are. Up above the world so high, like a diamond in the sky" (Jane Taylor). I'm talking about when people are moved on by God and press in, in prayer.

I'm talking about you start a lunchtime prayer meeting and suddenly, hundreds and then thousands start showing up; then you would know! And that's what happened in New York at the time of the awakenings. People just announced they would have prayer and the churches were more filled during the time of prayer than they were on Sunday. So what does that tell you? A Spirit of prayer started falling on people, and they started pressing into the things of God.

REVIVAL MUST BE YOUR NUMBER ONE GOAL

ALL IT TAKES IS JUST A FEW DETERMINED PEOPLE.

Revival can come when preachers make revival their number one goal. You can have a revival anywhere, anyplace, anytime, if you make it your number one goal. "We're going to have a revival or a riot! We are going to have a move of God! We're going to have a move of God, and I don't care where else God is moving on the earth. We're going to have a move of God, and that's it. And there's nothing that the devil can do about it. We'll swing the bat every which way but loose."

All it takes is just a few determined people. When Christians are willing to sacrifice time, money, effort, and energy, you're going to have revival.

CONDITIONS FOR REVIVAL ARE RIPE TODAY

Personally, I think things are ripe for revival right now! Just looking at the world in general, I think things are ripe today. Thank God for what He did in the 1990s, but I believe things have come full circle.

If I look at the "weather system," and the patterns and the high pressure and the low pressure, we are ripe for another great move of God to shake America.

If you hunger and thirst after righteousness, you will be filled (Matthew 5:6). "Draw nigh to God, and he will draw nigh to you," (James 4:8). This is something done from the heart of man, not something just agreed upon with your natural mind saying, "I'd like that." This is something that you cry out for from your innermost being. It's that deep calling unto deep that I have referred to earlier (Psalm 42:7).

I am not talking about a touch. Many have been touched. I'm talking about a transformation and a change. I'm talking about from the inside out, when people look at you and say, "There's something different about you." They can see it in your eyes. They can hear it in your voice.

God will not force Himself on anybody. He only comes when He's wanted. You can feel the tangible power of God. It is as tangible as when you put your finger in a light socket.

"Lord, let the fire of the Holy Ghost come, let the lightnings of God come, let the storms of God come even now, and let the fire fall on all those reading this. In Jesus' Name, I loose the anointing right now!"

KEEP THE FIRE BURNING

It is up to you to not only make sure the fire is burning, but to keep it burning. You're the guardian of your heart. You have to stoke that fire every day. Make sure there is fresh wood on the fire. Make sure that nothing comes to put the fire out. Make sure that your heart is always burning with a passion for the things of God.

You must press in to be God's storm system—to be His hands, His mouthpiece, His feet, and to carry the lightnings of revival.

12

REVIVAL BEGINS WITHIN

It's All About the Heart

We are to be continually being changed. Second Corinthians 3:17–18 says, "Now the Lord is that Spirit: and where the Spirit of the Lord is, there is liberty. But we all, with open face beholding as in a glass the glory of the Lord, are changed into the same image from glory to glory, even as by the Spirit of the Lord."

If that verse said, "We are changed into glory," you could look at it and say, "Well, it's just a onetime thing. I got saved and baptized and filled with the Holy Ghost, and the glory of God came on me, and it was all just wonderful and great. I've now been saved for forty years, I've been in the way for forty years," and you could talk about what happened years ago. But this is not just something that happens and takes place once in your life; it's a *continual* process of being changed.

I know that some people would say, "But why can't God just do it all? Why does it have to be a 'from glory to glory' thing? I really would like Him to just get it over and done with. Can't He just do it all now? Every time He changed me before, it's been uncomfortable. And I know that every time He changed me, I've said, 'Ouch,' and I knew what was going to take place during the process of change, and I thought, *Oh no! Not that again!*"

But the bottom line is that you could not receive all that Heaven has for you at one time. God has to do it little bit by little bit. And besides that, the human heart is too big for just one touch. One touch will begin the change, one touch will begin the process, but this is an ongoing process that will not end until the day that you see Jesus face-to-face.

FROM GLORY TO GLORY

> REVIVAL IS NOT AN EXTERNAL THING. IT'S NOT SOMETHING HAPPENING "OUT THERE." REVIVAL BEGINS WITHIN.

We've been changed from "glory to glory" (2 Corinthians 3:18). The measure of glory that you received in days gone by opens you up for the measure of glory that is still available for you. And the moment you get to the place when you're not hungry and you're not thirsty, where you think you've arrived, you will cool off. That's why revival moves and it's almost as if it goes around and people get it, and then they cool off; they wane and wax cold. Then others catch the fire and they go on. It's very rare that you find people who fall in the fire and stay in the fire, and you see them five years from now, ten years from now, and that passion and that fire is still burning and you don't have to say, "Oh my! What happened to him? He cooled off!"

Revival is not an external thing. It's not something happening "out there." Revival begins within. It starts deep down inside the heart of an individual who is hungry and desperate, and you never lose that hunger or that desperation. You are hungry and you get hungrier and hungrier and you get more and more desperate.

People say, "Come on, now; haven't you got it yet?" No! My God, I'm just getting started in this thing. I'm not going to get past, "As the deer pants for the water brooks, So pants my soul for You, O God" (Psalm 42:1, NASB). I'm going to keep panting for the water. Lord, I'm hungry for You. I'm thirsty for You. I am desperate for You. I want more of You. I want more of You now than I've ever wanted it before. In fact, there is room now in my heart for more of You than there was before. Build in me a bigger capacity to receive more of You.

"He must increase, but I must decrease" (John 3:30). I am nothing, He is everything. Because you can't break open your "alabaster box" and pour perfume on the head of Jesus without getting some on you (Luke 7). You'll leave smelling of the fragrance of the Lily of the Valley and the Rose of Sharon (Song of Solomon 2:1). So, wherever you go, people will look at you and say, "My! Where have you been?"

A CHANGE OF THE HEART

> IT'S EASY TO RENEW THE MIND WHEN THE HEART IS CHANGED.

The modern-day Church thinks that revival has just got something to do with the mind. We believe in the renewing of the mind; the Bible tells us about the renewing of the mind (Romans 12:2), but what purpose is there in renewing the mind when the heart is fouled up?

You can renew your mind till the cows come home, till the moon turns green, and the monkeys chew tobacco. It's easy to renew the mind when the heart is changed. I believe in the renewing of the mind; we preach on the renewing of the mind, but before you even begin to renew your mind, you had better have something happen in your heart!

There are people in churches all over the world, going to church every Sunday, sitting and saying, "Amen. Hallelujah," and they are renewing their minds, but their hearts are all fouled up!

They give a mental assent to the fact that Jesus is Lord—"I'm a Christian"—but inside their hearts, there's something wrong. They haven't even been converted, because when you get converted, when you really, genuinely, get saved, something happens; it's different. I know that we are not to judge people's salvation, but I have met some preachers and I have thought, *My God, are they really saved? Can they really be saved and do that?*

Ezekiel 36:25–26 says, "Then will I sprinkle clean water upon you, and ye shall be clean: from all your filthiness, and from all your idols, will I cleanse you. A new heart also will I give you, and a new spirit will I put within you: and I will take away the stony heart out of your flesh, and I will give you an heart of flesh." Many of God's people have got a heart that's so hard, but when Jesus comes, He takes that hard heart and He makes it soft.

Some people think that if you have a soft heart it's a sign of how weak you are, "Look at that—I saw a grown man cry!" We should have hearts that are eighteen inches thick to criticism and praise (because both will kill you) but paper-thin to the needs and hurts of others. "I'll take out the stony heart" God says, but it is up to every individual to grow concerned about their own heart.

Don't sit and judge yourself by your intentions when your actions are slipping by and look pretty bad. You can't put your husband or wife's heart on the altar; you have to come and put *your* heart on the altar.

It's like the song that says, "Not my brother, not my sister, but it's me O Lord, standin' in the need of prayer" ("Standing in the Need of Prayer," African-American spiritual). *You* need to hear this. *You* need it. Someone says, "Oh I tell you, my brother-in-law really needs to hear this message, pastor."

"That's my mother-in-law sitting back there, pastor; she desperately needs to hear this."

"Thank God I brought my wife; she needs to hear this message."

No! It's got nothing to do with your husband, your wife, your mother, your father, your sister, your aunt, your uncle, or your cousin; it's got to do with *you* and *your* heart and laying *your* heart on the altar and saying, "Oh, God, come with your fire and come and do a work deep on the inside of me. Come and let the fire fall and burn out all the dross, because I want that which is pure. I want that which is holy."

THE FIRE OF GOD PURIFIES THE HEART

> REVIVAL IS A THING THAT HAPPENS WITHIN; IT'S NOT WITHOUT.

When the fire comes, it burns out all the dross. Now, somebody says, "But Brother Rodney, I am born-again. I'm saved, I love God, and I don't snort cocaine. I don't smoke marijuana; I don't drink alcohol; I'm not into perverted things." No, but you walk around full of pride. You're full of unforgiveness; you are full of bitterness; you are full of jealousy; you are full of competition; you are green with envy; you are full of gossip and full of slander.

The hidden sins of the heart are not apparent to many because people are so used to judging the outward things. And nobody like the Church can judge the outward things!

Lucifer, when he fell, did not fall because he ran off with the organist. He fell because of pride, and pride begins in the heart. We need a soft heart, a tender heart, a humble heart, a pure heart, and that's why we need revival.

Someone says, "Well, we've had revival," but we need to *continually* have it and we need to constantly maintain a pure, humble, teachable, repentant, and soft heart.

Revival is a thing that happens within; it's not without. You can put on all the outward displays, but inside, you are rotten to the core. And that's why you've been to many revival meetings, and you've seen people touched, but they didn't get a change.

If you haven't had a change, then it should be your number one goal this year, by the special grace of God, to have a touch from the Holy Ghost that is totally life-changing and life-transforming. And you have to grow concerned about yourself, because most of the time others are not going to grow concerned for you. They may say, "That person is heading for trouble," but they really couldn't care less. They'd come to your funeral, shed a few tears, but two weeks later, they'd forget about it.

The Bible tells us to work out our salvation with fear and trembling (Philippians 2:12) and in Hebrews 3:12, talking to the Church, says, "Take heed, brethren, lest there be in any of you an evil heart of unbelief, in departing from the living God."

In other words, they were with the living God, but now they have departed from the living God, and he said, "Take heed lest there be in you an evil heart of unbelief." The heart is the thing that must be dealt with. The Lord told me this at the outset when revival broke out. When we started off, we were really in the healing ministry. We would go around praying for the sick, and I still pray for the sick, but I got tired of praying for the sick because I would pray for the sick and they would get healed, but six months later they died or were sick again. I went to the Lord and said, "What's the problem? Why is this happening? I don't want to waste my time praying for people and they get healed but then they get sick again." And He said, "*It's because you're dealing with the fruit. You need to deal with the root. You need to go and lay an ax to the root of the tree. The problem is the heart.*"

EXHORT ONE ANOTHER, DAILY!

You have got to get into the heart of the matter and the matter of the heart. The Bible says, "Exhort one another daily" (Hebrews 3:13). So how often do we have to have this happen? Daily! Not once a week, or once every six months at a campmeeting or special conference. It's "daily exhort one another"—daily!

Hebrews 3:13: "But exhort one another daily, while it is called To day; lest any of you be hardened through the deceitfulness of sin." If somebody who wears shoes all the time takes their shoes off and walks across the parking lot, it will be painful for their feet. They'll walk and the little gravel pieces will press in and every step will be painful. Why? Because their feet are soft and tender. But if they walked barefoot daily, if they walked out there in the worst conditions, then there will come a day when they can just go strolling through gravel and can walk on all kinds of things, and it won't even affect them. Other people wouldn't be able to walk, but they'd just be strolling along, "What's wrong with you, tenderfoot?" Their feet have become hardened; their feet have become calloused.

If your feet are not protected, they will become calloused and hardened, and likewise, if your heart is not protected, it will become calloused and hardened. The Bible says that we are to protect our hearts with all diligence, for out of the heart flows the issues of life (Proverbs 4:23). You have to protect your heart, and the Bible says to daily exhort one another so that you don't develop a hardened heart and get an evil heart of unbelief (Hebrews 3:13). Do you know of Christians who were so on fire for God that you could see the light of God shining in their eyes, but when you look at them now, you know that something went wrong somewhere? They've got a hardened heart, and you really don't want to be around them because if you get around them for any length of time, you feel like you need to go take a shower. And even if you took a shower, after that you'd need to go shower one more time!

What happened? Were they born-again? Yes, they must have been born-again (some of them at least) to have had the fire of God on them, and the light of God shining through them. But what went wrong?—they didn't protect their hearts. Because daily your heart is exposed to the elements; daily your heart is exposed to criticism; daily your heart is exposed to the lust of the flesh, the lust of the eyes, and the pride of life, and if your heart is not protected, your heart will get hardened. And it's not something that happens just overnight.

If your heart is not protected, then what happens is that your heart becomes seared; your conscience becomes seared. That's why you ask yourself, "How can they do what they do?"

YOU HAVE GOT TO GET INTO THE HEART OF THE MATTER AND THE MATTER OF THE HEART.

A VESSEL MEET FOR THE MASTER'S USE

Jesus is looking for a soft heart; He is looking for a tender heart. Because it's a soft heart and a tender heart that can be used by Him, not just once, not twice, not three times, but on a continual basis. And when I studied the passage of scripture that talks about, "If a man therefore purge himself from these, he shall be a vessel unto honour, sanctified, and meet for the master's use, and prepared unto every good work" (2 Timothy 2:21), I realized that when you have a soft heart, the Master is going to use you, He's going to use you for the banquets and bring you out when all the guests are there and put you in the middle of the table.

KEEP A HEALTHY SPIRITUAL HEART

It does not matter how on fire you are right now; you need to heed the warning of the Spirit of God and make a decision, and purpose in your heart by the special grace of God and by God's help every day, "I'm going to be changed from glory to glory, to glory, to glory, until the day that He comes to take me home. The moment even a little attitude comes and rises up. I'm going to judge it; I'm going to jump on it like a chicken on a Junebug. I'm going to jump on that attitude. The moment unforgiveness arises, I'm not even going to let it settle in and take root. No! I cannot afford that!"

Your heart is so precious because the precious Blood was shed for your heart. It's the Blood of Jesus that makes your heart precious. In the natural, we may watch ourselves physically. We may watch our diets and make sure that we keep our cholesterol levels down and that we exercise and we eat right, so that our hearts can keep beating and that our arteries do not get clogged up. Because if your arteries are clogged up, you're going to have a heart attack or you're going to have a stroke.

Yet spiritually, there are many who sit in church and their hearts have become clogged up and they've had a stroke and they can't even lift their hands and worship. Their hands can't even go to their back pockets to get an offering out anymore. They've had a 'stroke;' they can't even shout, "Amen."

I watch people during the time of worship. They just stand and look; they're not even singing; they don't even open their mouths. You want to run down and grab them and shake them till their false teeth rattle and say, "What's wrong with you? Don't you realize that you're in the presence of the King of kings and the Lord of lords? Why can't you open your mouth? It doesn't matter if you can sing a tune. It doesn't matter if you can't keep a tune or hold a tune. My God, just croak! Make a joyful noise unto the Lord, and lift up your voice and praise Him and give Him glory!" But they can't because they've had a heart attack spiritually. That's why revival is necessary to come and to jump-start their hearts again and get them to beat and pump life into their beings. The Bible says, "A merry heart doeth good like a medicine" (Proverbs 17:22).

Somebody says, "You can't be your own heart doctor." Yes you can. In this case, you can be your own heart doctor.

JUDGE YOURSELVES

You have to ensure your heart stays tender and you must judge yourself. Have you ever had things on the inside of you, and they started rising up and you thought to yourself, *I don't even know where that came from. But I'll tell you what, I don't like it and I don't want it,* and you dealt with it?

That's why parents need to ensure that a child's heart stays soft and tender. And the only way to do that is there's a certain spot on a child's anatomy, the backside, that must be ministered to on a regular basis. Somehow, that surface of the body, not the ear, not the head, not the shoulder or the chest, but that strip across the buttocks seems to be connected to the heart, so that when correction is felt, it tends to flip the switch, and immediately, repentance doth come!

Why do you think teenagers and young people are hurting themselves? There's such a high percentage of teenagers and young people who are beating themselves and cutting themselves and hurting themselves and for many it's because they are looking for correction; they are looking for discipline. Somebody has not disciplined them.

The Bible says if you spare the rod, you hate the child (Proverbs 13:24). My daddy loved me; my mama loved me; they loved me so much! I'm thankful they loved me so much!

Now, somebody might say, "Well, the Lord is not going to do that. God won't come and spank you." That's not what the Bible says. The Bible talks about the "chastening" of the Lord (Job 5:17; see also Psalm 94:12; Jeremiah 10:24; Proverbs 3:12; Hebrews 12:5–6). If you think the Lord doesn't spank you, then obviously you haven't had a spanking.

I know some people don't believe what I'm saying, but they haven't read the Book of Hebrews. I never knew there were so many illiterate people in the Body of Christ who have never read the Word. "Well, come on, Brother Rodney. God doesn't spank His children." Then why would He tell you to spank your children? If you are His child, and you open yourself for correction, then yea verily, thou shalt receive a spanking! But that spanking is not to kill you.

For "we have had earthly fathers who disciplined us and we yielded [to them] *and* respected [them for training us]. Shall we not much more cheerfully submit to the Father of spirits and so [truly] live? For [our earthly fathers] disciplined us for only a short period of time *and* chastised us as seemed proper *and* good to them; but He disciplines us for our certain good, that we may become sharers in His own holiness. For the time being no discipline brings joy, but seems grievous *and* painful; but afterwards it yields a peaceable fruit of righteousness" (Hebrews 12:9–11, AMPC).

If we would judge ourselves, then we would not be judged. But when we are judged, we are chastened. So don't wait for the spanking from above. Deal with yourself, and put your heart in a place where it is vulnerable to the Lord. Say, "Lord, whatever attitudes arise, whatever things are not of You, I don't want them in my life, I don't care what you have to do to get them out, but I want them gone, and I'm giving you full permission. I don't care how humbling it is; I don't care what other people think about me, but I want a heart that's pure. I want a heart that's tender. I want a heart that's soft, and I want You to come and do work on the inside of me. And I'll obey You. I'll do whatever You want me to do."

If you had come to our house when our children were being disobedient, we didn't care if we had guests or not; we would take the children in a side room, and you'd hear this noise coming through from the next room! It just happened to be that you were there the day that the judgment was meted out! And there was weeping and wailing and gnashing of teeth.

But when you meet some Christians and you wonder why they are looking the way they are, you wonder why they're so depressed, maybe they're just so disobedient that they are in a place of chastening half the time.

AVOID A ROOT OF BITTERNESS

> YOU HAVE TO BE CAREFUL NOT TO ALLOW YOUR EARS TO BE THE LID OF A GARBAGE CAN WHERE PEOPLE CAN COME AND JUST DUMP THEIR RUBBISH IN YOU. IF YOU DON'T, THEN WHEN YOU GO AWAY, IT WILL HAVE AFFECTED YOUR SPIRIT AND THEN YOU'LL KNOW SOMETHING'S HAPPENED–THERE WILL BE A ROOT OF BITTERNESS SPRINGING UP.

To keep a soft and tender heart, you must also not let a root of bitterness spring up. I know someone will say, "Oh, Brother Rodney, change the subject; move on to something else," but read Hebrews 12:12–15. This is the Word of God: "Lift up the hands which hang down, and the feeble knees; And make straight paths for your feet, lest that which is lame be turned out of the way; but let it rather be healed. Follow peace with all men, and holiness, without which no man shall see the Lord: Looking diligently lest any man fail of the grace of God; lest any root of bitterness springing up trouble you, and thereby many be defiled." Normally, it takes somebody who's been offended and a root of bitterness springing up in them, who will then go around the church, polluting others.

It takes one bad apple to poison the whole bunch. That's why you'd better be careful if you meet anybody in church and they are running their mouth and they are criticizing and you think they've got an angle that you might not know of. Be careful that you don't open yourself to their poison and receive a root of bitterness that comes straight from them to you, because you might not have the whole story. And as angry as they might be, and as justified as they might be, or think they are, they are wrong.

You have to be careful not to allow your ears to be the lid of a garbage can where people can come and just dump their rubbish in you. If you don't, then when you go away, it will have affected your spirit and then you'll know something's happened—there will be a root of bitterness springing up.

Be careful. In fact, it would be better for you to warn that individual and say, "Be very careful what you're saying right now. You'd better pray; you'd better hit your face, and you'd better see God."

He says in Hebrews 12:15 (AMPC), "Exercise foresight and be on the watch to look [after one another]." So, we need to look after one another. If you see your brother or sister, and they are heading in the wrong direction, you say, "I'm just telling you right now, this is dangerous ground, and you are heading for trouble."

If I saw you walking on the riverbank and you were heading for a nest of water moccasins, what kind of an individual would I be to let you walk right in the middle of that nest? Would it look like I loved you?

So you have to warn people; you have to tell them. They might get upset with you," but at least you warned them of the error of their ways.

A TENDER HEART KEEPS YOU IN THE PLAN AND PURPOSE OF GOD

Continuing in Hebrews 12, it says:

> See that no one falls back from and fails to secure God's grace (His unmerited favor and spiritual blessing), in order that no root of resentment (rancor, bitterness, or hatred) shoots forth and causes

> trouble and bitter torment, and the many become contaminated and defiled by it. That no one may become guilty of sexual vice, or become a profane (godless and sacrilegious) person as Esau did, who sold his own birthright for a single meal. For you understand that later on, when he wanted [to regain title to] his inheritance of the blessing, he was rejected (disqualified and set aside), for he could find no opportunity to repair by repentance [what he had done, no chance to recall the choice he had made], although he sought for it carefully with [bitter] tears.
>
> VV. 15B-17 AMPC

"What are you telling me, Brother Rodney? Are you telling me that that I could cross a line? Are you telling me that I could come to that place?" I'm warning you now by the Spirit of God that if you don't protect your heart and keep your heart pure, there could come a time when you will miss the plan and the purpose of God for your life.

As Esau lost his birthright, so you could miss the plan and the purpose of God for your life. Even though he cried and repented with tears, he couldn't get it back. It was finished; it was gone. Be careful; this is not a game. This is not a game; it is holy!

> For you have not come [as did the Israelites in the wilderness] to a [material] mountain that can be touched, [a mountain] that is ablaze with fire, and to gloom and darkness and a raging storm, and to the blast of a trumpet and a voice whose words make the listeners beg that nothing more be said to them. For they could not bear the command that was given: If even a wild animal touches the mountain, it shall be stoned to death. In fact, so awful and terrifying was the [phenomenal] sight that Moses said, I am terrified (aghast and trembling with fear). But rather, you have come to Mount Zion, even to the city of the living God, the heavenly Jerusalem, and to countless multitudes of angels in festal gathering, and to the church (assembly) of the Firstborn who are registered [as citizens] in heaven, and to the God

> Who is Judge of all, and to the spirits of the righteous (the redeemed in heaven) who have been made perfect, and to Jesus, the Mediator (Go-between, Agent) of a new covenant, and to the sprinkled blood which speaks [of mercy], a better and nobler and more gracious message than the blood of Abel [which cried out for vengeance]. So see to it that you do not reject Him or refuse to listen to and heed Him Who is speaking [to you now]. For if they [the Israelites] did not escape when they refused to listen and heed Him Who warned and divinely instructed them [here] on earth [revealing with heavenly warnings His will], how much less shall we escape if we reject and turn our backs on Him Who cautions and admonishes [us] from heaven?
>
> HEBREWS 12:18-25 AMPC

I could carry on reading this chapter and actually, I encourage every single one of you to take the whole of the Book of Hebrews and read it. Just take whole chapters. It's a New Covenant book. But we don't play with this New Covenant. We don't play with the grace of God. If you want the anointing of God, you can have it and not only have it, but you can live in it.

CHECK YOUR SPIRITUAL TEMPERATURE

> CHECK YOUR TEMPERATURE; YOU ONLY WANT TO BE RUNNING A HIGH FEVER—A HIGH FEVER OF HEAVEN!

As you judge yourself, you must also continually check your spiritual temperature. It's one thing to have the anointing today, but will you have it tomorrow? Will you have it next week? Can you maintain the glory of God in your life? You can't have the glory and the things of the world; you can't have the glory and sin; you can't have the glory and the ways of the world. You have to choose. That's why this is a 'leaving everything and following Him.' "I have decided to follow Jesus, no turning back, no turning back" (Simon Kama Marak. Formerly attr. to S. Sundar Singh).

In the Book of Revelation, Jesus talks to the Laodiceans and He says, "I know thy works, that thou art neither cold nor hot: I would thou wert cold or hot. So then because thou art lukewarm, and neither cold nor hot, I will spue thee out of my mouth" (Revelation 3:15–16). He's talking to the Church, and He said you are lukewarm. We've got to check our temperature. You should walk in the door of the church and grab a thermometer and check. That's what church is there for. Check your temperature; you only want to be running a high fever—a high fever of Heaven!

You don't want to be lukewarm; you don't want to be cold; you want to be hot. Hot is when you love not your life unto death, nor the world; you don't care (Revelation 12:11). The things of Heaven mean more to you than anything else. Lukewarm, He says, is when you're "rich, and increased with goods, and have need of nothing" (Revelation 3:17).

That's when you have everything, your church is now accepted, and everybody comes. It was on fire in the days when you were persecuted and called a cult and they wrote up about you in the newspaper, and they attacked you, and people spoke all kinds of evil things against you, and you had to fight for your very existence. But now, your church is kind of accepted and the mayor of the town comes. Everybody loves you, and all the sports figures come and the top singers come, and your church is just wonderful and an accepted thing—and you are now LUKEWARM! You have need of nothing. Don't you know you are wretched, you are blind, you are naked (Revelation 3:17)? How can a church become wretched and blind and naked? When it starts to cool off and it allows its temperature to drop.

We've got to keep our temperature checked. If you find yourself going along for six weeks and you feel your temperatures cooling off, go to https://www.revival.com/ and check out where we are. Then jump on a plane, come on a bus, train, or automobile, and get into a meeting. Just make sure that you keep yourself on fire. You can log onto revival.

com, watch us every night on TV for The Stand, watch us on YouTube or Facebook, or order some DVDs and just get saturated in it. But don't allow yourself to cool off.

FIGHT TO KEEP A TENDER AND PURE HEART

You have to guard your heart and fight to keep a tender heart. If you've been around this ministry for some years, you will have heard me talk about these principles. We have to grow up and mature past this attitude of, "I've heard that before," because you're going to hear it again. Some of you have been running around and your hearts are not tender. You do not know how hard I have fought to keep my heart soft. You do not know the struggle. You do not know the fight. I look back over the years, and I remember times when it took everything inside of me to hold the course. It's one thing to have things coming to you from the world and you can deal with that, but when it comes from the Church family, when it comes from people within the Body, it's very hard to deal with. I can tell you that there were times when it was touch-and-go.

Only by the grace of God, only by the special grace of God, am I here to celebrate over 40 years in the ministry. I have people thanking me, but I feel nothing; they could be talking about somebody else because it's all by the grace of God; it's only by the special grace of God. I know we happen to be heading up this ministry, but you might as well be talking about somebody else. That's why I give in the offering. That's why I keep going and keep preaching and proclaiming, because it's really not our ministry; it's His ministry. It's all because of Him.

How can a beautiful dish sit on the dinner table and brag to the guests, "Look at me; look at me. I'm carrying the lamb stew?" How can the teapot come out there and say, "Look at me, carrying this mint tea. Look at me?"

Give me a break. None of us can brag of ourselves. We are just vessels. God pours it in us, and we are just there to pour out. That's all we are. It's Him, and all glory goes unto Him.

Have you fought to keep your heart right and pure? It is a fight and if it's not a fight, then I can tell you that you are probably sitting reading this with a hard heart right now. It's a fight.

You have to decide, "I will NOT walk in unforgiveness. I will NOT walk in bitterness. I will NOT walk in pride. I WILL forgive. I WILL walk in love. I WILL have nothing to do with sin in any form. I WILL be holy. Sin, bitterness, unforgiveness, pride, get away from me. Get away from me!" It's a fight.

Imagine that you are all dressed up and you're going to go to some banquet and ball. The ladies are all dressed up in flowing gowns, with beautiful light, pale colors, and the men are all in tuxedos. If somebody ran into the room who looked like they had come out of the swamp, covered in swamp mess, and they started grabbing hold of you and flinging their arms around you, what would you do? You'd say, "Get away! Get away from me. You are messing me up. You are getting your dirt all over me!"

Yet in church, some old swamp thing comes out, full of his mess, and he puts his arm around you, and the next thing, you're having him over to your house. You haven't even checked him out. He's dirty and he's stinky, and before you even know it, you stink just like him. And then you go off and start your own church, the Church of the Smelly Swamp Things.

You think that's funny, but that's what happens spiritually. You wouldn't allow somebody all dirty to just come in, but people do it all the time. You have to protect your heart.

It's a fight to stay in revival. There are certain preachers I can't hang out with. I'm not criticizing their ministry, but I had to make a decision a long time ago that if I walk with them, I will have to compromise everything I preach. You have to protect your heart. This is one of the root messages of revival.

DON'T JUST WATCH OTHERS IN REVIVAL–JUMP IN!

I watch people. I have even watched people come into The River Church, Sunday after Sunday, and they think they are in revival because they come to The River, but they are not in revival; they are in some swamp. I watch them come and sit, and they watch people coming under the anointing, and yet they themselves have never come under the anointing. They're just sitting there. They've never been touched by the power of God. They just say, "Well, I go to The River." But they never got *in* it. I want to ask, "What's your problem? Why haven't you got in it? You should be under the water." But they just come to sit on the bank. They just come to watch other people in the River.

Because I'm the pastor, I'm nice, but in revival I'm not that nice. I'll be all over you. I'll be out there in the pew, grabbing you and shaking you. On Sundays I'm nice. "Let them be. Let Swamp thing be," but I've had about as much of it as I can take. They sit there on Sunday and look like death warmed over—you Swamp thing.

When you hit the doors of our church, you should be in an attitude of prayer, you should be hungry, you should be pressing in, and you should be in a place of worship. Somebody says, "You are requiring too much of me." Well then, find another place of worship. There are plenty of them in town, and our buses will take you there on Sunday mornings!

I know people will say, "That's because you're not really a pastor." No, I'm a heart checker! Sometimes I stand here on Sunday mornings and I wonder why some people even came. I look out and think, *I don't know why they came today. They're not even here.* Because people, especially when they sit near the back, think I can't see them. But I can see their faces.

I had a man come and sit in the front row of one of my meetings wearing dark glasses in the evening service! It's one thing if you have an eye problem and you need help, but he didn't need help in that way. The man was wrong. He was a phony, and he didn't want me to look in his eyes because he was afraid of what I might see.

DON'T BLOCK OFF ANY AREA OF YOUR HEART

If you want revival, you cannot block areas of your life from God. When you go to a true doctor, you are taken into a room and you are examined. And the true doctor's going to check you properly. In order to be checked, sometimes you're going to have to "expose" yourself! And spiritually, there are some people who just don't want to go that far. But you have to allow the Lord in every area of your heart. Nothing sacred, nothing hidden. Don't put up a No Entry sign; don't block off any area of your heart. You have tell God, "You're going to the deep and hidden parts of my heart. I want to change. I'm hungry for You. I'm thirsty for You. I want You; I want You alone. I don't care what it takes."

That's the person who's going to have an encounter with God. That's the person who's going to be changed from glory to glory. That's the person who's not going to be up and down, but will be a constant, just rising up more into the glory, brighter and brighter, until the day that they stand before Him in robes of white.

When we go to the world, we go with the simple message of salvation and the love of God and the mercy of God. But then we bring the message of revival to keep them in the fire. When we come to the church, we bring the message of revival to bring them back to their first love, to fall in love with Jesus all over again. Different meetings, still by the Spirit of God. Not all meetings are the same.

I'm not trying to get everybody saved reading this, but I'm trying to keep you saved. Sometimes the easiest thing you ever do is get people saved; it's so hard to keep them saved. Only the fire of God can keep people in their place. In our meetings, as you sit in the divine atmosphere of the Spirit of God, you will notice a change on the inside of you. Your heart will begin to soften more and more and become tender.

The moment you say, "I have need of nothing," you are lukewarm. I've even had ministers tell people close to me say, "I just can't sit through one of your services." Meanwhile, they go around and conduct "revival meetings" of their own but they can't sit through one of my meetings! Why can't they sit through one of my meetings? How was it that my 81 year old father could sit through everything? He didn't want to miss anything, and when there was not a meeting going on at The River, he would come to me and say, "When's the next meeting?" He would take the DVDs home from the services, and watch them back-to-back for days and days. I believe my parents went through every DVD we had five times!

Was it because I'm his son? I don't believe that for one moment. I know he and Mom loved me, but he was just locked into the anointing because that's where he lived. He was just locked into the presence of God.

If I invited you to my house for a meal and you couldn't sit through the meal, you would be trying to offend me. The food we are dishing up cannot be rubbish because we have some of the finest chefs cooking for us. And so, we know the food's good, but if you told me that you couldn't sit through the meal, you just had a little bit of the salad and then ran out, and you never even got to have the special dessert that the chef prepared, then something is wrong with you.

Because you might not realize this, but I do not just have a service; it is a meal. The majority eat, but there are one or two people who just sit and they don't even touch their plates. For the whole service, they didn't even pick up their fork and they definitely didn't pay anything for the meal! They used the time of the offering to go to the toilet. They grabbed the offering envelope and stuck it in their pocket and put nothing in it.

I wonder how big is their offering envelope collection is at home? Don't take an offering envelope if you're not going to do anything with it; you're a liar! It's amazing how people's bladders work right at the time of the offering, and it's amazing how people hide behind their children—"Johnny needs to go." Johnny didn't need to go, it is just that the parents needed to get out of the heat!

BE A CARRIER OF REVIVAL FIRE

YOUR FIRST LOVE. DO NOT LEAVE READING THIS BOOK WITHOUT YOUR FIRST LOVE. DON'T LEAVE WITHOUT THE JOY OF YOUR SALVATION; DON'T DO IT. YOUR LIFE DEPENDS ON IT. I PRAY THAT EVERYONE WOULD HAVE A TOTAL HEAD-ON COLLISION WITH THE HOLY GHOST.

You have to say, "Come, Holy Spirit; do it in me." Look down deep on the inside of yourself, regardless of who you are, or what your station is in life, or how long you've been in the ministry. Do you think I'm saying this just for the sake of it? You can't preach these things without them shaking through your very being. If I was just bringing a message, I could give it to you and be unaffected by what I was bringing. But when you bring this message, burnt in the fire, birthed in the Holy Ghost, it stays with you; you can't get away with that.

"Blessed are they which do hunger and thirst after righteousness: for they shall be filled" (Matthew 5:6). "Draw nigh to God, and he will draw nigh to you" (James 4:8), but just because you're sitting reading this it does not mean to say you are drawing nigh unto Him. Your life has to be transformed.

Peter's life was totally transformed from having "foot and mouth" disease (because that's what he had), to being used of God on the Day of Pentecost and proclaiming that great message. What you have to understand is that it's not just about some emotional outbreak; it's about the fire of God doing a work in the heart of an individual, that God does a work through you, not just in your neighborhood, but in your city, town, state, nation, and that you carry the fire of revival. Because when the fire and the Holy Ghost revival starts within you, you are a container: you carry it, and it breaks out wherever you go.

People might criticize me; they might say I am crazy, but they can follow me around the world and they'll see that wherever I've gone, fire has broken out. They can try to work it out. "How did that happen? How did that come to pass?" But when the fire of God begins to burn, there's no devil in hell that can stop it, and he cannot put it out.

I see the fire of God spreading across Europe. I see the fire of God shaking the whole of continent of Africa, I see the power of God shaking the whole of Asia. I see the fire of God shaking North and South America. I see the fire of God shaking Australasia, and from the Arctic to Antarctica.

It's true that God finds a vessel and puts His fire in, but sometimes, that vessel has only yielded two, three, four, five years, six years, ten years, and then He has to find another vessel—why should you be replaced? You need to stay on fire.

Can't you just be the vessel that He wants you to be? You might be 85–90 years old, but if you're a vessel of honor, on fire for Him, He will still pull you out and put you on the dinner table.You are still a carrier of revival fire.

Do not leave reading this book without your first love. Don't leave without the joy of your salvation; don't do it. Your life depends on it. I pray that everyone would have a total head-on collision with the Holy Ghost.

13

REVIVAL IS NOW AND IT'S NEW

A Fresh and New Thing

The hard thing about revival is that it is a "new thing," but people like the "old thing," and they don't want to change. Isaiah 43:18–19 says, "Remember ye not the former things, neither consider the things of old. Behold, I will do a new thing." But you cannot have the old and the new, you have got to make a choice.

When Elisha followed Elijah, he wanted that double portion anointing, but he could not receive the double portion anointing until he got rid of his old anointing. That's why he took his mantle and threw it away. Don't keep your old mantle, tear it up so that nobody else can wear it. Get the new thing that God is doing.

YOU HAVE TO CHANGE YOUR WAY OF THINKING

> YOUR WAY OF THINKING CAN EITHER SET YOU FREE OR HOLD YOU BACK IN BONDAGE.

In order to receive the new thing, you have to change. Looking back over the years in our ministry, it was almost every three months God would tell me, "You're going to have to change again." I'd say, "But, Lord, I just did that!" And that change was not about the pulpit; I'm talking about things in the natural, behind the scenes, just my way of thinking.

Your way of thinking can either set you free or hold you back in bondage. Because your mindset is going to lock you in. And a lot of our mindsets are locked in because of religion and tradition. We think with the religious mindset; we think with religious tradition. God wants to do a new thing, but because we won't allow the Lord to even change our way of thinking, we can't go to the next level and we can't receive what Heaven has. So don't be afraid to change, because the new thing is going to bring about change.

I touched on this earlier, but one of the biggest struggles you're going to have about change is family members and close friends who have known you for a long time. They don't want you to change because when you change, you threaten their very existence and their status quo, and they'd like you to remain as you are. There are communities in the United Kingdom and in Australia where if you are raised in that community, you go to the local school, you go to the university there, and if you move out, it's death for you, "How dare you leave your heritage?"

But when God calls you, He always calls you *out* of something. Like when he called Abram, He called him out of something and said, "Get out of your home country. Get out of where you are. Leave it behind" (Genesis 12:1, paraphrased). There comes a time when you just have to say goodbye. Not because you don't like the people there, but because God is doing a new thing.

> WHEN GOD CALLS YOU, HE ALWAYS CALLS YOU OUT OF SOMETHING.

YOU CANNOT HAVE THE NEW AND KEEP THE OLD

> THE THINGS OF THE SPIRIT ARE NEVER FORCED, AND YOU DON'T HAVE TO FORCE THEM.

You can't have the new and keep the old. You can't have the new as a place that you visit occasionally, "I'll stay with the old because it's comfortable. I know it; I'm familiar with it." God says, "I'm going to do a new thing" (Isaiah 43:19), do you want the new thing? A new thing is always fresh. Have you ever had Krispy Kreme donuts? You need to get the donuts when the light is on. Why? Because it's a new thing. It's fresh! When the light is on at Krispy Kreme, that's when the cars pull in, because they know it's fresh. And when God does something new, it's always fresh; it's not stale. There's nothing worse than last week's donuts!

As I've traveled around the world, I've been to a lot of restaurants, and when they bring a bowl of bread rolls, I pick up a bread roll and tap it with my knife to check for freshness. In fact, each bread roll gives a distinct sound, and you know you're in trouble when the bread roll goes, *chink!* I've called many a waiter over and said, "Hey, could you give me a fresh roll, please?" There's nothing like new and fresh—like putting on that new, fresh, clean shirt, or a fresh, clean pair of socks.

I like the new thing God does. I like the fresh thing God does, and He's always new and He's always fresh. "I will do a new thing; now it shall spring forth" (Isaiah 43:19). That's why I love the things of the Spirit, because the things of the Spirit "spring forth." Even the word *prophesy* in the Hebrew means "to bubble forth, to tumble forth, to spring forth."

The things of the Spirit are never forced and you don't have to force them. They come out like they're springing forth. "Spring up, O well, within my soul" (L. Casebolt). It's that life of God that is always fresh and bubbling, and flowing and running, and pure and holy and new

(Numbers 21:17; John 4:14). That's why you don't have to be stale and old and hard like "last week's donut!"

I meet a lot of preachers, and I can see they are "last week's donut." The only good thing is maybe they've got a little bit of icing on and you can get a little bit of sweetness from the outer edge of the donut. But other than that, you don't want to take a bite!

THE FIRE OF REVIVAL BRINGS AN OASIS IN THE DESERT PLACES

IN THE MIDDLE OF THE DESERT, IN THE MIDDLE OF THE WORST PLACES, GOD WILL USE PEOPLE WHO WILL CARRY THE FIRE OF REVIVAL.

When revival comes, it makes everything fresh and new. God says, "I will even make a way in the wilderness" (Isaiah 43:19). That tells me that it doesn't matter what that place looks like. It can be the worst desert place, but when revival comes, it's going to spring forth a mighty oasis, with palm trees, rivers, fountain springs, luscious green grass and birds. In the middle of the desert, in the middle of the worst places, God will use people who will carry the fire of revival. There are a lot of people who want God to send them to the nice places, but God's going to send you to the worst places. We've ended up in some of the worst places on the planet and when I got there, I found out that it was the hardest place, the worst place, where crime rates were the highest! I said to the Lord, "Well, thank You very much! This is just great!" He replied, "*Why do you think I sent you? I sent you so that you can allow this new thing to spring forth, so that the river can flow in the desert and the palm trees can grow!*"

What you have got to understand is that you are leaving an oasis behind you everywhere you go. You become the person who deposits an oasis. You dig a well, and the water starts to flow; the people start to come. You plant the palm trees, and they come for the shade.

And then people come to say, "Thank you. Thank you so much. We were dying from thirst until you came, but you dug a well and it began to flow. In fact, what started off as a little stream has now become a river, and oh, how refreshed we are! And we come daily to sit by the banks of the river and put our feet in and get into the water, and we bask in the sunlight of God's love. We sit under the shade of the palm trees and drink the coconut juice."

I cannot tell you how many places we've gone to, and during the very first meeting, you'd think we had a mass funeral! Sunday morning at a new church that had never had revival, you'd think people had died! You'd think that at any moment, they were going to wheel out a coffin and you'd find out that it was God who died last night! It had to be because of the way they were in mourning—everybody was sad. But we'd come in with the life of God, with the Word of the Lord and the presence of God, and then the freshness of Heaven would come and begin to touch the hearts of the people.

I'd watch their faces begin to change over Sunday, Monday, Tuesday, Wednesday, Thursday, and Friday. By Friday night, the whole place was shining. People's eyes were sparkling; there was a spring in their step. They were raising their hands; they were shouting, "Hallelujah! Glory to God!" It was like night and day. You couldn't even believe it was the same place. We'd even look and say, "Is this the same place we showed up a week ago? Is this possible? Can these be the same people?" And that oasis, as it springs forth, will not only impact the very spiritual atmosphere and the climate of the region, but it will impact the economy and the politics of the region to really bring about a change.

I can do a tour of America, and every place we've been and had a revival for an extended period of time, the area has changed. When we first went in there, there might not have even been a nice hotel; there might not have been good restaurants, but today, you can go around that church, and whether that church is flowing in revival or not, whether that church is even there today or not, the whole area around it has brand-new developments, new banks, new hotels, and everything is springing up. The fallout of revival to the community is one of blessing and prosperity.

Someone says, "What happened there?" We had a meeting, the power of God fell, and the fallout is like a nuclear blast over the neighborhood and over the whole area. It's just a pity the church didn't receive it. The world received it and they don't even know why they're getting blessed.

CARRIERS OF REVIVAL ARE THE DIFFERENCE

> YOU MAKE THE DIFFERENCE; YOU BRING THE DIFFERENCE. IT GOES WITH YOU. WHEN YOU WALK IN THE DOOR, THE VERY ATMOSPHERE CHANGES.

Revival begins within, stays within, and is contained within the heart of an individual. And a person carrying the fire of revival is going to bring an impact no matter where they go. You can drop them anywhere in the world with nothing and come back three years later and you'll see there's an oasis. They've got a church, a Bible school, a television ministry going out, and they have one of the largest cattle operations. That is what will happen if your mind is open and you're open to the plan and the purpose of God. That's the difference that we make when we carry the fire of God!

Now, if you're a religious person and you're so narrow-minded that you can look through a keyhole with both eyes, you limit God, and you just think it is all about a Sunday-morning, one-hour dry-cleaning service. In by 10 a.m. out by 11 a.m., three hymns, three "hers," take up the offering and preach from the *Encyclopedia Britannica* or the *Reader's Digest*, and then pronounce the last rites and the benediction. Then everybody goes home just as dead as they came! If that's what you're doing, you're not going to impact anything! In fact, whatever is out there is going to impact you!

You make the difference; *you* bring the difference. It goes with *you*. When *you* walk in the door, the very atmosphere changes. When *you* walk in the room, when *you* walk in an area, everything changes, by virtue of who is dwelling on the inside of you. "Greater is He that's in you" (1 John 4:4, paraphrased). Because God is going to use *your* mouth, *your* hands, *your* feet, and it's "out of *your* belly" (see John 7:38), not somebody else's belly.

Now, if your belly will not respond, then God will use another belly. That's why some of us have to have more belly than others—to carry enough supply for others as well! It's not fair that some of us have to carry more of a supply so that others can be nourished and be fed and be blessed.

REVIVAL IS NOW!

> REVIVAL IS A NOW THING AND IT'S A NEW THING.
> IT'S ALWAYS NOW AND IT'S ALWAYS NEW.

Revival is a new thing, it's a now thing and it's always now and it's always new. If it happens today, it's now and it's new. If it happens tomorrow, it's now and it's new. If it's not happening, then it's something that happened in days of old, and all we can do is talk about it, and look at a photograph and think back: *Oh, how wonderful that was. I remember the move of God back in 1919. I was saved and sanctified and filled with the Holy Ghost back in 1920, and then I leaked out in 1921!*

There was one song we sang when I was a little boy in Pentecost—I don't know who wrote it—that goes, "Bring back those happy, those happy days, when the Holy Ghost fell on every face," and it was always singing about the past. Another goes, "When we all get to Heaven, what a day of rejoicing that will be" (Eliza E. Hewitt). So we're either singing about the day when we get to Heaven, or to bring back those happy days!

When you wake up in the morning, *you* determine what kind of day you're going to have, "I'm just going to have a day of revival today! 'This is the day that the Lord has made. I'm going to be glad and rejoice in it' (Psalm 118:24, paraphrased).' I don't care that I've just received three phone calls that are totally adverse!"

THE ANOINTING AFFECTS EVERY AREA OF YOUR LIFE

The Holy Spirit will affect and change every area of your life. When He pours out His anointing, it's fresh rain in your ministry. When the He pours out the anointing, it's fresh rain in your business. It's fresh, it's *fresh*. When the anointing of God comes on you, it'll make you a better father, a better mother, a better housewife, a better parent, a better preacher, a better teacher, a better advocate, attorney, solicitor, CPA, business owner. It makes you a "better" because you have the Holy Ghost; you have the Spirit of God.

You'll be the best vacuum cleaner salesman both sides of the Mississippi! It's fresh bread, fresh oil, new wine, living water! The Bible doesn't say, "Stale bread, rancid oil, vinegar, and swamp water!" No, it's fresh bread, fresh oil, new wine, and living water (see Psalms 92:10; Proverbs 3:10; John 7:38). The psalmist said, "I shall be anointed with fresh oil" (Psalm 92:10).

God says, "I will do a new thing; now it shall spring forth" (Isaiah 43:19). It frustrates me when I get around preachers and they'll sit around discussing and start asking each other, "So, what's God saying? What's God doing?"If you're hooked up with the Holy Ghost, you don't have to ask, "What's God saying? What's God doing?" It amuses me that every time we have crossed over to a new year, if you listen to those preachers, it is as if God was saying something different! It was especially so when we transitioned from 1999 to 2000. Everything was "Y2K," generators, and lima beans.

There were people who had so many beans stored up that the natural gas alone could run a whole city for a week! I saw preachers on television saying, "For your generous love gift this month, we'll send you free and postpaid this new generator along with a twelve-month supply of lima beans. Get your Y2K supplies while they last." And everybody was running around in fear.

Do you know what we did the first week of 2000? My wife, my kids, and I flew to Istanbul Turkey, where Pastor Corey Erman has a River church and Bible school, and we had a week of meetings. There was nobody on the plane because everybody said that at midnight, all the computers would stop and planes would drop out of the sky. So, I said to my wife, "I wonder where we could go in the world that's really a place we shouldn't go. Let's go to Istanbul, Turkey." And we had a great time!

THE ANOINTING IS ALWAYS FRESH

The anointing is always refreshing. Someone says, "But Brother Rodney, I'm tired." It's got nothing to do with how you feel in the natural. We all get tired; we all get worn-out; we all overcommit ourselves from time to time—especially if you're me! I find myself trying to book three days in one day, and then when I get to that day, I think, *Who did this? What idiot booked this?*

I can't get several weeks into one week. I've done that before, and it's not a good thing! But God says, "I will do a new thing" (Isaiah 43:19). God is doing what He's always done, but it's always new. When I see somebody come forward to get saved, it's a new thing. It's new for them. I might be aware of it, but that moment of them getting saved is new. When I see somebody getting healed, it's a new thing. When I see somebody getting delivered, it's a new thing. When I see somebody getting full of the power of God, that's a new thing. It's always new, always fresh. I said this before, that there has never been one time in all these years that I have walked out and seen the move of God and said, "Oh my, not that again! I'm tired of that. Let's do something else." I've never said, "Oh no! Another day of joy and freedom, another day of liberty. If only we could go back to Egypt. Let's hear the crack of the Egyptian whip one more time. Let's spend one more night with the frogs."

YOU MUST FLOW WITH THE HOLY GHOST

> REVIVAL IS WHATEVER THE HOLY GHOST WANTS DONE, WHENEVER HE WANTS IT DONE, THROUGH WHOMEVER HE WANTS IT DONE, AND HOWEVER HE WANTS IT DONE.

Revival is whatever the Holy Ghost wants done, whenever He wants it done, through whomever He wants it done, and however He wants it done. In order to be a part of the new thing, you have to make a decision to be a part of the new thing that God is doing in the earth today, and you have got to humble yourself. Because in order for the new thing to take place, you can't come with any preconceived ideas, and that's very hard. It's easy for people like me, but it's very hard for others who want to have everything planned and mapped out.

It's easy for me because I don't have to have anything planned out. You could leave the next week blank and it wouldn't bother me because something's always going to be happening, and it'll only happen when it happens. Somebody says, "Well, when will you know about it?" When it happens!

When we came to the U.S.A., the Lord spoke to me and He said, "I don't want you to book up in advance." And I said, "Lord, why? Other people do. They book up and you can look at their itinerary and you'll see everywhere they're going to be. I'd like to let people know where I'm going to be." And He said, "If you do that, you're going to miss out on what I'm going to do, because when you go to a city, I'm going to open up another city to you right from that city. But if you are booked up ahead, you won't be able to do it because you've got everything planned out. I want you to trust Me, and I want you to trust Me totally!"

I remember in 1991, we had flown back from Africa and I had one week of meetings—just one week of meetings that I'd set up. When we landed, we did the meetings, and then when they finished, I had a tentative schedule to fly down and go to another city, but the pastor called me at the last minute and canceled the crusade. So I was in the hotel, and at that time, I had my administrator and his wife and kids traveling with me. I had my mom and dad and then myself and my wife and my kids, and we were all in the hotel rooms, just sitting there. I believe it was the Days Inn in upstate New York, just north of Albany, in a place called Clifton Park.

It was Saturday morning, and the crusade had finished Friday night. It was about 11:00 a.m. and the checkout time was 12:00 noon, and my mother called the room. "Where are we going? The cars are packed. Where are we going?" I said, "I don't know yet." She said, "Well, son, check-out is in half-an-hour. Surely we need to know where we're going." I said, "Mom, the guy canceled on me, and I don't know where the Lord wants me to go, but in half-an-hour we'll go somewhere. We're going to go north, south, east, or west. I don't know where yet, but when I know I'll tell you!"

So, I put the phone down and no sooner had I put the phone when it rang and it was a friend of mine from California that God uses prophetically. He said, "Where are you in the world?" So, I told him. He said, "There's a friend of mine who has a church about two hours south of you that you need to go to. I felt led to call you this morning just to tell you to go there." I said, "Well, I don't even know the guy." He said, "It doesn't matter. You call him right now."

I called the guy on the phone and said, "I just had a call from this minister (and I told him who it was), and he said you were two hours south of me, and I've just been up here and had a whole week of meetings." He said, "Yeah, I've heard about you, but we don't really want any guest speakers right now. We've had a lot in lately, and they were not of any help, and I don't particularly want to have a meeting."

I said, "Well, I obviously don't want to come if you don't want me, but this minister just told me to give you a call. I'm about to leave town and I'm heading out, so it'll kind of be now or never, because I probably won't be back in this area. If it doesn't happen now, I'm not coming back."

So, he said to me, "You know, I've never really heard you. I've heard *of* you but never really heard you. I tell you what: you just come down and you do tomorrow morning, and only tomorrow morning. Then, if God moves, you might do tomorrow night, but right now, it'll be tomorrow morning; that's it." So, I said, "Fine," put the phone down, and called my mom and said, "Get in the car; we're heading south!"

The power of God hit Sunday morning. It was like a bomb went off, and we stayed three-and-a-half weeks! Over two-and-a-half thousand people in the Hudson Valley were touched by the power of God.

That's how we conducted our ministry for many, many years. If you look at our calendar today, you'll see very little on there, because we are conducting our ministry in the same way. There are some things at intervals because these are key events that we have to plan. But I just wait on God.

Someone says, "Well, God will tell you." Yes, He will, but He's not going to tell me just because I want to know! Sometimes too, I find that it's better not to tell anybody anything because the less people who know about it, the better it is. Some people have connections with the devil, and then they tell the devil and he finds out what's going on! You don't want to tell too many people because of their connections!

When we were on our 300-city tour in 2019/2020, if we had not followed the Holy Ghost we could have ended up in the midst of a lockdown in a foreign country and unable to come back to the U.S. for possibly months, if not longer. The Holy Ghost has guided us to make 'unscheduled' stops, hold impromptu meetings all by divine appointment. And this is going to become even more critical as we move into these end-times. We can only go where He tells us to go and do what He says to do, when He says to do it. Nothing more, nothing less, and nothing else.

I figured it out this way: I don't know what God has for this year. I know it's going to be better than last year, but I also realize that if I don't know what's going to happen this year, then neither does the devil! And before he knows it, suddenly I'm in a city and there's nothing he can do about it. He doesn't even have time to form a resistance movement!

I talk to preachers who say, "I'm booked up for the next five years," and I think, *Oh, how terrible that must be! What a boring life to be booked up for the next five years. That must be yawn, yawn, snore, snore, boring, boring!*

I'm also booked up—I just haven't made the bookings yet! Someone says, "How can you live like that?" But that's why I'm always having a new thing. Our staff, bless their hearts, are the greatest people of faith, because they just have to follow. And when people say, "What's Pastor doing now?" they answer, "We're not too sure; we'll tell you when we know!" And basically, I don't really know right now. My wife doesn't even ask anymore. She says, "Just give me a few days' notice."

It's a new thing! Fresh! You should not have a stale day. The reason why people never walk in this new thing is because they say, "Well, this is the way we do it around here. This is the way we've done it for years." So, when they cry, "Oh God, give us a new thing," He says, "I can't give it to you. You won't let Me do it."

YOU MUST HUMBLE YOURSELF

THE WAY UP IS THE WAY DOWN. I AM NOTHING. HE IS EVERYTHING

To walk in the new thing, you really have to humble yourself. I've got a great story on humility: I was hunting in the African bush and I was tracking a blue wildebeest. He was a huge brute, a beautiful trophy animal. When you hunt in Africa, you get up right before the sun even gets up. At 5:30 a.m. you have a cup of coffee, grab your rifle, and you're gone so when it's just starting to get light, you are there.

I started walking, and in the bush, there are certain kind of bushes with different kinds of thorns. There's even a bush that in the Afrikaans language is called the "Wait-There-a-Little-Bit Bush," because if you get caught in it, you're going to wait there a little bit. You can pull out of it, but it kind of attaches itself to you. I was tracking this animal and as I was running in between the bushes, the thorns were scratching and my arms were bleeding. Not profusely, but they were scratched. It was hot, and there were the sounds of the African bush, and you don't know what you're going to come up on! You can come up on anything, from something that could eat you, to something that could squash you.

I had probably walked about seventeen miles, and by 3:00 p.m., it was so hot and I was thirsty. I said to the guy who was tracking that I needed a drink. The trackers are so good. They will tell you what animal came through and how long ago he came through. They can pick up the dung and tell you what the animal is and what it ate—unbelievable things!

The tracker told me, "About half a mile up, there is a spring, and you can get some water at the spring." So, I made it over to the spring, and I looked and there was a water hole, but the water hole was dirty because animals came to drink and they relieved themselves all around the edge, I thought, *My God! I can't drink that!* He said, "No, there's a pipe that runs over there and a well that pumps the water out. Just go to the pipe and there is clear water that comes out of the pipe. You don't have to drink from the water hole." So, I went over and I bent down to pick the pipe up and as I lifted the pipe up to bring it to my mouth, the water stopped coming out of it.

I put the pipe down and the water started flowing again. So, I bent lower down, but as I lifted the pipe up, the water stopped. And I heard this in my spirit: *Lower, lower.* Here I am, in the African bush; it's so hot; I'm thirsty, so I kneeled down and lifted the pipe up, but again, it stopped. I put it down, and the moment it was on the ground, the water flowed out. I heard again, *Lower!*

I got on all fours and picked up the pipe, and the moment it was lifted, it stopped. I put it down and it flowed. I heard, *Lower.* So, I lay right down with my face on the ground, and I started drinking from this pure water, and I started to laugh. I laughed and got beside myself, and the tracker said, "What are you laughing at?" I said, "I just got a message: If you want the pure water, you have to go lower. You have to go lower. You have to humble yourself." I didn't want to get dirty. I didn't want to get dirty with the muck. But the only way to get the pure water was to go lower!

You can come to church all dressed up in your suit. You want the new thing that God is doing, but you say, "I'm not going to get messy. I'm not going to get down there." But you are thirsty for that water, and you've been in the bush for so long, and you're tired and your muscles are aching. You need that water, and the only way to get it is to go lower.

You must go lower. You must go *lower*. The power of God fell on me, and I had revival right there in the bush. I never did find that blue wildebeest; he just kept alluding me, but I got a message from Heaven on how to drink the living water!

You must go lower. There's enough to drink; you've just got to find the right place. It's messy around where you drink, but even among all the mess, the pure is right there. You've just got to know how to get to it. People have come to our meetings and said, "This is too messy. We don't like this. This is not dignified." Well, you have to go lower. You just have to go lower. The way up is the way down. I am nothing. He is everything (John 15:5).

You have to determine, "Whatever it takes, I'm going to do it. Whatever I have to do, whatever I have to change, I'm going to do it." Have you ever thought for one moment that God could be leading you in a totally new way? Different from what has been done before, and you don't have to find out the pattern? Just because somebody said, "That's the pattern of doing things," it doesn't mean to say that that's the way God is going to do it.

Back in 1896, the patent office coming out of New York sent out the word to everybody not to bring any new inventions because everything that could be invented had already been invented. Oh, how wrong they were. How wrong they were!

God says, "I will do a new thing" (Isaiah 43:19). Well, what new thing can He do? You have to stay humble to see it; you have to humble yourself. You've got to be willing to change.

CHANGE MUST HAPPEN ON THE INSIDE FIRST

Change happens inside first; then it happens out there. It's inside, then outside. You can change the outside, you can get yourself a toupee, you can have liposuction, you can do all of what needs to be done, but that's not going to change your circumstances.

You can change where you live, you can change the car you drive, change your clothes, and some have changed marriages. But everything is still the same. It's got to happen on the inside. The change must take place on the inside.

I've already mentioned those hidden things of the heart. So many people want the anointing but they don't want to change. They want revival but they want it along with their own agenda. "We don't want revival to mess up our church." And that's not the way things are going to be.

"A way in the wilderness, and rivers in the desert" (Isaiah 43:19). Many are waiting for circumstances to change. However, when it happens on the inside of them, then it's going to happen on the outside of them. Circumstances have to change on the inside before they change on the outside. "Oh, Brother Rodney, I'll be happy when everything changes," but it has to happen on the inside.

THE NEW THING WILL CAUSE UPHEAVAL IN EVERY AREA OF YOUR LIFE

> THE HISTORY BOOKS ARE WAITING TO BE WRITTEN ABOUT A PEOPLE WHO WILL TOTALLY ALLOW REVIVAL TO HAVE ITS WAY IN THEM, AND WHO DO NOT EVEN CONSIDER THE CONSEQUENCES, AS IT MIGHT COST THEM THEIR LIVES.

I'm going to say something now that some people are probably not going to be overjoyed to hear, but if you want this new thing and you want this fresh thing, then you'd better get ready for an upheaval in every area of your life. I'm talking about an upheaval. I'm talking about from one moment to the next you might not even recognize yourself. You'll find yourself in a different city, a different town. I'm talking about a *total* upheaval. If you're ready for that, then you can get ready for the new thing. Otherwise, you'll just keep having the old thing.

Every time I prayed, "Oh, God I want to change," it was an upheaval, and through the upheaval, I was saying, "Lord, what's this?" He'd say, "It's what you've been praying for. I'm positioning you. I'm getting you ready for the next level of what I'm about to do." It's not going to be business as usual, and there's never going to be a dull day, and it's not going to be boring!

If you could predict what's going to happen the next three months, then you're not hanging out with the Holy Ghost! Because He'll surprise you, you'll be shocked; you'll be astounded and you'll be blown away.

That upheaval might start in the area of relationships, which I have mentioned earlier. Some people will be offended and walk away. They don't want to change, and they don't want you to change either. Some associations might change. Some people come around you for the wrong reasons, or with ulterior motives; they are there to take and they are not part of the solution. They are there just because they don't know any other way than "reach out a hand and take." But when revival comes, it's going to strip everything away. It's going to strip away the flesh. It's going to strip away the carnal things, and only that which is of the Spirit of God is going to remain.

It's not the same old, same old, it's a new thing. It's fresh. It's exciting, and there is never a dull moment, and you don't know what God's going to do.

"Well, why doesn't He tell me?"

"Because you wouldn't like it!"

"What's He doing now? He's ruining my life."

"No! Haven't you asked Him for change? Haven't you prayed for change? Well then, trust Him that He knows what He's doing!"

Trust Him that He'll bring you out. Abraham was wondering when

God told him to leave his country and go out. He didn't even know where he was going. God didn't tell him where to go. Abraham was looking for a city "whose builder and maker is God" (Hebrews 11:10). And we are to have the faith of our father Abraham to just step out and to boldly do what God's told us to do, to boldly go where no man has gone before, to brave new frontiers.

The history books are waiting to be written about a people who will totally allow revival to have its way in them, and who do not even consider the consequences and it might cost them their lives. In other words, you counted the cost before you even went into it. "If this takes everything I've got, I'm in, boots and all! I'm in with both feet, and wild horses couldn't drag me away. I'm not going to stop until the day I stand before God, and I hear these words: 'Well done, thou good and faithful servant'" (Matthew 25:21).

A new thing, a new thing! That new thing might cause great persecution. That new thing might cause great upheaval, but rejoice! Measure how that new thing is going by how much persecution you are receiving. If you're not being persecuted, you are probably still holding onto the old thing! (And I'm not talking about your husband or wife now!)

A NEW THING IN YOU, A NEW THING THROUGH YOU

It's new; it's fresh; it springs forth! You might feel that you are in a desert, but God can make you an oasis. God wants to do a new thing. "Behold. I make all things new" (Revelation 21:5). The Lord says it will spring forth. It's going to *spring* forth, you won't have to force it and you won't have to try to make it happen. It's going to *spring* forth and you don't have to help a spring. What God has for you is a thousand times more!

It's not going to be the "old donut" anymore. No more licking the sugar on the outside and reminiscing about the donut and when it used to be fresh. God says, "I'm doing a new thing." Blessed be the name of the Lord.

Remember: when Jesus was around people, they went "walking, and leaping, and praising God" (Acts 3:8). Why? Because of the new thing.

It springs forth. "Out of your innermost belly will flow rivers of living water" (John 7:38, paraphrased). *Rivers* of living water! It's only as you allow God to do the new thing *in* you that He can do the new thing *through* you. The new thing cannot happen out there till it happens in you.

If God doesn't do a work in you, then how is He going to do the new thing? God's operating table is on the floor of many of our meetings. I know some people see what happens in our meetings and they think it is just craziness, but they can't see what the Lord's doing on the inside. They can only see what's happening on the outside. People have walked out of our meetings and you meet them a year, two years, or three years later, and they'll tell you:

"I started a new ministry, and God's used me around the world."

"I started a new company. It's exploded."

"Ever since that day that the fire of God hit me and I ran around the building, everything broke loose."

God does it differently in everybody. It's a new thing, but only the humble shall drink.

14

THE LAST-DAY MOVE OF GOD

Great Joy in the City

Let's look at two passages of Scripture. Firstly, Acts 2:12–17:

> And all were beside themselves with amazement and were puzzled and bewildered, saying one to another, What can this mean? But others made a joke of it and derisively said, They are simply drunk and full of sweet [intoxicating] wine. But Peter, standing with the eleven, raised his voice and addressed them: You Jews and all you residents of Jerusalem, let this be [explained] to you so that you will know and understand; listen closely to what I have to say. For these men are not drunk, as you imagine, for it is [only] the third hour (about 9:00 a.m.) of the day; but [instead] this is [the beginning of] what was spoken through the prophet Joel: And it shall come to pass in the last days, God declares, that I will pour out of My Spirit upon all mankind.
>
> VV. 12-17 AMPC

I feel that this scripture really describes the reaction to the move of God. The multitude were all beside themselves with amazement and were puzzled and were saying one to another, "What can this mean?"

Secondly, Acts 8:4–8:

> Now those who were scattered abroad went about [through the land from place to place] preaching the glad tidings, the Word [the doctrine concerning the attainment through Christ of salvation in the kingdom of God]. Philip [the deacon, not the apostle] went down to the city of Samaria and proclaimed the Christ (the Messiah) to them [the people]; And great crowds of people with one accord listened to and heeded what was said by Philip, as they heard him and watched the miracles and wonders which he kept performing [from time to time]. For foul spirits came out of many who were possessed by them, screaming and shouting with a loud voice, and many who were suffering from palsy or were crippled were restored to health. And there was great rejoicing in that city.

REVIVAL IS NOISY

> THERE IS NO SUCH THING AS A QUIET REVIVAL.

There was great joy in the city! There was great *joy.* There is no such thing as a quiet revival. There has never been a quiet revival because even if it happened, you would never hear about it. A revival is noised abroad. When there's great joy in the city, everyone is going to know about it.

The great joy that you see in our meetings has been happening on a continual basis since April, 1989. We had been praying and crying out for God to move. We were desperate. All it takes is one person desperate for the things of God—and we were invited to a church in upstate New York, a little town called Clifton Park.

The pastor said to me, "I want you to come in and conduct a series of meetings and start Sunday morning and then go Sunday night all the way through Friday night, but," he said, "I want you to have morning services during the daytime as well." I was shocked and surprised because I'd never heard of any pastor in America who wanted to have two meetings a day. At that time, it was really hard for us to have an extended meeting. We wanted to have meetings Sunday morning, Sunday night, and then do Monday, Tuesday, and Wednesday nights, but they usually didn't want us to have a Monday night meeting because at that time, I didn't know about Monday night football in America and how people like to stay home and watch football on a Monday night.

But this pastor said, "I want you to run Sunday through Friday night and then do the morning services during the week." When I heard that, I nearly dropped the phone, I was in a state of shock. I thought, *I believe something's going to happen this week!* He said to me, "What will you be speaking on in the morning time?" And it was quickened to me by the Holy Ghost to speak along the lines of the subject of the anointing.

Now, every place that we go into, I always dedicate the Sunday mornings to sharing my testimony of how the Lord touched me with the fire of God in July, 1979, and I was hit by the power of God and was drunk in the Holy Ghost for three-and-a-half days. And every time I would share along those lines, the power of God would be poured out and the manifestation of the power of God that was poured out was glorious. But that was only really when I shared my testimony. Then Sunday night, Monday night, Tuesday night, Wednesday night, God would move in a limited way. So now, this was the first time ever that we were having morning services and I was speaking on the subject of the anointing. The church had about 250 members, and on Monday morning, I was surprised when sixty people showed up.

That might not sound like a lot of people to you, but back in those days, sixty people on a Monday morning was sixty more than we'd ever had before. Tuesday morning, a hundred people showed up, and I said to my wife, "Something's happening!" One hundred of the 250 members showed up on a Tuesday morning. These people were hungry, and I knew God was going to move in a supernatural way.

I was preaching from the book of Luke 4:

> And Jesus returned in the power of the Spirit into Galilee: and there went out a fame of him throughout all the region round about. And he taught in their synagogues, being glorified of all. And he came to Nazareth where he had been brought up: and, as his custom was, he went to the synagogue on the sabbath day, and stood up for to read. And there was delivered unto him the book of the prophet Esaias. And when he had opened the book, he found the place it was written, The Spirit of the Lord is upon me, because he hath anointed me to preach the gospel to the poor; he hath sent me to heal the brokenhearted, to preach deliverance to the captives, and recovering of sight to the blind, to set at liberty them that are bruised, to preach the acceptable year of the Lord.
>
> VV. 14–19

I was just minding my own business, reading the scripture, and the very atmosphere of the room suddenly changed. It felt like the room became electrically charged—it felt like angels of God were walking among us—the air was holy. And while I was speaking, people got hit in their seats. Some were weeping; some were shaking; others were laughing uncontrollably with great joy. Some were falling out of their seat. And as a minister who's used to public speaking, that takes a lot of getting used to, because if people do not keep totally quiet, you can't concentrate on your train of thought.

It is so distracting when you're trying to preach and there's a noise and you have to preach above the noise of the crowd. The only reason I'm able to do it nowadays is because I've spent many years practicing in revival services around the world. And for the most part, I can now pretty much hold it together—somebody has to be the Rock of Gibraltar in the middle of the storm! So no matter what happens in the meetings, I can keep looking and watching. I'll be the one in that meeting who will keep it together.

The glory of the Lord filled the house, and the power of the Lord was made manifest. And what broke out that Tuesday morning service in April, 1989, started off like a little stream, but it grew and grew and grew. And now, it has spread to the nations of the world.

THE HOLY SPIRIT FALLS UPON ALL FLESH

> THERE'S NO SUCH THING AS BEING CONSERVATIVE WHEN THE FIRE OF GOD GETS ON YOU; EVERYTHING'S GOING TO CHANGE.

People told me back then that it would blow over, and they were right—it's blown over the whole world! You can't stop the wind of the Holy Ghost. Preachers have blocked the wind, but it just blows somewhere else. But I don't want it to go somewhere else, I want it to breathe right here, "like a mighty rushing wind" (Acts 2:2 ESV). That's the Book of Acts. "This is that which was spoken by the prophet Joel. And it shall come to pass in the last days, saith God, I will pour out of my Spirit upon all flesh" (Acts 2:16–17). "All flesh" means *all* flesh because that's what all flesh means. That means Scottish flesh, Norwegian flesh, Finnish flesh, Dutch flesh, American flesh, African flesh, African American flesh, Turkish flesh.

Philip went and preached Christ, and there was great joy (Acts 8:5–8). The passage does not say there was little joy. It does not say they just smiled at one another. It says there was *great* joy in the city. Great joy. "I bring you good tidings of great joy" (Luke 2:10). Joy! It's that walking and leaping and praising God kind of joy. I'm talking about your head anointed with oil and your cup running over joy (see Psalms 23:5). I'm talking about beside yourself joy.

That's why the multitude were amazed and bewildered. That's why they were wondering because the disciples looked like they were drunk, and Peter said, "These are not drunk, as you suppose" (Acts 2:15 NKJV). They were drunk, just not as you suppose. At nine o'clock in the morning, the glory of God was made manifest.

God is pouring out blessings that cannot be contained. He's already doing it. There's no such thing as being conservative when the fire of God gets on you; everything's going to change. Don't just sit and watch it. When the Spirit of God falls, respond to the Spirit of God. This is not made-up. If this was just something that we made happen, don't you think that I would be tired of it by now from April, 1989? No, it's real, God is still touching people and people are being born every minute who need a touch. But as many as are born, a skeptic is among them, and they have offspring!

God is still pouring out His Spirit on all flesh, He has never stopped. No matter what people in the Church say, He has never stopped pouring out His Spirit upon all flesh.

Somebody says, "Well, you couldn't pay me to behave like I was drunk." When the Holy Ghost touches you, you'll do it for free!

This anointing is to set the captives free. This anointing is to bind up broken hearts. This anointing is to heal and deliver. But you can't have the way of the world or the things of the world, *and* have the anointing.

Someone says, "Is it really necessary, all this excess joy?" Well, that's what happened the Day of Pentecost. So, if you have a problem with that, then you really need to go talk to the Head of the Church of the Lord Jesus Christ, because He told the disciples to go tarry at Jerusalem until they had been endued with power (Luke 24:49). Then on the Day of Pentecost, the wind came, the fire fell and the devils trembled in the pits of hell.

That's why the devil hates this Pentecostal revival. He hates it; he can't stand it. He does everything he can to try to stop it. He mocks it, he stirs up the people against it and they make up lies about it. But you can't stop the flood of the Holy Ghost; you *cannot* stop it. "There was great joy in that city" (Acts 8:8). And the best is yet to come. Blessed be the name of the Lord!

15

REVIVAL SIGNS AND WONDERS

Getting Man's Attention

WHEN GOD POURS OUT HIS SPIRIT, IT IS IMPORTANT TO REALIZE THAT IN ORDER TO GET MAN'S ATTENTION, GOD MOVES WITH SIGNS AND WONDERS. THEN NO ONE CAN DENY THAT HE'S IN THE HOUSE.

Revival signs and wonders are very important because that's how the Church started. If God started the Church a certain way, then that means that's what He wants. The Bible tells us in Acts 2:1–4, "And when the day of Pentecost was fully come, they were all with one accord in one place. And suddenly there came a sound from heaven as of a rushing mighty wind, and it filled all the house where they were sitting. And there appeared unto them cloven tongues like as of fire, and it sat upon each of them. And they were all filled with the Holy Ghost, and began to speak with other tongues, as the Spirit gave them utterance."

Acts 2:6 begins, "Now when this was noised abroad," and as I said before, there has never been on record a quiet revival. The Bible says, "The multitude came together, and they were astonished and bewildered" (vv. 6b–7, paraphrased). God comes as signs and wonders.

When you look at it, you say, "I wonder what that is." People walk into my meetings and say, "Well, I've never seen this before." If you had walked in the Upper Room that Day of Pentecost, you would have never seen that before either.

So when God pours out His Spirit, it is important to realize that in order to get man's attention, God moves with signs and wonders. Then, no one can deny that He's in the house.

When you come into God's presence, God will touch you, and when you leave, you'll know that He's alive. You're not going to go to a place where God is supposed to be and He didn't even show up—or if He did, it was for a minute.

The Bible says, "Now when this was noised abroad, the multitude came together, and were confounded, because that every man heard them speak in his own language. And they were all amazed and marvelled" (Acts 2:6–7). When God moves, you get amazed and you marvel!

Now look at Acts 2:12 (AMPC): "And all were beside themselves with amazement and were puzzled and bewildered, saying one to another, What can this mean?" If you come into one of our meetings and the power of God hits the place, you might ask, "What does this mean?"

But the Bible goes on to say in Acts 2:13–15 that Peter stood up with the eleven to explain, because some joked about it and some derisively said that they were simply drunk and full of intoxicating wine.

When you come to our conferences and campmeetings, or go to a series of meetings, you get filled up to the top, and then there's just a little splash and it runs over the side. The psalmist says, "You anoint my head with oil; my [brimming] cup runs over" (Psalm 23:5 AMPC). So, you see a manifestation of a cup that's running over.

There are people who don't even have a cup—their cup was stolen. They have to get a new cup so that God can begin to fill it up. But that's one thing about the Lord: He knows how to fill your cup. He knows how to fill it to the top, and He knows how to fill it to running over.

Peter heard what the people said about them being drunk, and he stood up "with the eleven, raised his voice and addressed them: You Jews and all you residents of Jerusalem, let this be [explained] to you so that you will know and understand; listen closely to what I have to say. For these men are not drunk, as you imagine, for it is [only] the third hour (about 9:00 a.m.) of the day" (Acts 2:14–15 AMPC).

DRUNK, BUT NOT AS YOU SUPPOSE

They were still drunk, just not as you imagined. Now, you can sit in my meetings and just watch, or you can sit and drink, because there's living water for every single person and there is new wine for every single person.

I've had people tell me, "I don't need this," but then they go home to pop pills! They say, "I don't need this," but then they go to see their psychiatrist next week; "I don't need this," but then they need some shock treatment; "I don't need this," but then they need some more methadone; "I don't need this," but then they need Prozac; "I don't need this," but then they need Zoloft.

A touch from God is God's psychiatry. Peter said, "For these are not drunken, as ye suppose, seeing it is but the third hour of the day. But this is that which was spoken by the prophet Joel; And it shall come to pass in the last days, saith God . . ." (Acts 2:15–17). The Amplified Classic Edition says, "This is [the beginning of] what was spoken through the prophet Joel. "He didn't say this was the end; we are not of them that are called "cessationists," who believe that everything stopped with the last apostle. We don't believe that, we believe the Bible. We believe what the Word of God declares: that Jesus Christ is the same yesterday, today, and forever (Hebrews 13:8). If this was good for the early Church, then it is good for the latter Church.

EVERYONE NEEDS THIS POWER TODAY

> THE PRESENCE OF GOD IS IMPORTANT. YOU CANNOT MAKE IT THROUGH THIS YEAR WITHOUT THE POWER OF GOD AND WITHOUT THE PRESENCE OF GOD.

This Upper Room meeting was designed by Jesus, the Head of the Church. We, the latter Church, need it just as much as the early Church needed it and you can try and make all the excuses you want to.

Don't come to my meetings Sunday after Sunday and sit like a bump on a log when everything is available to you. Imagine going to a restaurant week after week but you don't eat any of the food; you just sit there and listen to the music, but you don't eat anything and you don't drink anything. Are you on an extended spiritual fast? Have you now risen to the place where you've attained it and it is beneath you now? The presence of God is important. You cannot make it through this year without the power of God and without the presence of God. I don't care who you are, I don't care how educated you are, I don't care what your social standing in life is.

Every single man, woman, boy, and girl needs God's presence, needs the Holy Spirit, and needs to be filled with the Spirit of God. That's not even negotiable. I don't care if your grandfather was Smith Wigglesworth. I don't care if your great-grandfather was the Apostle Paul. You need the Holy Spirit, and you need His presence in your life. You have to enter in. You can sit and watch or you can enter in. You can sit, watch, and nod your head, "That's right, Pastor, that's right. Amen." You can raise your hands, but it's about entering in; it's about yielding. It's about letting the Lord come and do what He wants to do.

Peter said, "This is the beginning of what was spoken through Joel, that it shall come to pass in the last days, saith God, 'that I will pour out my spirit upon all flesh'" (Acts 2:16–17 paraphrased). All flesh means ALL flesh. This is God speaking through the prophet Joel. Somebody says, "This is an option." Yes it is, but you have to make a choice: You can either live the low life or you can live the high life, and God's plan is for everyone to live the high life.

SOUL-WINNERS ARE THE BIGGEST DRINKERS

> YOU CAN MEASURE THE NUMBER OF SOULS COMING IN THAT YOU BRING TO THE LORD BY THE AMOUNT OF SPIRITUAL DRINK YOU'RE DRINKING.

Pastors Eric and Jennifer Gonyon would be the first to tell you that everyone who is a soul-winner has been touched by the fire of the Holy Ghost because Jesus said, "You're going to receive power to be witnesses" (see Acts 1:8). We watch people on fire and they are winning people to the Lord. The moment they stop winning people to the Lord, you know that they leaked out; you know that they stopped drinking. The biggest soul-winners are the biggest drinkers. That's a fact. You can measure the number of souls that you bring to the Lord by the amount of spiritual drink you're drinking. If you win just one person to the Lord every now and then, you probably just have a little sip. You open the wine and smell it, but that's all you do. But when you get full of the new wine, you can't help yourself. You become a blabbermouth and you have to tell.

Someone says, "I'll get somebody else to do it." Don't get somebody else to do your job. At The River Church and River University, we are training people to win the harvest and bring in the harvest, but *I'm* personally winning the harvest. *I'm* out there behind the scenes, winning the harvest.

GOD IS A GOD OF SIGNS, WONDERS AND MIRACLES

When the Holy Spirit came, He came with supernatural power to the Church. That supernatural power gives us the ability to be witnesses unto Him in Jerusalem, Judea, Samaria, and to the uttermost parts of the earth (Acts 1:8). In Tampa, Brandon, Sarasota, the Keys, and Grenada, and it just keeps going and heading out. Supernatural power, supernatural gifts, supernatural wisdom, supernatural prayer, supernatural guidance, everything supernatural!

Jesus' ministry was a supernatural ministry that had signs and wonders and miracles, and I don't believe it's coincidental that the first miracle He did was when he turned water into wine. And He's still going around turning water into wine, because the Word of God is the water, and if you drink enough of that, He'll come and turn your water to wine. Supernatural blessing, supernatural provision, all of God's supernatural abilities are available to every single one of us. That's why He said, "I'm not leaving you alone; I'm not leaving you comfortless. I'm going to come to you . . . These works shall ye do and greater works than these shall ye do, because I go to My Father" (John 14:18; 14:12 paraphrased).

REVIVALS ARE ALWAYS REVIVALS OF THE SUPERNATURAL

WE HAVE TO CONTEND FOR THE SUPERNATURAL.

From Genesis to Revelation, the Bible is a supernatural book. The twenty-first century must flow in the power of God because there are generations of people who have never seen the power of God. They wouldn't even know that God moved in that way.

Every revival of the past of any notability was a revival of the supernatural. If we just go back over the last few hundred years, from Finney, Wesley, Cartwright, Edwards to the Cane Ridge revival in Kentucky; the Welsh revival in 1904; the revival in Topeka, Kansas, 1905; the Azusa Street revival, 1906; the healing revival of 1947–48 through the 1950s, they were all revivals of the supernatural. They were all revivals of signs and wonders.

We have to contend for the supernatural. If we don't, others are not going to do it. We *must* do it. We must contend for the supernatural because signs and wonders are for *today*. People getting saved, healed, delivered, receiving the baptism in the Holy Ghost, operating in the gifts of the Spirit, and people falling under the power—it's for today! The supernatural where people go into trances (and that is scriptural—Acts 10), see visions, have dreams, are overcome, weep uncontrollably under the power of God and are filled with joy unspeakable. And if the noise of the joy bothers you, what are you going to do when you get to Heaven? Look for a quiet place? No, it's, "Well done, thou good and faithful servant. . . . Enter thou into the JOY of thy lord" (Matthew 25:21, emphasis added).

EXPECT TO SEE SIGNS AND WONDERS

When the glory of God, the wind and fire, the wind of the Holy Spirit, the fire of the Holy Spirit comes, we *expect* to see signs. Everywhere we go, I preach the Word and I expect to see signs. I expect God to confirm His Word with signs and wonders. It's not about me doing something; I'm just the vessel that brings the Good News. But behind the message of Good News are always signs following: "And these signs shall follow them that believe; in my name shall they cast out devils; they shall speak with new tongues; they shall take up serpents; and if they drink any deadly thing, it shall not hurt them; they shall lay hands on the sick, and they shall recover" (Mark 16:17–18). The Bible says, "And they went forth, and preached every where, the Lord working with them, and confirming the word with signs following" (Mark 16:20).

Acts 8 says Philip, who at that time was a deacon, went down to Samaria and preached Christ unto them, and there was great *joy* in the city. The whole city heard because unclean spirits came out, crying with a loud voice. People were set free; people were healed; people were delivered. If Philip, the deacon, needed the power of the Holy Ghost, then you and I in this day, and this hour that we're living in, need the power of the Holy Ghost! And not just once or twice at a campmeeting, not just at some ministry retreat or some special camp that is being held, but *every time* we get together, we should come with an expectation of God's presence and what He's going to do.

There are new people coming in all the time who need a touch from God. Somebody could be there with a terminal disease that needs a breakthrough, but because we don't contend for the supernatural, there's no balm in Gilead for them (Jeremiah 8:22). Someone has got to stick their neck out. Somebody, even in the face of persecution, regardless of what's said about them, has to stick their neck out and believe God for the supernatural.

The power of God's falling right now as you are reading this. Your miracle can happen *now*; your touch can happen *now*, because the Word of God is going forth, and God confirms His Word with signs and wonders following.

You are people of signs and wonders, because Jesus said, "These signs shall follow them that believe" (Mark 16:17). So, wherever you go, these signs shall be following you. Everywhere you go, in your workplace, in your home, in your car driving down the road, you're going to have the power of God.

We had a dear lady who came from Lakeland to one of our meetings at The River, and she said she got so hit by the power of God that when she and her friends left the meeting and were driving home, they suddenly found themselves going in the opposite direction.

So, they turned around and came back to stop at a gas station. They pulled in and it was around 1.00 a.m. or 2.00 a.m., and they were laughing, beside themselves. The guy at the gas station said, "Where have you been?" and they said, "We've been to church," and he disbelievingly said, "Yeah, right! You've been to church?" She said that what was supposed to be a 40 minute drive home became over a three-hour drive home! They were besides themselves.

You could come with depression, but in the presence of the Lord, you're not leaving with depression. You could come with a burden, but you're not leaving with a burden, because anything can happen and probably will. But you come with the expectation; you come because we are looking unto Him; you come to receive from Him. It's His goodness, His grace, His mercy, His love, it's His kindness to pour it out on us.

HE GIVES ABUNDANT LIFE

> JESUS WILL NEVER LET YOU DOWN, AND YOU'LL NEVER HAVE A LOSING SEASON WITH HIM. BECAUSE WITH JESUS, YOU'RE ALWAYS GOING TO THE PLAYOFFS AND YOU'RE ALWAYS GOING TO THE BOWL. IT'S ABUNDANT LIFE!

Even when we really shouldn't even get it, He still comes and He opens up the blessing, and He pours it on us. The rain of Heaven—His goodness and His grace comes down, because He loves you so much. He loves you too much.

Religion will stop you from getting the "too much." Tradition will stop you from getting the "too much." Jesus comes and He gives you more abundantly. "The thief cometh not, but for to steal, and to kill, and to destroy: I am come that they might have life, and that they might have it more abundantly" (John 10:10). Abundant life! Abundant life! Too much life! Somebody says, "How are you doing?" You reply, "Too much life!"

You have to jump in the river of God. Don't sit with your toe in and then pull it out. Somebody needs to throw you in upside down. What are you trying to protect? It's about opening your hearts. There are people who think that those who get touched by God don't have much, and the elevator doesn't go all the way to the top floor. They are a hamburger short of a Happy Meal, or the lights are on but nobody's home! But no, there are people with extremely high mental ability and capacity who receive a touch from God because they've just opened their hearts to get what God has. No matter how big your head is, you have to open your heart. You can have a big head and a little tiny heart. But God wants to give you a big heart to receive what He wants to do with you and through you, because He wants to give you abundant life, too much life.

We've had all sorts of people coming to our meetings. We had a captain of a US aircraft carrier, and he ended up on the floor. We had one of the leading brain surgeons in America fall under the power of God. We had somebody from NASA come and the power of God hit him, but you don't have to be a captain or a brain surgeon or a rocket scientist to receive from God. You can be an ordinary person. We have had attorneys and doctors in our meetings, but you don't have to be an attorney or a doctor of medicine to receive because God's not just giving His power to educated people.

We had a lady come to our meetings who is an ordained Presbyterian minister who had a church in California of over a thousand people, but then God visited her with the baptism the Holy Ghost and sent her to Haiti, where she built many churches all over the country. She's not crazy. Somebody says, "She must be drunk, then." Well, she is not drunk but not as you suppose. She's just very, very filled with the Holy Ghost!

I am talking about receiving heavenly things, and we should get excited. When somebody gets handed the keys to a new car or expensive gift, they don't stand there passively and say in a monotone voice, "Thank you very much." So, if we get excited about the natural things, what about spiritual things? I'm talking about grabbing hold of the things of God in Heaven! I'm talking about getting excited about Jesus and how awesome He is.

And don't use the excuse of it being a cultural thing, because we've traveled to over 90 countries in the world (at the time of this book), and I've seen Japanese excited about Jesus, Koreans excited about Jesus, Dutch excited about Jesus. And I know Americans have the ability to get excited about Jesus, because I watch them at the football matches and see how excited they can get. But I tell you that Jesus will never let you down and you'll never have a losing season with Him. Because with Jesus, you're always going to the playoffs and you're always going to the Bowl. It's abundant life! It's too much life!

16

THE END-TIME, LAST-DAY, MOVE OF GOD

The Upper and the Lower Springs

I feel led of the Lord to close this book by looking at two aspects of the end-time move of God. I'm going to start with the first one now, and then we'll cover part two later in the chapter. This is a prophetic message that I originally preached in 2005 about what is to come.

We've dealt with how to have revival, we've talked about revivals of the past, we've talked about what the Lord has done, but let me project ahead in the Spirit and talk to you about what is about to come on the earth. And I want to talk to you about two aspects of it. The first is going to be the end-time financing of the Kingdom of God, and the second will be the end-time move of God.

1. THE END-TIME FINANCING OF THE KINGDOM OF GOD

About nineteen years ago, I believe it was in February, 2003, the Lord laid on my heart to bring a message that was not really original to me. Most of my messages the Lord will drop in my spirit, and He will give me a phrase or something, and it will come in my spirit. But I had spent a lot of time with Brother Reinhard Bonnke the previous December and had traveled with him in November to the nation of Nigeria. And that really grabbed ahold of me because if you've never stood in a crowd of 750,000 people at one time, you have no concept of it.

I'm not talking about 750,000 people "evang-elastic-ally," speaking! They map the field out and all the poles are spaced and that's how they counted the crowd. It was the same man who counted the crowd for us in the crusade we had, so we knew, to almost within 5,000 people, how many we had there. In fact, on the last night, he said we conservatively had 115,000, but, he said, "Pastor, it could have been closer to 130,000." Because there's a way of measuring the field, and when you walk, you gauge the density per square meter or yard, and it was up to nine people in some places! They were packed like sardines!

One night at this crusade with Brother Reinhard, I believe, it was in Obumushu, Nigeria, there were people as far as the eye could see. I was sitting on the platform, and I said, "I want to go see what it's like at the back of the field." So, I just left the platform and walked through the crowd. It took me forty-five minutes to get to the back of the field, and when I turned around, the platform looked about one-foot wide and I could not even see Brother Reinhard standing there. I could hear the voice but could see no man. I thought it was biblical, hearing a voice and seeing no man!

Then, it took me about another forty-five minutes to get back through the crowd. In fact, I took a wrong direction. Somebody says, "What do you mean? Couldn't you see the platform?" I took the direction I thought would get me back to the platform, but it took me into an area that was so dense with people that I could not move. I was blocked everywhere. In between the people, the children were lying, sleeping on the floor. So, I had to backtrack twenty minutes and then come around another way. I'm talking about people as far as the eye could see.

Brother Reinhard and I would have lunch together every day and we would talk about the finances and what it takes to conduct a revival of that magnitude. And I know that there are some people who don't believe in mass crusade evangelism, but we do one-on-one evangelism *and* mass crusade evangelism. Thank God for all the others who are winning the harvest and bringing the harvest in. However, it would be great if everybody was winning thousands to the Lord every year, but they're not. The fact of the matter is, some might only win ten in a year.

If you are a River member, your numbers will be much higher than the average person because we train people to go and win the harvest and bring the harvest in. If you hang around Pastors Eric and Jennifer Gonyon, you'll know. If Pastor Jennifer goes through a drive-through, by the time she's given the order to the time she's collected the hamburgers, the guy is born-again, baptized in the Holy Ghost, and is sowing an offering back in the ministry and has actually enrolled in the first year of Bible school!

But not everybody is going to do one-on-one evangelism. Neither is everybody going to do mass crusade evangelism, but everybody can be a part of the Gospel. And people have asked me, "What would you do if you weren't called to preach?" I would be in business, which I am right now anyway, but I would be in business, making as much money as I could, to fund the end-time harvest. I want to be a part of sharing the eternal harvest on that day when I stand before the Lord. I do not want to get to Heaven and find out that there was more that I could have done, but because I was lazy, I didn't do it.

THE GOSPEL IS FREE, BUT IT COSTS MONEY TO GET THE JOB DONE

It all comes down to the talents (see Matthew 25:14–30). To the one, God gives one talent, to the other He gives three, and to other He gives five, and we are to multiply what God has entrusted to us. Somebody's got to go, but somebody also has to fund it.

Something that really struck me was Brother Reinhard was talking to me about the very first time he was in Lesotho, which is a kingdom nation inside the borders of southern Africa. He was there as a missionary, and he would start out on the streets, playing an accordion. We call them squash boxes—as long as you keep squashing them, they keep making a sound. This is how it is in Africa: if you have a guitar or accordion, and you stand in the middle of the street and just squash the box and sing, crowds come. Before you know it, twenty minutes later, you have a hundred people, and then you start preaching. That's how I learned to preach in the foothills of the Transkei.

And later on, in the first year of ministry, I went right in the middle of Hillbrow, which was at that time the most densely populated square mile in the world. We would preach in a place called High Point. Motorbike gangs would try to ride over us; they would bring the bike ride onto the sidewalk and buzz it right by while we were standing there, proclaiming the Good News—if you can't preach on the street, don't try to get in the pulpit.

Somebody says, "I don't have a place to preach." Then something is seriously wrong with you! Are you blind? Someone says, "I feel called to ministry but I just don't have a place to preach." There are places to preach everywhere you go! I don't know how many of our members at The River Church have gone into a restaurant and grabbed the microphone, and asked the manager, "Can we just pray for the troops?" Everybody wants to pray for the troops, so they all bow their head—250 people in the restaurant praying for the troops, and then the River member says, "While your head is bowed, if you don't know Jesus, then make Him your Lord today; ask Him into your life. Say, 'Jesus, come into my heart.'" So, at the restaurant, 250 people make Jesus Lord of their life.

You may say, "Well, those kind of people are not in my church." Thank God! Because if they went to your church; they probably wouldn't win souls!

So when Brother Reinhard and I were talking, he spoke about the struggle he had financially. The rent on his office space was R50 (ZAR), or £50 at that time. Just R50, but he was walking through, praying over that R50 like it was a million dollars and crying out to God, "Where is the R50 I need? I have got to pay it." And then he said to the Lord, "Is this how it is going to be for the rest of my life? I'm going to have to fight and wrestle in prayer over R50?"

Because when you go out on the field, the first thing to realize is that it is going to cost you money. Nothing is free. The Gospel is free, but it costs money to get the job done. Somebody is going to have to pay the bill.

Everyone has heard about Charles Grandison Finney, but what you didn't know is that Charles Finney had some crusades that were paid for by two brothers, named the Tappan brothers. They owned a publishing company in New York, and they came to him and said, "All your crusades will be funded by us. Don't you worry about it," and they paid for all the buildings and rented everything.

Not everybody knows about the Tappan brothers—of course, now they do, because I'm talking about them! But nobody at that time knew about the Tappan brothers; they only knew about Finney, but when you get to Heaven, the Tappan brothers will share in the harvest, along with Charles Finney.

GIVE WITHOUT STRINGS ATTACHED

But any funding must be given without strings attached. I have a problem when people with means want to give money and they always want to dictate where the vision is going, and how the vision is going to go. People should go where the anointing is and say, "I'll lay my treasure here; you do with it whatever God tells you to do," and not try to dictate the vision!

If God has called you in an area of business, then that's your vision—to make money. But don't come and tell me what my vision is, and don't come and tell me how to win souls—because I know how to win souls! Just come and lay your treasure down and say, "Do it!" And don't do it with any strings attached, because I'm not attachable. I'm very detachable!

So Brother Reinhard said to the Lord, "Is this how it's going to be done from now on?" And the Lord spoke to him and said, "No! In the last days, things will change."

THE UPPER AND THE LOWER SPRINGS

> THE LORD SAID, "THE UPPER SPRINGS ARE THE FINANCES, AND THE LOWER SPRINGS ARE THE ANOINTING, AND IN THE LAST DAYS, THE TWO SPRINGS WILL COME TOGETHER. THE TWO STREAMS WILL COME TOGETHER, AND THERE WILL BE A FLOOD." AND THAT FLOOD IS GOING TO BE THE EMPOWERMENT FOR THE END-TIME HARVEST.

God gave him a passage of Scripture out of the Book of Judges: "And Othniel the son of Kenaz, Caleb's younger brother, took it: and he gave him Achsah his daughter to wife. And it came to pass, when she came to him, that she moved him to ask of her father a field" (vv. 13–14a). So Achsah was getting married, and she asked her dad for a field. When we are working in the ministry, we are working in a field—the mission field, or you could call it a vineyard.

The passage continues, "And she lighted from off her ass; and Caleb said unto her, What wilt thou? And she said unto him, Give me a blessing: for thou hast given me a south land; give me also springs of water. And Caleb gave her the upper springs and the nether springs" (vv. 14b-16). So, she talked about two areas of water that she wanted: she wanted the upper and the lower springs.

The lower springs are not evident. Did you know that the whole of Florida has water right under it, and it's not that far down? Sometimes it is just a foot or two feet underneath but you can't see it. However, the first rains will bring the water table right up, and that's why everything gets swamped.

There are other parts of the country where it can rain and rain and everything sinks away and there is never a problem, but not in Florida! We are low-lying, and the water table is up high. You could be walking along and not know that there's water one foot below you—there's a spring underneath—the lower springs.

And then there are the upper springs. Achsah said, "You've given me the field, but give me the upper and the lower springs."

The Lord spoke to Brother Reinhard and said: "The upper springs are the finances, and the lower springs are the anointing, and in the last days, the two springs will come together, and there will be a flood." And that flood is going to be the empowerment for the end-time harvest.

I believe, and I prophesy, that we stand on the brink of the two streams coming together—all the anointings have been released. The Lord said to me, "All the end-time anointings for the last-day move of God have been released in the earth, but the finances have not been released like they are supposed to be released." God wants to empower His people. God wants to empower every single person reading this with the supernatural ability to get the job done.

THE ANOINTING CANNOT BE BOUGHT

I remember years ago, in 1987, when I first was coming to America, at the beginning of the year, financially, whatever I had was gone. I had a 1969 Mercedes-Benz 280 SE with a sunroof. But the paint had oxidized, the tires were bald, the steering wheel was bald, and the springs were split. The springs would stick out and pinch your backside. On the steering wheel, the power steering would work, and then it wouldn't, and when you accelerated, it would make a terrible noise. It was very embarrassing. I would drive down the highway and the horn would sound for no reason. Then the thing would just backfire at the most inopportune time. Terribly embarrassing! When I put the air conditioning on, huge snowflakes came flying out!

If I hit a bump, the window would disappear into the door panel. So, I could be driving down the road, and anything could go wrong. I could drive down the road and try to take a corner, and suddenly, the power steering didn't work. I was fighting with the steering wheel, trying to turn the corner. Then I would be on the highway, and the horn just sounded and the guy in the car next to me looked at me, and I'd try to explain, "No, no, it's not you; it's this car!" Then I found myself punching the dashboard—"You bad car!"—because the guy next to me is angry with me and thinks I sounded the horn at him.

Then the worst was pulling into a church to go and preach, and the car backfired. The deacons dived for cover because they thought it was a drive-by shooting! That's not funny. And it was really bad when I'd pull into the parking lot, switch the ignition off, get out of the car with the keys in my hand, but it would start up again! *Carrung, carrung, carrung, boom!* And I'd stand there and look at the people, and I'd just shrug my shoulders.

The water would fill up in the sunroof, and when I put my foot on the brake, the water would hit the back of the sunroof and run down the back of my neck. When I got to the church, if I took my jacket off, I had a rust stain running down my back. But here I was—called to preach to the nations of the world, I'm going to rent arenas and stadiums, I'm going to preach the Gospel to the nations of the world, and everybody would look and say, "Yeah, right!"

I eventually prayed the car would get stolen. And you won't believe what I did. One night, I left the keys in the ignition on purpose, and prayed that it would not be there in the morning. I walked out in the morning and it was gone. I was so happy. But something said to me, *Just walk to the end of the drive.* I walked to the end of the drive, looked up the road, and there it was! The thief had stolen the car and was driving it away, but in his mind, he must have been thinking to himself, *If I get back to the hideout with this, they are going to kill me. This is the worst thing I've ever stolen in my life!* And so he just parked it and left it running. It was just kind of ticking over, but he had ripped the tape deck out and then disappeared!

Then in April, 1987, I received an invitation to come to America on what I called "my first missionary journey to America," because God called us as missionaries to America. I think some people forget that. The other day I was talking to a pastor and I said, "I'm coming into your area," and he said, "Well, why do you want to come into my area? Stay in your area!" I said, "Pastor, I love you, but you obviously don't remember what I'm called to do. I'm called to America. I'm coming to your area! I didn't know your name was on the town." He said, "You're already in Tampa. Why do you come over here?" I said, "Because it's part of my calling." He said, "As long as God *has* called you to come here." I said, "Yes! He did when He said, 'Go to America!'" Tampa is just our world headquarters and base. God said, "Go to America," and there are fifty states in America.

After I received this invitation to America, a very wealthy man, a multimillionaire, got to hear about the invitation, and he called me up and said, "I really want to meet with you and have lunch." And I thought, *Oh my! This could be an answer to prayer; he's going to help me. He heard about me going to America, and he's going to help me. That's phenomenal. I don't have any money; I've got a car falling to pieces; by the second or third of the month I've got no money, and I've got Kirsten and Kelly, and Kenneth just about to be born.*

He told me to meet him at a beautiful restaurant. The steaks were unbelievable. I'm telling you right now, the steak was phenomenal. It just melted in your mouth. They had a Roquefort salad and it was like nothing you've ever eaten in your life.

I pulled up to the restaurant in my old beat-up Mercedes-Benz—thank God, it didn't backfire! I parked the car, got out, and he pulled up in his Bentley. We walked in and we sat down at the table. He had his son with him, and he started to talk to me. "I heard you're going to America." I said, "Yes." He said, "I'll tell you what: I just feel that I want to pay for you." I was thinking, *My God! This is it! I mean, this is the launching. My God, the Lord is making the way!*

He said, "Yes, I'm going to pay for you, pay your hotel, and give you spending money." I thought, *How good can it get? This is unbelievable.* And then he said to me, "The only thing I ask of you is that I will pay for my son to go with you and then, whatever night you preach, you give him the other night." And my heart sank immediately, I felt sick in my stomach. I thought, *How can he do that to me? He knows how bad I want to go. He's going to pay, he's going to pay my ticket, he's going to pay my hotel and give me spending money, but I can't do it.* He was talking about giving me tens of thousands of dollars; he strung the numbers out. He said, "The only proviso is that you have my son preach every second night," and I put my fork down. I was halfway through the steak, and the steak had just become the worst cow I've ever eaten in my life. I looked at him and I said, "Sir, let me just say, I really appreciate that you want to do that, but I can't." He said, "Why not? I'm going to pay the whole way." I said, "I cannot because this has been a dream of mine. The Lord spoke to me when I was a young boy. I like you, I like your son, but I don't really know him that much, and I've never even heard him minister. I've been in the ministry since 1980, and I've been waiting for this for so many years. I'm not prepared to share every second night with your boy. To be honest with you, he needs to just go out and prove himself in the ministry." And the guy got mad at me. They had planned to order dessert because they had already said to me that I had to try certain dessrts, but they finished their meal and left me sitting at the table.

I looked through the windows as their Bentley headed off down the road. I finished, (because I wouldn't waste a piece of steak), and I went out and I got into my car, and I started crying. I drove off down the road, and I said, "Lord, this is totally unfair; this is wrong. This is like dangling a carrot in front of me and then pulling the carrot away." I said, "Lord, you know, I don't even have the money to go to America. I can't even do this trip. This man dangled a carrot in front of me. Why is this? Lord, he's got all the money. I've got a ministry, but I don't have any money." And the Lord said to me, "Son, you have got to understand something: he might have the money, but he can't buy a ministry. You've got a ministry and I'll give you all the money!" And those tears of sadness turned to tears of joy because the Lord laid the foundation to firstly never look to anybody as a source of supply.

THE LORD IS YOUR SOURCE OF SUPPLY

> DON'T JUST THINK THAT BECAUSE YOU'VE GOT THE MONEY, YOU'RE GOING INTO MINISTRY. BECAUSE MINISTRY COMES WITH THE ANOINTING; IT DOESN'T COME WITH MONEY.

I want to say this to all the traveling ministries, that if you base your ministry on somebody feeding you, you are going to be in big trouble when they pull the plug on you!

You'll hit the skids; the wheels will be pulled. They'll fund you while you play ball and you do what they tell you to, but the moment they think you're not going the way they think you should, they'll pull the plug on your funds, and you'll be up a creek with no oar. It's better to go slower and to build strong in your faith, walking with God, trusting God, and no man being your source. If God speaks to somebody, fine. If He doesn't, fine, don't worry about it. The Lord is your number one source of supply. I know of ministers who are out of the ministry today because they were plugged into one person, and the plug got pulled, and then they had nothing to operate with.

I'm not trying to chase away people who have money, but I'm not going to be dictated to by people with money. If they have a vision to reach the lost, that's fine; then find out where God's put you and get behind that ministry, and fund it.

If you want to go into the ministry, then go into the ministry, but pay the price. Don't sit on the fence and don't just think that because you've got the money, you're going into ministry. Because ministry comes with the anointing; it doesn't come with money. You can buy a church, you can do the building up, you can get up to preach but you'll be as flat as a pancake. Some people think that just because they have got some money they have got a ministry, but it doesn't work that way. It's the anointing, the anointing!

DO NOT BE BOUGHT

Ministries are being manipulated by people with finances. Your job is not to manipulate; your job is just to put the finances in. Riches are fleeting, but the anointing remains. And besides that, Jesus said, "I'll build my church, and the gates of hell will not prevail against it" (Matthew 16:18, paraphrased). People give you money; then they think they are doing you a favor—"Look what I've done for you." But they are not your source, God is your source and you must keep Him as your source.

So, the Lord really spoke that to me. He said, "You don't have the money but you have a ministry, and I'll give you the money." It's been a long journey, from the month of January 1987, to this time, and it has been a learning process.

That's why, whenever we give funds, we tell people, "There are no strings attached." Now, I have told people, "We are going to bless you, but this is not for the ministry; it is for you personally," because I know some people who are always dumping money in the ministry, and God wants to bless them but they will not listen. I have told them, "I forbid you to put this in the ministry!" That's the only time I'll put a stipulation on it, but it's because it is for that person's good, because they don't know how to receive. People need to learn how to receive. They might be good givers, but they don't know how to receive.

Let me give an example: Let's say that a pastor and wife are burning themselves out and the wife says to me, "We have been trying to go on vacation for a long time, but every time we get blessed, he gives all the money away, and then we can't go on vacation." Then I'll say, "Okay, fine. I'll take care of that. We will sort that out. Here are the finances. This cannot be used for the ministry. It can only be used for a vacation. Do you promise me?" Then they are forced to go away and take a rest—a much-needed rest.

That's why many ministers have lost the anointing, because they've been bought. Somebody paid them to shut up. You cannot pay me enough money to shut me up. I'm not going to change, I only change when Heaven changes me!

Everything you have comes from Heaven and when God requires something of you, then you just hand it over and do what the Lord tells you to do. The Bible says that the believers came in, and they put themselves at the disposal of the apostles. They said, "I'm here to serve you. I have resources. Where do you need it the most? I want to sow it into where it's needed the most" (Acts 4:32–37). That's the way to do it. Not, "We'd like to build a youth facility in the name of my late mother, the Henrietta Walker Auditorium for Youth Advancement." There are so many pews dedicated to people. I sat in a pew a while ago and saw a plaque that read "In loving memory of sister whoever." I thought, *Did she die and they buried her under here? What is this?*

I'm saying this for a reason because the amount of finances that I'm speaking about is not millions. Someone says, "Well, I've got a couple of million." Well, that's peanuts! "I have got $10 million." That's peanuts! I'm talking about billions. I'm talking about a flood. When you talk about a flood, you are talking about an unlimited supply, because the Lord said, "You shall lend to many nations, but you shall not borrow" (Deuteronomy 15:6 NKJV).

> THE AMOUNT OF FINANCES THAT I'M SPEAKING ABOUT IS NOT MILLIONS. I'M TALKING ABOUT BILLIONS. I'M TALKING ABOUT A FLOOD. WHEN YOU TALK ABOUT A FLOOD, YOU ARE TALKING ABOUT AN UNLIMITED SUPPLY!

YOU MUST HAVE A PURE AND HUMBLE HEART

I don't personally believe that there are many people in the Kingdom who can handle what is about to happen, because if your heart is not pure, the money that ends up being power will destroy you. In fact, it would not be the will of God to just give people unlimited supply because they couldn't handle it. It would destroy and ruin them. If you just dumped millions of dollars into every ministry, there'd be every crazy idea going on—water parks and even statues of the preacher that speak when you come in to their church; it's the truth!

But God is not into waste, and we're going to give an account of every dollar spent. And don't think the preacher is going to be the only one giving an account of every dollar they spend. Why do you think that the preacher must be held responsible for every dollar he spends, but you, out there in the marketplace, can spend your dollar on anything you want?

I've got news for you: you will have to give as much of an account for what you've done with your dollar as the preachers will. You had better believe it!

Everybody will be held accountable on that day. You're going to be held accountable for what you did with your time, you're going to be accountable for what you did with your talents, and you're going to be accountable for what you did with your treasure. Every single person will stand before God by themselves and give an account of what they did with their time, their talents, and their treasure.

God will not just drop unlimited funds on people. It will only be for the ones who have pure hearts, who have totally died to self, who don't have any ego involved, and have hearts are just sold out for the Kingdom of God. Otherwise, it will elude you.

SUPERNATURAL FAVOR

When the children of Israel left the land of Egypt, they stripped the Egyptians. What is about to happen is a stripping of the Egyptians. I'm not talking about stealing it from them. I'm talking about the favor of God being so on you that they just hand it over. They won't even know why they're doing it; they'll just turn loose of it. The favor of God is on you. They'll start to say no, but end up saying yes to you, and you won't see that there is a ten-foot angel that has them in a headlock, making them nod their heads!

When you leave and go down the road, they are left asking, "Why? What did I do that for?" It's because of the favor of God on you. Favor is something money can't buy, and that's something I have right now: favor.

God has just blessed us with favor, supernatural favor. We have it, favor!

We have many people come and work around the ministry and they say, "We have worked around many places, but we can't believe the favor you have." We have extreme favor; we have high doses of favor and right now as you are reading this, you are getting contaminated with favor. Whether you believe it or not, it is favor, supernatural favor.

When Jesus needed the donkey to go into Jerusalem, He told the disciples where the donkey was tied up. The donkey was somebody's fixed asset, and Jesus said, "Loose it and bring it here" (Matthew 21:2–3, paraphrased). And there's an anointing in these last days coming on the Body of Christ to turn to the fixed assets and say, "Loose it and bring it here. The Master hath need of it." Remember, He said, "If they ask you, 'What are you doing?' say, 'The Master hath need of it.'" The anointing is on you to loose the fixed assets and bring them into the Kingdom for the end-time harvest of souls.

When we were in Soweto, South Africa, we were with Bishop Matula, who was one of the key pastors of support in the city of Soweto. And we are thankful to the bishop and first lady of the wonderful church there for supporting this ministry when we went into Soweto. But two nights out from the crusade, I was $150,000 short.

And really, what we should have done was run for another week, but to do that, I would have needed probably over half a million dollars and as it was, I had to borrow the other $150,000 to finish out the crusade. But I said, "If we could have gone another week, we could have ended up with a quarter of a million people, or even 300,000 to 400,000 saved—the word was spreading so fast." The only problem that people had was transportation. We would send the bus into a region and the bus would pack with 120 people and leave 400 people standing, crying their eyes out because they couldn't get on the bus!

Talk about breaking your heart. I cried out to the Lord. From Soweto I said, "Oh, God, we cannot have these crusades and borrow money. We have to come to a place where these things are paid in full, when we can go in unhindered."

THE FLOOD OF FINANCES AND SOULS

In order for the Body of Christ to walk in this abundance, it means that every single person reading this, and more, are going to have to be extremely blessed! And I believe that we are standing on the brink of the two streams coming together—the upper and the lower springs—creating a supernatural flood for the funding of the end-time harvest, so that we can reap the greatest harvest of souls that the world has ever seen.

I believe that 2005 was the year of the launching and the culmination of what God promised us, and I prophesied that back in 2005! Today, I see it coming to pass, so that we can go marching through the nations of the earth and we can see whole countries, whole cities, whole towns, whole villages saved in a matter of days. I'm talking about a quickening. I believe this is it! This is it!

Just obey God and do what He says. Whatever God says, I do it; it doesn't bother me. But that's why the Lord will entrust finances to me, because He knows I'll do what I need to do with it. When we got the eighty-three-acre property here at The River, (now over ninety acres), the institution that funded us at that time, looked at our finances, and said, "We've been working with ministries for twenty-five years, and we have never found a ministry that spends so much money outside of themselves with no benefit back to themselves. We feel you deserve the property."

Yet, these were the same finances that we couldn't use to even buy twenty computers! We had just had the crusades at New York and Shreveport and almost bankrupted the ministry! My wife and I had to mortgage our house and stick $300,000 in. Thank God we had it, so we could finish that crusade in Shreveport, Louisiana.

I'm not crying, I'm just trying to tell you that whatever it takes, we are going to get the job done. Whatever it takes, whatever the sacrifice, whatever the Lord says to do, we are going to do. Of course, we have now paid off the property completely and paid in full for the building of the pavilion and the new sanctuary, and are totally debt free.

STEP OUT AND GOD WILL MEET YOU

You must step out in faith and when you do, God will meet you. Now when we did the crusade in Soweto, I previously mentioned that I had to borrow $150,000. We had already planned another crusade for Durban, but because of that, I immediately said to Pastor Eric Gonyon, "Just cancel the other crusade.We can't go into another crusade; that's another half a million dollars, and there is no way we can do it." And then, (I believe it was a Wednesday morning) I was standing at The River preaching, and I came under conviction. The Lord said to me, "Every time I've told you to do something, you have never had the money to do it. And now, because you're celebrating twenty-five years in the ministry, you are going to suddenly change?" He said, "Go ahead and book the Durban crusade. I'll meet you."

The Lord quickened to me, and said, "There is an urgency about Durban." We had a pastor of a leading church in the city of Durban call us and say, "Please come. We need help." And then one of the leading evangelists, put the crusade together. He spoke with the pastors, and because of Soweto, there was a momentum already building in the city of Durban. We stepped out in faith and when we stepped out in faith, God met us.

SUPPORT YOUR OWN MINISTRY, AND OTHERS

We lead the charge. I don't make it public, but my wife and I are in the top ten givers to the ministry, and most years, we are number one. There have been one or two years that somebody passed us, but only by a few thousand dollars. My wife and I believe in this ministry. That's why we fund this ministry, because we know what we are doing with the money.

This is good ground. This is good soil. Do you think I'm stupid? I know where to sow seed. I find a field that's producing and I get behind it. I'm behind this ministry. I'm a supporter. I'm the number one partner and supporter of this ministry because I believe in what we're doing.

I'm believing God that the day will come when I personally will put millions of dollars into this ministry. We believe God for extra funds to come in, and I'm praying all the time for seed to sow.

We went to preach one place and the pastor came up to me said, "The Lord just spoke to me to give you $10,000, but not to give it to the ministry, but to give it to you personally." I put my hand up to take it, and my wife grabbed it. I said, "What are you doing? And she said, "Oh, I've been believing for $10,000 to sow into the ministry!" I was left thinking, *There goes the $10,000!* She had already pledged it to the ministry! The guy had just come to me to give it to me personally, and not for the ministry, and she grabbed it and off it went!

We are believing God for seed to sow. I want to say this to every minister: you need to be the number one supporter in your ministry. If you don't believe in the ministry, why should somebody else support it? And then, from your ministry, you need to support others.

Even back in 2005 when I preached this message, on average every year, we sowed about a million dollars into other ministries, and the current figure is far higher. Both 2020 and 2021 were record-breaking years of sowing into other ministries and in 2022, we sowed over $7 million into other ministries. The combined seed over those three years was $20 million USD!

The Lord has also laid on our heart to support many of the older folk in the ministry. Many of them are in their late seventies and eighties. And we have been supporting them on a monthly basis. I want to create a fund to look after the men of God have served the Kingdom well and we can then totally underwrite and look after them. We have been in different places of the world, and we are taking care of different ones there. Someone says, "Why would you do that?" Because I know the sacrifice that they have made.

I remember one man who impacted my life so much, I grew up under his ministry. I went to his deathbed about six months before he died when he was eighty-nine. What a powerful man of God! The day I arrived, the denomination had just sent him a thank you card with, I think, $10 or $20 in it and a little pen and pencil set that you could buy for $19.95. I almost burst into tears.

I called him "Rev" or "Doc," and I said, "Rev, I just came to tell you that I love you and I want to appreciate you for the impact you've had on my life." Because when I was a little boy of five, six years of age, I would come to the meetings, and people would be just flying under the power of God. He would fast a hundred days a year! He would have what he called a "Wall of Jericho," where the "walls" would fall down. This was where you would get in a line and walk along like a wall, and he would have his hands raised, and people couldn't even walk within ten feet of him. Boom! Boom! Boom! They would fall under the power of God. And the last night of every crusade, he would have this "Wall of Jericho" service.

I said to him, "The Lord spoke to me to do something." Now, he'd been lying, eyes closed, looking like he was dead, but now he kind of opened one eye and he leaned over and said, "What did He tell you to do?"

I thought, *Typical evangelist. He's almost dead, but you mention an offering, and he starts raising up!* I said, "The place where you are staying is not adequate"—because it had a flight of stairs and had no elevator. He had fallen several times and hurt himself, and that's why he was in the condition he was in. I said, "We're going to find you a nice place with an elevator, where you can live the rest of your life out. I am going to buy you that place."

I told him that I was going to give him a certain amount each month, and then I said, "When you go, it will carry on for your wife; we will look after her," because they had no children and nobody supporting them. So, he opened up one eye and he looked at me and said, "If you do that, I'll live. If you don't, I'll die." So, I started laughing and said, "So, in other words, you living and dying is all on me?"

But the Lord enabled us, and we bought her a beautiful place. Sadly, he never did get to move into it because he went home to be with the Lord six months later, but we did not miss a payment and we paid the home off.

Someone says, "Well, why would you sow into a ministry that's passed?" Because I have to. I have to because of the legacy that he left and the fire that he instilled in me as a little boy. How can I say thank you enough?

WE HAVE A RESPONSIBILITY BACK TO THE KINGDOM

Somebody says, "Why are you telling us all about what you give? You are going to lose your reward." No, I've already got my reward. That's why I can tell you now, my reward has already come in. I won't tell you what I'm doing now because I don't want to lose my reward on that one! When my reward gets in on that, then I might tell you what's happened, but these are things that happened a long time ago. I'm sharing with you because everybody needs to realize that we have a responsibility back to the Kingdom.

Yes, we have to look after the poor, but not everybody is poor. Yes, to look after the widows, but not everybody is a widow. But we are to help people, and to help the ministry.

When I was growing up, my dad was a wonderful example of this. He had a business and one time, it rained for sixty days and totally destroyed the business. Things were tight, but when the evangelist came through town, my dad and mom went down and bought him four new tires for the car. They used their vacation money. Over the years, I watched them give. They were always giving, always looking after people, always looking after the poor, always looking after the needy. You can't live seeing that as a kid and then grow up and not do the same. I would say, "Dad, what are you going to do?" He'd reply, "Oh, we are going to put new tires on the preacher's car, son."

My dad dreamed for years of funding the end-time harvest. And everything he dreamed of and everything he spoke of, we are going to see happen and come to pass.

I know that some people might say, "Well, this has got nothing to do with revival." It has more to do with revival than you can ever know. Because the laborers are crying in the field. Do you know the cry that came up from Soweto?

I cried out to the Lord, and I said, "God, you know and I know that this is not even right. We could have continued this meeting." Soweto would have collapsed under the weight of the explosion of the power of God. We were days away from it, but we had to pull the plug because of one thing—MONEY!

THE FUNDING OF THE END-TIME HARVEST

> I SEE A DAY COMING WHEN THERE WILL BE NO RESTRAINT, THERE WILL BE NO RESTRICTIONS, THERE WILL BE UNLIMITED SUPPLY TO GET THE JOB DONE.

But I see it changing. I see a day coming when there will be no restraint, there will be no restrictions. There will be unlimited supply to get the job done. We can go into a city and stay a month, two, three, four, five months! And if the radio station doesn't like it, we'll buy the station, and if the TV station gives us problems, we'll buy the TV station, and if the newspaper doesn't like it, we'll shut them down!

I believe we are standing on the brink of the greatest harvest of souls that the world has ever seen. I am teaching something here that is going to be one of the major arms of funding the end-time harvest, because we are living in the costliest age of human history.

I see us going back to New York City, renting Madison Square Garden, and paying cash for it. It is going to come again. In 1999, we were six weeks in the Garden. Watch what's going to happen. New York City has not seen the last of us.

We just dropped a Holy Ghost bomb in 1999, and we are going to go back and reap the harvest. Because I remember walking the streets of Manhattan and I saw the Blood of Jesus running up and down the streets of Manhattan. I saw New York being shaken by the power of God.

I see Los Angeles shaken by the power of God. I see the great city of Chicago shaken by the power of God. I see the city of Detroit shaken by the power of God. I see the city of Miami, Florida, shaken by the power of God. I see Tampa shaken by the glory of God, I see the city of Atlanta shaken by the glory of God. and what God is going to do is put people together where we can strategize. We will go in, like a planned mission, and take the enemy out.

I see at The River, an office high-rise with three floors, with computers monitoring revivals that are taking place around the world. We will have evangelists on the field, totally funded right out of our R.M.I headquarters. They won't have to worry about the funding. They will come running and say, "Where's the next crusade?" And we'll say, "We need you right now. We need you in India right now! The field is already there. Can you do it?"

"Yes, I can,"

"Get on a plane; here is your ticket. Go!"

Oh yes, it is going to happen. Why? Because God's army is the only army that's totally disjointed and everybody does their own thing. Somebody has to grab ahold of the vision and strategize, and sit down like a general and plan a military offense. "We'll attack in this area; we'll take Scandinavia and then we'll move in and we'll take Italy, and then we'll move in and take Egypt, and then we'll move in and take this nation." Somebody has to plan it. Imagine if we targeted a nation and flew in a hundred evangelists in ten days, and every town, city, and village and had a crusade. In ten days, it would be over!

We can crush nations. We can shake nations. We can take nations. We can possess nations! I might have known some of these things in the Spirit years ago, but I didn't know how to do it. But now, I know how to do it and I can see it.

Honduras is 112,492 square kilometers. It's a small country about the size of North Carolina with six million people. We can take Honduras in a matter of ten days. If we take a hundred fiery, flaming, Holy Ghost evangelists and fund every crusade, we can shake Honduras and then just march through Central America. Listen, you might think I'm crazy, but I'm not. I might be a lot of things, but I'm not crazy.

Evangelists are trying to reinvent the wheel, trying to outdo this one, trying to cut this one off at the pass, trying to get there before this one, and it's a zoo! But it's about to change where the separate armies are going to become *the* army. We are going to work together, and we are going to submit one to another. Somebody says, "How do we do that?" It's all by the anointing. Not just because somebody has a plan, but because of the anointing.

When the anointing increases to such a place where people are dissatisfied with doing their own thing, they will just come and say, "Everything I have and everything, I am, I place it here. What's next?" Isn't that what happened in the early Church? People sold things and they came and just put it at the apostles' feet and said, "We just put it here." This is going to happen again, and that will give way to the greatest outpouring of the power of God known in the history of this planet. Greater than anything you've ever seen or heard about.

The two streams are coming together, the anointing and the finances, for the financial and the spiritual harvests. We are going to take from the devil and we're going to hurt him in two areas: we are going to take his money and we are going to take his people. Glory to God!

WHEN THE ANOINTING INCREASES TO SUCH A PLACE WHERE PEOPLE ARE DISSATISFIED WITH DOING THEIR OWN THING, THEY WILL JUST COME AND SAY, "EVERYTHING I HAVE AND EVERYTHING, I AM, I PLACE IT HERE. WHAT'S NEXT?"

2. THE END-TIME MOVE OF GOD

I've already covered the first aspect of what is about to come on the earth, (the end-time financing of the Kingdom of God), and the second one is the end-time move of God. This last day, end-time move of God is going to be a coming together of the former and the latter rains, where the harvest shall be so great that there will not be room in the churches to fit all the people. You will not be able to build buildings big enough to house the people. Where they are building all these big stadiums, we will possess them. Rejoice when your city builds a football stadium, because the Church will possess it!

THE GLORY OF THE LATTER HOUSE

> WHAT WOULD HAPPEN IF GOD WOULD SO PROSPER THE CHURCH THAT PEOPLE WOULD COME TO CHURCH TO GET THEIR FINANCIAL NEEDS MET AS WELL?

When the glory of God fell in Wales, football teams were disbanded. When the glory of God falls in Tampa, the Buccaneers won't even be able to play. This is a culmination of everything that was prophesied. The glory of the latter house shall be greater than of the former house (Haggai 2:9). The former house was Solomon's Temple. Do you know how glorious the former house was? The Queen of Sheba came and passed out; she fainted! I really think she fell under the power. She just came and fainted because the glory was so great. And God says that the glory of the latter house will be greater than that of the former house. That means you ain't seen nothing yet.

You've heard me tell you this before, and it's quickened to me again by the Spirit of God: Could it be possible that people would come to church in the end-time move of God to not only get their spiritual needs met but to get their financial needs met as well? That God would so prosper the Church that this could happen?

What would happen if you had such a pool of resources that you couldn't even give it away? Even if you sat and wrote out checks to help pay off people's debts, and you gave away $186 million in a day, by the same night it would have already replenished itself and you couldn't give it away?

Some years ago, I was standing in front of the mighty Niagara Falls, and as I was standing and watching the water going over, the Lord said to me, "That's what I have for the Church in the way of blessing, but the Church is standing there with a little glass, trying to get ready to receive what I'm going to do! They're not ready for what I'm about to do, because I'm sending a flood to the Body of Christ."

It's huge! But some of you are not ready; you've got to change your mindset; you've got to change your mentality. Some people here in Florida, if they just get a new trailer and they pick up a new coon dog, they're happy. My God, you have got to change your whole mindset. There's no room to receive it—blessings coming from every side. No room to receive it. The Church rising up, empowered by the Spirit of God, to do *exploits* in His Name.

It's time to reap the harvest, and it's time to reap the harvest in an unprecedented fashion. No lack! More than enough provision to fulfill your vision. Whole nations!

What the Lord is just looking for is people He can trust. Don't sit and say, "I'm not sure if God could trust me." He probably can't. But rather, say, "God, You can trust me; go ahead and test me. Put me to the test. You can trust me. You can trust me, Lord. I won't fail you. I'm not going to let You down."

If my son wants something from me, the worst thing he can do is say, "Well, I'm not sure if you can really trust me." Because I'd reply, "Son, I probably can't, seeing that you brought that up!" But when he comes to me with a convincing story and says, "Dad, I'm your son. I love you. You can trust me. Come on. Turn it loose." I'll say, "Okay, here's the test." And then, as he's faithful and proves himself, increase comes and the blessing comes.

> IT'S TIME TO REAP THE HARVEST. IT'S TIME TO REAP THE HARVEST IN AN UNPRECEDENTED FASHION.

THE SHAKING OF THE NATIONS

David took the lion and then he took the bear, and God said, "Fine. You can take the giant." I'm talking about a supernatural quickening. You see, most times when people talk along these lines, all they talk about is houses, cars, and jets—give me a break! That's got nothing to do with it. You will be so blessed you will not even know what to do with what you are blessed with. I'm talking about funding the end-time harvest. I'm talking about shaking nations.

"He that hath an ear, let him hear what the Spirit saith" (Revelation 2:17).

With this final move, I see a city hit by the power of God. Everywhere people go, there are traffic jams. I see stadiums filled. I see television mobile units tracking and mapping the move of God, and I see it broadcasted around the world. I see news reporters saying, "A crazy thing happened. An ambulance pulled up, and a person totally damaged from a car wreck was hit by the power of God and jumped up and took off running." I see hospitals being emptied. I see deaf schools being emptied. I see blind schools being emptied. I see mental institutions being emptied, all because somebody, full of the fire of the Holy Ghost, went in there and set them free, turned them loose.

I see railroad stations jammed with people as trains come into town, carrying those full of the glory of God. I see airports jammed, traffic jams, upheaval, whole cities shut down by the glory of God. Someone says, "Do you really think this is going to happen?" If Nineveh could repent, then God will give us another Nineveh. God will show us a city, and if He can give us one, He can give us two, and if He can give us two, He can give us three.

But besides that, do you think when it's all said and done that the devil is going to stand and look and say, "I won the majority of it?" There are almost 1.5 billion people in China, unofficially. Do you think the devil's going to claim most of China? Do you think he's going to claim most of India? I have got news for you, the Blood was shed for all of them. Now hear the word of the Lord as I gave it in 2005:

> For too long My people have limited Me and put Me in a box and brought Me down to their level and to their mentality, and their way of thinking. But in these last days, I'm opening up the hearts of many,

and I'm opening up their minds to begin to receive all that I will do in these last days, for I am able to do exceedingly abundantly above all that you can ask or think, according to My power that's working on the inside of you.

So do not limit Me, saith the Lord, and do not put Me in a box and say, "Oh, He shall only do this and do that and do the other thing." But oh, I shall do that which you haven't even heard of. I shall do that which even now we speak of things, but we speak of them in a shadow, but the substance of that which we speak of shall surely come.

And the glory of God shall be seen coming through ordinary men. Oh, hallelujah! For those that have lived humbly and walk pure before Me, they shall see and walk in the light of My great glory, for these are the days of the outpouring of the Spirit of God. These are the days when signs and wonders and miracles, that which was even spoken of by the prophet Joel, shall be in great manifestation upon the earth and seen among men, and they shall see it again and again and again and again and again. It shall not be just a smattering over here and over there. But oh, outbreaks everywhere. Everywhere! Everywhere!

Great, so great, so great shall be the move of God that some of you, even within eighteen months from now, twenty-four months from now, will have to pinch yourselves because you'll think you've died and gone to Heaven! It is now! It is now! Unusual signs, unusual wonders, to grab the attention of whole regions. Weather patterns will be stopped in their tracks, and they will say that they just disappeared off their screen. Unusual signs, unusual wonders shall be made manifest that will get national media attention in different countries and different settings. And with each nation, and with each region, there will be a key that will unlock the door.

"And I'll give you the key," saith the Lord, "to unlock the door for millions to come in to the Kingdom."

WE WERE BORN FOR SUCH A TIME AS THIS

> GOD MUST HAVE FELT THAT YOU HAD WHAT IT TAKES BECAUSE HE PUT YOU HERE IN THIS TIME.

Again, I say that I see Europe shaken by the fire of God. I see Europe shaken by the glory of God. The whole continent of Africa ablaze. I see the whole of Asia on fire. I see North and South and Central America shaken. Somebody says, "These belong to the devil." No, they don't belong to the devil—they belong to the King of kings, and the Lord of lords.

It is time for those who are truly liberators to go marching through the land—*tramp, tramp, tramp, tramp*—setting the captives free, binding up broken hearts. And you are the generation to fulfill this! You were born into the Kingdom of God for such a time as this (see Esther 4:14). You're it! You're it! YOU are IT!

God must have felt that you had what it takes because He put you here in this time.You were not born in the 1800s or the 1600s. You were born for this hour. We get to wrap this up, because Jesus saved the best wine until last (John 2:1-11). As great as what the Day of Pentecost was, you have not seen anything yet. And I tell you, the prophets of old would have given anything to have lived in this day. That's why these are not the "Days of Elijah." No, they are not. These are the days of the Holy Ghost! If I'm not mistaken, I believe Elijah only had eight notable miracles and Elisha had sixteen, because he had a double portion, so what are you talking about? These are the days of the Holy Ghost!

The only way you're going to receive what I'm telling you is if you drink of the New Wine. The drunker you get, the more you'll see it. You'll say, "I see it, I see it." But when you sober up, you can't. You cannot come with me on this journey and stay sober. Get totally drunk. Get drunk on the New Wine and you will dream of angels, sing new songs, and prophesy in your sleep.

THE ONLY WAY YOU'RE GOING TO RECEIVE WHAT I'M TELLING YOU IS IF YOU DRINK OF THE NEW WINE.

A HOLY GHOST TSUNAMI

Everything we've seen up to now is preparatory for what is about to come, and it shall come suddenly, like a Holy Ghost tsunami. And there is nothing the devil can do to stop it. Get ready. Get ready!

There will be no unused members in the Body of Christ, but everyone from the least to the greatest, from the littlest child among you to the oldest member shall be used by the Spirit of God.

That's why your whole concept has to change from everything happening in the pulpit, because this next wave of God will hit the marketplace. It's going to hit Wall Street. It's going to hit Congress. It's going to hit the Senate. The Holy Spirit is not sleeping.

It will be as "when the Day of Pentecost was fully come" (Acts 2:1), only it will be, "And when the day of [and you fill in your name in the blank] was fully come . . .". And then all of Heaven is going to break loose, and we're going to reap the greatest harvest of souls. Then we need to "get the heaven out of here!" When it hits, it'll be three, four years, and then—boom! We will be out of here!

There won't be any time for anybody to get flaky. There won't be any time for somebody to go off the rails. It will be BOOM—gone! Because we are getting ready for the return of the King. We are getting ready for the return of the King, and our King wins! Oh, yes! All hail, King Jesus! Hallelujah! Our King wins! Because the Blood is sufficient, the Word is all-powerful, and the Holy Ghost is still the Holy Ghost!

There will be places of worship open twenty-four hours a day. There will be teams leading worship just doing three, eight-hour shifts, and there'll be a constant flow of people coming through. The glory of God will be poured out. There will be ambulances pulling up on the parking lot because an epidemic broke out and hospitals are full. They won't know what to do, but someone will say, "If you just get the sick to that place, they'll get healed."

Now, you might say, "How do I know that these things are true?" All right, I'll give you a thing to test it out: when Mary showed up at Elizabeth's house and she greeted Elizabeth, John the Baptist leapt in her womb, and while I've been speaking, if something kicked on the inside of you, you know!

Finances without the souls is what they had in the 1980s. What they called "prosperity" was nothing more than "bless me." It's rubbish. We are not going to get the souls without the finances, so we need the two to come together, and we must have pure humble hearts.

> THERE WILL BE NO UNUSED MEMBERS IN THE BODY OF CHRIST, BUT EVERYONE FROM THE LEAST TO THE GREATEST, FROM THE LITTLEST CHILD AMONG YOU TO THE OLDEST MEMBER AMONG YOU, SHALL BE USED BY THE SPIRIT OF GOD.

SOULS MUST BE YOUR NUMBER ONE GOAL

You will always know if you are going the right way because you make souls your number one goal. That was Jesus' number one goal when He came to the earth. I don't care if you are a pastor, a teacher, someone who wants to disciple the church and make them grow—you have to have souls as your number one goal, because that was the Master's number one goal. "For the Son of man is come to seek and to save that which was lost" (Luke 19:10).

Souls, souls, the harvest, people—the only thing you can take with you when you leave this earth, is people.

There's so much more that I could say. I have many more things to tell you, but some of you can't even handle what I've already said. You have almost gone on a tilt. But the rest will unfold. God will show you. God will reveal it to you.

THE END-TIME ARMY OF THE LORD

The changes that are happening in technology are going to bring about a whole new wave. There is coming a change in television. I could go on because of the things that I've seen in my spirit and when I get under the anointing, what's about to happen pops on the inside of me. It's going to be like another Industrial Revolution except it is going to be a technological revolution. Have you already had something leap on the inside of you as you are reading this? Well, it shall surely come to pass.

Now I tell you what the Lord showed us in Shreveport. Shreveport was (in 2005) a town of 300,000 in 2005, and we saw 59,000 decisions, but the Lord showed us that with 59,000 out of 300,000 we could go into smaller cities of 5,000 and 10,000 and eat them for breakfast. Then we could go on to bigger and bigger cities. The Lord has already shown me that we will move into a city and there will be a spiritual "military camp" set up with 5,000 to 10,000 soul winners who have the capacity to lead hundreds a day to the Lord. Then at night, we will hold crusades. During the day there will be 5,000 to 10,000 soul-winners on the streets. I've already seen it; it's just a matter of time.

We'll go marching through. It's going to cause such an upheaval. You haven't seen anything yet. You talk about persecution? They'll have news media flying in from all over. We'll be arrested; we'll be thrown into prison, beaten. It'll be the Book of Acts all over again.

JOY IS THE VOICE OF THE END-TIME MARTYRS

> SOME WILL BE MARTYRS FOR THE FAITH. THAT'S WHAT THE LORD SAID TO ME. AND HE SAID: "THE JOY IS THE VOICE OF THE END-TIME MARTYRS."

Some of us will even be martyrs for the faith. That's what the Lord told me. And He said: "The joy is the voice of the end-time martyrs."

They will line us up in front of a firing squad, and we'll just stand there and say, "Go ahead. Make my day! Ha-ha-ha-ha. "For me to live is Christ, and to die is gain" (Philippians 1:21). There will be a report back that says, "Those people are crazy. We went to kill them and they all just sat laughing at us."

We will just say, "I see Jesus standing at the Father's right Hand" (Acts 7:55 paraphrased). Praise the Name of the Lord Jesus!

THE REWARD OF THE SOUL-WINNER

This flood is going to come to sowers of seed. I'll tell you one thing for certain: I believe that the people who hang around The River and hang around this ministry, when they get to Heaven, their treasure is so big up there that they are going to have to have thousands of angels just carrying their share! Because per capita, River members are going to have so much treasure. We show our members how to make a deposit, and some of them are depositing all the time in their heavenly bank accounts.

Now you might have got a little irritated with me down here, but when we get to the other side, you'll be grabbing me and kissing me. "Thank you, Pastor. Thank you, Pastor. Thank you. You showed me how to deposit treasure up here!"

There will not be one River member standing there with an empty pocket on that day. We're going to make sure they get all the crowns. They will be walking, arms outstretched, carrying them all—the soul-winner's crown, the victor's crown. I want them to be first at the prize-giving. There is not going to be anybody under this ministry looking at me with a sad face. Remember the Bible says, "God shall wipe away all tears from their eyes" (Revelation 21:4). Some people are going to be crying because they don't have anything. But not those under my care. Not on my watch! I'm not having them look across at me at the Judgment Seat of Christ and say, "You didn't tell me."

But in the meantime, there is work to be done. One day, we'll take five of those big Boeing 747s and take the whole River Church and take off to "destination unknown." People will come to the church building and there will be a big sign on the door that says, "GONE TO SAVE THE WORLD!"

POSTSCRIPT

If you have been blessed and challenged by this book, please write to us here at our Tampa office or email us at testimonies@revival.com

We would love to hear from you. If you were stirred up and challenged to change and allow God to do His work in you, we pray that God would use you in a wonderful way to touch a lost and dying world.

Write to:
Revival Ministries International
P.O. Box 292888 Tampa, FL 33687

You can also reach us at www.revival.com/prayer/testimony
or
call 1(813) 971-9999

For souls and another Great Spiritual Awakening in America, Dr. Rodney Howard-Browne

ABOUT THE AUTHOR

Drs. Rodney and Adonica Howard-Browne are the founders of Revival Ministries International, the River at Tampa Bay Church, and River University in Tampa, Florida.

In December of 1987, Rodney, along with his wife, Adonica, and their three children, Kirsten, Kelly, and Kenneth, moved from their native land, South Africa, to the United States called by God as missionaries from Africa to America. The Lord had spoken through Rodney in a word of prophecy and declared, "As America has sown missionaries over the last two hundred years, I am going to raise up people from other nations to come to the United States of America. I am sending a mighty revival to America."

In April of 1989, the Lord sent a revival of signs and wonders and miracles that began in a church in Clifton Park, New York, that has continued until today, resulting in thousands of people being touched and changed as they encounter the presence of the living God. God is still moving today—saving, healing, delivering, restoring, and setting free!

Drs. Rodney and Adonica's second daughter, Kelly, was born with an incurable lung disease called cystic fibrosis. This demonic disease slowly destroyed her lungs. Early on Christmas morning 2002, at the age of eighteen, she ran out of lung capacity and breathed out her last breath. They placed her into the arms of her Lord and Savior and then vowed a vow. First, they vowed that the devil would pay for what he had done to their family. Secondly, they vowed to do everything in their power, with the help of the Lord, to win one hundred million souls to Jesus and to put $1 billion into world missions and the harvest of souls.

When Drs. Rodney and Adonica became naturalized citizens of the

United States of America, in 2008 and 2004 respectively, they took the United States Oath of Allegiance, which declares, "I will support and defend the Constitution and laws of the United States of America against all enemies, foreign and domestic." They took this oath to heart. They love America, are praying for this country, and are trusting God to see another Great Awakening sweep across this land.

Believing for this Great Spiritual Awakening, Drs. Rodney and Adonica conducted Celebrate America D.C., a soul winning event. They preached the Gospel of Jesus Christ for fifty nights in Washington, D.C., and surrounding areas from 2014 to 2019. Through the evangelism efforts on the streets, in the halls of Congress, and the nightly altar calls, 58,033 individuals made decisions for Jesus Christ.

During Celebrate America, in July of 2014, at the Daughters of the American Revolution Constitution Hall, Dr. Rodney executed a restraining order against the structure that is holding America in captivity, binding it and rendering it powerless and ineffective, from the Supreme Court, to the White House, to the Executive Branch, Congress, and the Senate, in the Name of Jesus. He commanded the Church in America to wake up and for the people of God to come out of their slumber. He declared that it is time to take the land.

During the Covid era, Drs. Rodney and Adonica took a stand for the Gospel of Jesus Christ. As a result, Dr. Rodney was wrongfully arrested at his home on March 30, 2020, for holding a church service at The River at Tampa Bay Church on Sunday, March 29.

As a result of his arrest, Florida Governor Ron DeSantis declared attendance at churches, synagogues, and houses of worship to be an essential activity. Dr. Rodney's arrest freed up every church in Florida to meet. All the charges were dropped by the Thirteenth Judicial Circuit State Attorney on May 15, 2020, and the date of his arrest and criminal record were expunged by Circuit Court Judge John N. Conrad on February 22, 2021.

Drs. Rodney and Adonica continue to take a stand for the Word of God and for billions around the world whose right to worship freely was removed and has not been, or perhaps will never be, restored. The Stand nightly services have continued for over 1,200 nights, as they stand for their brothers and sisters around the world who cannot stand freely.

With a passion for souls and a passion to revive and mobilize the Body of Christ, Drs. Rodney and Adonica have conducted revivals and soul winning efforts throughout ninety-two nations with the 300 City Tour, Good News campaigns, R.M.I. Revivals, the Great Awakening Tours, and The Stand. As a result, over 45,558,739 precious people have come to Christ, and tens of thousands of believers have been revived and mobilized to preach the Gospel of Jesus Christ. For more information, visit revival.com.

CONNECT

Please visit revival.com or rodneyhowardbrowne.com for our latest updates and news. Many of our services are live online. Additionally, many of our recorded services are available on Video on Demand.

For a listing of Drs. Rodney and Adonica Howard-Browne's products and itinerary, please visit revival.com. To download the soul-winning tools for free, please, visit revival.com and click on Soul-winning Tools.

- **Like us on Facebook:**
  Facebook.com/rodneyadonicahowardbrowne

- **Follow us on Twitter:**
  @rhowardbrowne

- **Follow us on YouTube:**
  YouTube.com/rodneyhowardbrowne

- **Follow us on Instagram:**
  @rodneyhowardbrowne

- **Follow us on Rumble:**
  @rhowardbrowne

OTHER BOOKS AND RESOURCES BY RODNEY HOWARD-BROWNE

BOOKS

Kingdom Business
Leadership Principles
The Phantom Virus
Socialism Under the Microscope
God's Top Ten
Perpetual Harvest
Killing the Planet: How a Financial Cartel Doomed Mankind
The Anointing
The Killing of Uncle of Sam: The Demise of the United States of America
Thoughts on Stewardship
The Coming Revival
The Touch of God
The Gifts of the Holy Spirit
The Reality of Life After Death
Seeing Jesus as He Really Is
The Curse Is Not Greater than the Blessing
How to Increase and Release the Anointing
School of the Spirit
The Anointing
Manifesting the Holy Ghost
What Gifts Do You Bring the King?
Prayer Journal
Sowing in Famine

AUDIO CDS

Prayer Time
Weapons of Our Warfare
Becoming One Flesh
Faith
Flowing in the Holy Ghost
How to Flow in the Anointing
Igniting the Fire
In Search of the Anointing
Prayer that Moves Mountains
Accelerate
The Camels are Coming
Pray Without Ceasing Vol.1
Pray Without Ceasing Vol.2
The Touch of God
Mountain Moving Prayer
Having an Encounter with God
God's Mandate
The Anointing is Transferable
Dealing with Offenses
The Vow and the Decree
Whosoever Can Get Whatsoever
Run to the Water
Demonstrations of the Spirit and of Power
The Double Portion
More Than Laughter
The Hand of the Lord

Running the Heavenly Race
The Holy Spirit, His Purpose & Power
The Power to Create Wealth
Walking in Heaven's Light
All These Blessings
A Surplus of Prosperity
The Joy of the Lord is My Strength
Prayer Secrets
Communion–The Table of the Lord
My Roadmap
My Mission–My Purpose
My Heart
My Family
My Worship
Decreeing Faith
Ingredients of Revival
Fear Not
Matters of the Heart by Dr. Adonica Howard-Browne
My Treasure
My Absolutes
My Father
My Crowns
My Comforter & Helper
Renewing the Mind
Seated in High Places
Triumphant Entry
Merchandising and Trafficking the Anointing
My Prayer Life
My Jesus
Seeing Jesus as He Really Is
Exposing the World's System
Living in the Land of Visions & Dreams
Kingdom Business
Taking Cities in the Land of Giants
Spiritual Hunger
The Two Streams

MP3 CDS

The Phantom Virus
Socialism Under the Microscope
Killing the Planet: How a Financial Cartel Doomed Mankind
The Killing of Uncle Sam
The Touch of God: The Anointing
Knowing the Person of the Holy Spirit
The Love Walk
How to Hear the Voice of God
Matters of the Heart
Exposing the World's System
How to Be Led by the Holy Spirit
The Anointing
The Ways of the Wind

DVDS

Mountain Moving Prayer
How to Personally Lead Someone to Jesus
The Fire of God
Vision for America
Living the Christian Lifestyle
No Limits No Boundaries
The Curse is Not Greater Than the Blessing
God's Glory Manifested through Special Anointings
Good News New York
Jerusalem Ablaze
The Mercy of God by Dr. Adonica Howard-Browne

Are You a Performer or a Minister?
Revival at ORU Volume 1, 2 & 3
The Realms of God
Singapore Ablaze
The Coat My Father Gave Me
Have You Ever Wondered What Jesus Was Like?
There Is a Storm Coming (Recorded live from Good News New York)
Budapest, Hungary Ablaze
The Camels Are Coming
Power Evangelism
Taking Cities in the Land of Giants
Renewing the Mind
Triumphant Entry
Merchandising and Trafficking the Anointing
Doing Business with God
Accelerate

MUSIC

Nothing Is Impossible
By His Stripes
Run with Fire
The Sweet Presence of Jesus
Eternity with Kelly Howard-Browne
Live from the River
You're Such a Good God to Me
Howard-Browne Family Christmas
He Lives
Anointed—The Decade of the '80s
Live Summer Campmeeting '15
Live Summer Campmeeting '16
Haitian Praise
No Limits
Christmas Extravaganza At The River

THE RIVER AT TAMPA BAY CHURCH

The River at Tampa Bay Church was founded on December 1, 1996. At the close of 1996, the Lord planted within Pastors Rodney and Adonica's heart the vision and desire to start a church in Tampa. With a heart for the lost and to minister to those who had been touched by revival, they implemented that vision and began The River at Tampa Bay, with the motto, "Church with a Difference."

Over 575 people joined them for the first Sunday morning service on December 1, 1996. Over the years, the membership has grown and the facilities have changed, yet these three things have remained constant since the church's inception ... dynamic praise and worship, anointed preaching and teaching of the Word, and powerful demonstrations of the Holy Spirit and power. The Lord spoke to Pastor Rodney's heart to feed the people, touch the people, and love the people. With this in mind and heart, the goal of The River is:

To become a model revival church where people from all over the world can come and be touched by God. Once they have been not only touched, but changed, they are ready to be launched out into the harvest field with the anointing of God.

To have a church that is multi-racial, representing a cross section of society from rich to poor from all nations, bringing people to a place of maturity in their Christian walk.

To see the lost, the backslidden and the unsure come to a full assurance of their salvation.

To be a home base for Revival Ministries International and all of its arms. A base offering strength and support to the vision of R.M.I. to see America shaken with the fires of revival, then to take that fire to the far-flung corners of the globe.

To break the mold of religious tradition and thinking.

To be totally dependent upon the Holy Spirit for His leading and guidance as we lead others deeper into the River of God.

Our motto: Church with a Difference.

For The River at Tampa Bay's service times and directions, please, visit revival.com or call (813) 971-9999. Location: The River at Tampa Bay Church, 3738 River International Dr., Tampa, FL 33610.

RIVER UNIVERSITY

River University is a place where men and women of all ages, backgrounds and experiences can gather together to study and experience the glory of God. River University is not a traditional Bible school. It is a Holy Ghost training center, birthed specifically for those whose strongest desire is to know Christ and to make Him known.

The vision for River University is plain: To train men and women in the spirit of revival for ministry in the 21st century. The school was birthed in 1997, with a desire to train up revivalists for the 21st century. It is a place where the Word of God and the Holy Spirit come together to produce life, birth ministries, and launch them out. River University is a place where ministries are sent to the far-flung corners of the globe to spread revival and to bring in a harvest of souls for the kingdom of God.

While preaching in many nations and regions of the world, Dr. Rodney Howard-Browne has observed that all the people of the earth have one thing in common: a desperate need for the genuine touch of God. From the interior of Alaska through the bush country of Africa, to the outback villages of Australia to the cities of North America, people are tired of religion and ritualistic worship. They are crying out for the reality of His presence. River University is dedicated to training believers how to live, minister, and flow in the anointing.

The Word will challenge those attending to find clarity in their calling, and be changed by the awesome presence of God. This is the hour of God's power, not just for the full-time minister, but for all of God's people who are hungry for more. Whether you are a housewife or an aspiring evangelist, River University will deepen your relationship and experience in the Lord, and provide you with a new perspective on how to reach others with God's life-changing power.

Programs Include:

- River Bible Institute
- River School of Worship
- River School of Government
- River Bible Español

You can be saturated in the Word and the Spirit of God at River University. Since 1997, River University has graduated over 10,159 students (including our subsidiary schools). River University is the place where you will be empowered to reach your high calling and set your world on fire with revival. For more information about River University, please, visit revival.com or call (813) 899-0085 or (813) 971-9999.

RIVER SCHOOL OF THE BIBLE ONLINE

River School of the Bible is our online school to train up revivalists for the 21st century. It was started so that those who are unable to come to the school in Tampa, can receive this training and impartation, anyplace worldwide. It is not a traditional Bible school. It is a Holy Ghost training center, birthed specifically for those whose strongest desire is to know Christ and to make Him known.

This program provides quality Spirit-filled biblical instruction, academic training, and practical education to men and women called into the five-fold ministry or for those who desire to become better equipped in other areas of Christian service. Since 2018, over 100 students have graduated from the school. So, don't wait! God wants to raise you up to do great things for Him.

For more information please visit revival.com/rsb or email rsb@revival.com

GOD WANTS TO USE YOU TO BRING IN THE HARVEST OF SOULS!

The Great Commission, "Go ye into all the world and preach the Gospel to every creature," is for every believer to take personally. Every believer is to be an announcer of the Good News Gospel. When the Gospel is preached, people have an encounter with Jesus. Jesus is the only One Who can change the heart of a man, woman, child, and nation!

On the next page is a tool to assist you in sharing the Gospel with others. It is called, "The Gospel Soul-Winning Script." Please, make copies of it, fold it in the center lengthwise, and read it to people. As you read it to others, you will see many come to Christ, because as stated in Romans 1:16, *"For I am not ashamed of the gospel of Christ: for it is the power of God unto salvation to every one that believeth ... "*

Please visit revival.com, click on Soul-Winning Tools, and review the many tools and videos that are freely available to help you bring in the harvest of souls. It is harvest time!

JESUS SAVES • JESUS HEALS • JESUS DELIVERS

SOUL-WINNING — SCRIPT —

Has anyone ever told you that God loves you and that He has a wonderful plan for your life? I have a real quick, but important question to ask you. If you were to die this very second, do you know for sure, beyond a shadow of a doubt, that you would go to Heaven? [If "Yes"—Great, why would you say "Yes"? (If they respond with anything but "I have Jesus in my heart" or something similar to that, PROCEED WITH SCRIPT) or "No" or "I hope so" PROCEED WITH SCRIPT.]

Let me quickly share with you what the Holy Bible reads. It reads "for all have sinned and come short of the glory of God" and "for the wages of sin is death, but the gift of God is eternal life through Jesus Christ our Lord". The Bible also reads, "For whosoever shall call upon the name of the Lord shall be saved". And you're a "whosoever" right? Of course you are; all of us are.

continued on reverse side—

JESUS SAVES • JESUS HEALS • JESUS DELIVERS

I'm going to say a quick prayer for you. Lord, bless (FILL IN NAME) and his/her family with long and healthy lives. Jesus, make Yourself real to him/her and do a quick work in his/her heart. If (FILL IN NAME) has not received Jesus Christ as his/her Lord and Savior, I pray he/she will do so now.

(FILL IN NAME), if you would like to receive the gift that God has for you today, say this after me with your heart and lips out loud. Dear Lord Jesus, come into my heart. Forgive me of my sin. Wash me and cleanse me. Set me free. Jesus, thank You that You died for me. I believe that You are risen from the dead and that You're coming back again for me. Fill me with the Holy Spirit. Give me a passion for the lost, a hunger for the things of God and a holy boldness to preach the gospel of Jesus Christ. I'm saved; I'm born again, I'm forgiven and I'm on my way to Heaven because I have Jesus in my heart.

As a minister of the gospel of Jesus Christ, I tell you today that all of your sins are forgiven. Always remember to run to God and not from God because He loves you and has a great plan for your life.

[Invite them to your church and get follow up info: name, address, & phone number.]

Revival Ministries International
P.O. Box 292888 • Tampa, FL 33687
(813) 971-9999 • www.revival.com

THE RIVER AT TAMPA BAY CHURCH
ALTAR CALL

CELEBRATE AMERICA
WASHINGTON, D.C.
57,498 SALVATIONS

THE STAND | 1,200 NIGHTS AND COUNTING

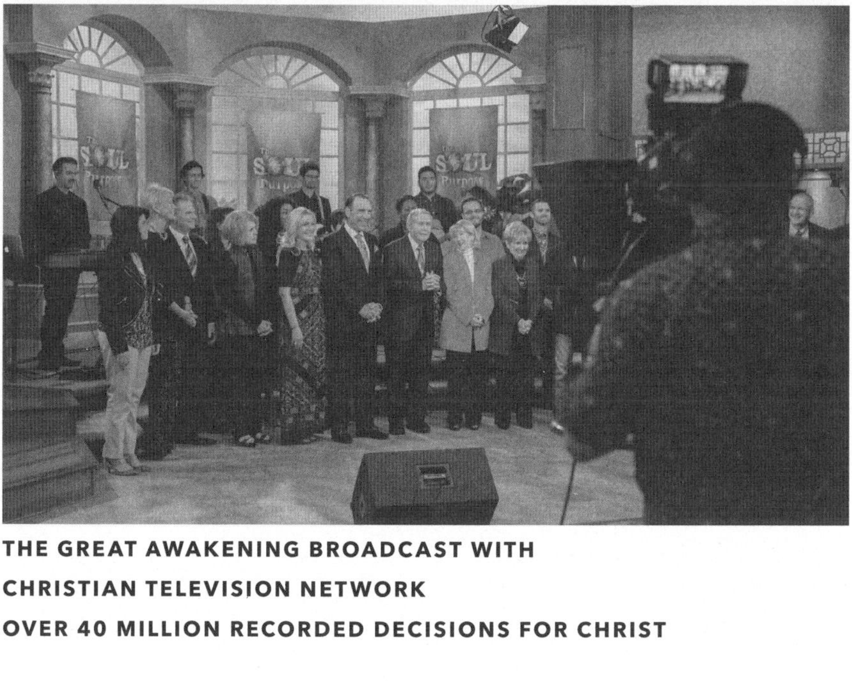

THE GREAT AWAKENING BROADCAST WITH
CHRISTIAN TELEVISION NETWORK
OVER 40 MILLION RECORDED DECISIONS FOR CHRIST

GOOD NEWS NEW YORK - 1999

MADISON SQUARE GARDEN

48,459 SALVATIONS

GOOD NEWS NEW YORK - 1999

MADISON SQUARE GARDEN

48,459 SALVATIONS

GOOD NEW SOWETO - 2004
SOWETO, SOUTH AFRICA
177,600 SALVATIONS

GOOD NEWS UMLAZI - 2005
UMLAZI, SOUTH AFRICA
286,750 SALVATIONS

SINGAPORE - 1995

THE EARLY YEARS

RODNEY, ADONICA, KIRSTEN, KELLY, & KENNETH

THE EARLY YEARS

RODNEY & ADONICA